From Sacral Kingship to Sacred Marriage

From Sacral Kingship to Sacred Marriage

A Theological Analysis of Literary Borrowing

Tom R. Roberts, Ph.D.

VANTAGE PRESS
New York

Cover design by Polly McQuillen

FIRST EDITION

Published by Vantage Press, Inc.
516 West 34th Street, New York, New York 10001

Manufactured in the United States of America
ISBN: 0-533-14492-2

Library of Congress Catalog Card No.: 2002096140

0 9 8 7 6 5 4 3 2 1

To my beloved wife, Barbara, without whose love and support this publication would not have been possible

Contents

Acknowledgments

This writer wishes to acknowledge all of the precious souls who have contributed so greatly to my path thus far in my academic and spiritual progress.

I owe a great debt to my first academic mentor, Dr. Charles V. Dorothy (Ph.D., Claremont Graduate School, *Dead Sea Scrolls and Their Relationship to the Book of Esther*). It was from his love and belief in my academic potential that began my journey into the scholarly realms. One of the first doors he opened was the Egyptian enthronement rituals and their relationship to the Book of Psalms. This Prince of Preachers instilled in me a confidence that would lead me to higher ground from each open door that my subsequent professors would open.

Another giant step was taken when Phyllis Tryble personally introduced me to the work of Tikva Frymer-Kensky, a Semitic scholar who has challenged some of the feminist writers by saying that the battles with the Semitic god demonstrate the dominant monad was seen as a male figure. Phyllis added a wealth of inspiration and encouragement at her lectures when I met with her at Pacific Lutheran University.

One of the most amazing persons who truly is a gentleman and a scholar of the first magnitude is Dr. Desmond Ford, who has provided some of the information in this dissertation regarding the theology and the structure of the Book of Revelation, with a wonderful emphasis on the balance of the Law/Gospel paradigm.

Next in my journey was John Warwick Montgomery, at Faith Lutheran Seminary, Tacoma, Washington, where he lectured on Christian Apologetics. He impressed upon those of us who knew him to always defend the Faith with a spiritual, rational, and scholarly explanation.

It was my great privilege to have studied under the direction of Dr. Joseph Wherry, with his emphasis on Eastern Church theology, which gave me a more well-rounded and balanced view regarding the history and the theological development of the Christian faith.

My sincere thanks go to Dr. William Koch, who was my mentor from Holy Family Seminary of Tacoma, Washington, who greatly enhanced my understanding and knowledge of the schools of psychology integrated with his understanding of pastoral counseling techniques. He also has a wealth of information regarding Reformation Theology and Lutheran Dogmatics.

Another very special friend and colleague is James Vineyard, M.Div., who brought into my world a broader understanding of liturgical theology and worship practices.

One of my personal heroes is Dr. Leroy Mikels, who is cited in this dissertation in regards to the kenotic forms that he studied in pursuing his Th.D. It was his love and understanding that began my undergraduate degree program and to whom I will be forever indebted.

It is my great pleasure to acknowledge Pastors George Allen and Robert Belton of Covenant Bible Seminary for their love and encouragement during my undergraduate studies in Pastoral Theology and Church History. From them I learned the qualities and character of an anointed pastor.

Dr. Joseph Battistone, author, pastor, and professor (Andrews University), whose encouragements and insights in the Apocrypha, such as the Ascension of Moses and the relationship of pastoral administration and Christian Education was a great inspiration to me at the beginning of my Ph.D. studies.

Dr. Samuele Bacchiocchi, whose tremendous zeal and personality has inspired me and our many discussions of his experiences at Gregorian University in the Vatican in Rome have been extremely valuable to me in my critique of Early Church historical sources.

I also wish to thank my advisor, Dr. Father Stephen Thomas, for his patience regarding the completion of this dissertation through the many changes in school administration as well as the personal setbacks we have encountered over the last seven years. His understanding has been especially valuable, as he has negotiated on my behalf with Hellenic Orthodox University for the completion of this degree program.

It is also with the deepest of thanks and heartfelt gratitude that I acknowledge Dr. Roy Blizzard for contributing greatly to my knowledge of the Jewish faith and its impact on the Early Christian Church. Roy has been an invaluable professor, as he unlocked so many Middle Eastern concepts and made them live in my memory by his excellent teaching.

And last but not least is my beloved wife, Barbara, whose editing skills have proved to be priceless in critiquing this manuscript and her sacrifices over the last several years as she has stood next to me through the rewards and hardships so that this dissertation could be faithfully presented. Without her love and support, this dissertation would have been much more difficult to produce.

Introduction

For a number of decades, publications had been written regarding the relationship between the Old Testament canon and Egypt. The contributions of these publications have been significant, and they are often cited in modern literature. One of these early publications was Sir Flinders Petrie's *Egypt and Israel* (1911) as well as Abraham Yahuda's *Accuracy of the Bible: The Stories of Joseph, the Exodus and Genesis Confirmed and Illustrated by Egyptian Monuments and Language* (1934).

Since that time, however, little has been written about the subject of the relationship of Israel and Egypt until a 1985 publication by Sarah Israel-Groll entitled *Pharonic Egypt: The Bible and Christianity.* The primary reason this relationship is no longer emphasized is that many scholars today are unconvinced that the Hebrew prophets and sages had a thorough knowledge of Egyptian society, but rather the biblical writers employed literary techniques from an earlier Persian Period of the seventh to the fifth centuries B.C., such as the story of Joseph as well as other Mesopotamian literature. Scholars such as Redford also claim there is little Egyptian coloring in the Exodus account and that the Egyptologist would soon sense that it was anachronistic.

However, others, such as Wilfred Lambert, are calling for a balance on this subject. He believes that ancient parallels can also been found among the Canaanites as well as the Egyptians, the Hurrians, the Hittites, and the early Greeks. In recent decades, editions as late as 1997 have been published of John D.

Currid's work entitled *Ancient Egypt and the Old Testament,* which reveal the trade routes between Egypt and Israelite society. He shows that the cultural interchange between those nations was greater than was previously believed. These patterns existed at two levels; first, the literary borrowing of ancient expressions and universal themes, which were later formulated into the canon of the local community and, second, temple patterns which were employed by each culture.[1]

On the validity of the exodus story itself, Dr. John Bright states as follows:

> "b. *The Exodus.* Of the exodus itself, we have no extra-Biblical evidence. But the Bible's own witness is so impressive as to leave little doubt that some such remarkable deliverance took place. Israel remembered the exodus for all time to come as the constitutive event that had called her into being as a people. It stood at the center of her confession of faith from the beginning, as is witnessed by certain ancient poems (Exodus 15:1–18) and credos (Deut. 6:20–25; 26:5–10; Josh. 24:2–13) that go back to the earliest period of her history. A belief so ancient and so entrenched will admit of no explanation save that Israel actually escaped from Egypt to the accompaniment of events so stupendous that they were impressed forever on her memory."[2]

At present there is no archaeological or historical data that gives us any direct knowledge of the Exodus or of many other stories from the Book of Genesis. However, it should not be overlooked that there does seem to be some Hebraic influence upon Egyptian society as well as Egyptian influence on Israel. Some of the controversy is in dating the campaigns of Joshua, as well as many other debates regarding who were the sea peoples of the period. It is not highly likely that the sea peoples in their conquests would have been Israelites, due to the fact that they feared the sea and actually employed sea-faring rites before the crossing of any major body of water. Ezra 8:24 is such a passage indicating this rite. Some scholars have suggested that an early exodus occurred during the 18th Dynasty of Egypt circa 1447 B.C. and a second great exodus took place circa 1250 B.C., with the conquest of Canaan completed in about 1220 B.C..

> Garstang espoused the traditional 1400 B.C.E. date for the conquest of Canaan, based upon 1 Kings 6:1: "In the four hundred and eightieth year after the people of Israel came out of the land of Egypt, in the fourth year of Solomon's reign over Israel . . . he began to build the house of the LORD." The chronology at the time for Solomon's accession was 970 B.C.E., so the fourth year would be 966 B.C.E. The time of the exodus would be calculated by adding 966 and 480, giving a date of c. 1446 B.C.E. Subtract from this the 40 years of wilderness wandering and a date of 1406 B.C.E. or 1400 in round numbers is reached for the conquest. Thus the discovery of a 1400 B.C.E. city at Ai supported the traditional time accepted for the conquest and confirmed the biblical account of the capture of Ai as related in Joshua 7–8, to the satisfaction of Garstang's church-oriented financial backers.[3]

At first glance a biblical scholar may ask the question what impact does the dating of the Exodus have on our study regarding when the conquest of Canaan took place? In response, this writer is attempting to establish the extent of Israel's relationship with Egypt by the thirteenth century B.C.E. The campaigns of Canaan would also add credence to the cultural interchange between Israel, Egypt, and Canaan, especially if there was more than one exodus of Israelites out of Egypt between 1447 B.C.E. and 1250 B.C.E. John J. Bimson explains:

> It should be noted that various destructions did occur in the 12th century, e.g., at Beth-Shan, c. 1150 B.C., and that there is nothing to distinguish the second half of the 13th century as the time of a "main wave of destruction"; throughout the 14th, 13th

and 12th centuries, there were periodic destructions of cities in Palestine. Furthermore, no cultural change occurred in the second half of the 13th century, which could be said to definitely attest to the arrival of the Israelites at that time. . . .[4]

Scholars such as Dr. Hester, who once held to the 18th Dynasty dating of the Exodus, now concede that a 1250 B.C. second Exodus is entirely possible due to the fact that this is the earliest archaeological dating that we can assign the Israelites for entering Canaan, and most scholars have reconstructed the chronology of Joshua and Judges to this scenario.

Tell-el-Amarna Letters—These letters, discovered in 1887–88, were written on clay tablets in Babylonian cuneiform by prominent officials in Palestine to the Pharaohs of Egypt about 1300 B.C. Their value lies in the description of life in Palestine about the time of the Exodus. In these letters the word *Habiri* (Probably Hebrews) occurs.[5]

The evidence also suggests that the Canaanites were in the zenith of cultural influence over invading peoples. Could there be a connection between Canaan's dominant cultural presence that led Israel to use a Canaanite pattern in the construction of their temple due to the fact that Canaanites held a culturally superior influence over the region? Postulating from the hypothesis of a later Exodus that would have taken place during the campaigns of Pharaohs Rameses II and Seti I, we may rely again on John Bimson:

In conclusion, we must say that the archaeology of Palestine for the 13th and 12th centuries provides no convincing evidence for a conquest or settlement of the land by incoming Israelites during that period. To interpret what evidence there is in terms of an Israelite settlement of the land involves a large subjective element and risks becoming a circular argument (i.e., dependent on prior assumption that the Exodus and Conquest should be dated to the 13th and 12th centuries B.C.).[6]

Scholars such as A. H. Sayce and R. Peterson have dated the reign of Seti I or Sethos I as circa 1319–1304 B.C. of the XIX dynasty, builder of the temple at Adydos.[7] The bias of some progressive scholars against the Exodus event is shown by their reliance on the lack of archaeological and historical evidence, which they use as a basis to dismiss the Exodus event altogether as a folktale and are able in their own thinking to write off the relationship of the biblical patriarchs with Egypt as well.

It is this writer's conviction, after examining the evidence of cultural influence flowing in all directions that it is highly unlikely that any of these nations existed in a cultural vacuum and it would be intellectually naive to assume that any of these nations were left out of the Mesopotamian literary traditions. I will concede the fact that Israel's literary traditions probably didn't have as much impact as the neighboring great empires until a much later period of time, possibly under the united Hebrew monarchy.

> Literary works throughout the ancient world, especially in the ancient Near East, share motifs and forms, Proverbs, hymns, disputations, and prophecies appear in the literature of cultures influenced by the Hebrews. But direct influence of one literary text upon another is often difficult to prove. The Egyptian maxims of Amenemope, which found their way into the Book of Proverbs, are a conspicuous exception. Other influences certainly are possible, such as Persian and Babylonian influences on the Book of Esther, or the Greek forms of historiography on the Acts of the Apostles. But the way specific forms and texts travel in societies where literacy is restricted to the few is complicated.[8]

This complication is due to two basic facts: one, the sophisticates who would journey from culture to culture only taught students who would study under the great teachers. However, it was possible for national leaders within the royal courts to obtain such information by the hand of the leader's scribe, who would write international correspondences, which books such as Jeremiah may well include. So most of the information that was passed along through international correspondence stayed at the top of the social strata, with few exceptions, such as the king or leader's issuing an edict to be followed by the people or an announcement of war.

Two, outside of the king and priestly classes, it is believed few citizens in the general populace could read or have general access to the origins of these traditions, which were borrowed from other cultures. And it is generally accepted that the majority of the citizenry didn't travel beyond their local vicinity unless they were fleeing great distress in their nation, such as famine or persecution, with the exceptions being military conscriptees, merchants, or religious teachers who traveled to engage other sages in the wisdom traditions. With this cultural interchange, through the scribes of the king's courts as well as the Hebrew sages and the traveling wisdom teachers, the literary traditions were developed and maintained within this cultural milleau.

The purpose of this dissertation is to provide an evaluation of the data utilizing broad scholarly support to create as accurate a picture as possible of the relationship of the literary traditions that played such major part in developing one major cultural literary tradition from which the local writers in each culture would draw and make contributions. This is a feeble attempt at best due to the fact that we have such a small amount of fragmentary evidence that has been transmitted to us via these literary traditions. It is my sincerest hope that the readers of this dissertation will be inspired and mentally stimulated to do further work in this challenging arena.

From Sacral Kingship to Sacred Marriage

1 The Origin of Monotheism

From the Genesis of biblical monotheism, the community of Faith, whether Jewish or Christian, has assumed that the belief in a monotheistic deity did truly originate with Israel's belief in Yahweh. There is also the contemporary position that the theory of primordial monotheism suggests Israel's belief in one god grew according to an evolutionary historical model and originated in Israel late in antiquity. One of the catalysts advancing this position, Diana Vikander Edelman, states as follows,

> A belief in the creation of heaven is not attested before the exile; the conviction that heaven and earth are created by gods is an insight of Babylon mythology with which Judah became acquainted only during the exile. In the HB, a real theology of creation can only be found in exilic and postexilic text.[1]

However, modern scholarship opens the possibility of some of the Egyptian Pharaohs, particularly Imhotep, proclaiming a belief in a monotheistic deity. What influenced this belief is still unknown. However, two theories thrive. One is that the ancient Shepherd Kings may have been Hebrew in origin, and during their rule in upper Egypt at the time of Joseph's saga, may have influenced the Pharaohs with their Hebraic monotheistic religion. The other theory advances the notion that all ancient Near Eastern cultures at one time worshiped monotheistically and some cultures gave way to animism, while others drifted into polytheism due to the fact that the one god seemed to be so unknown. But the fact that we still do not know which culture influenced the other to begin this dynamic process of intercultural population.

> Few scholars would deny the near-identity of the Hebrew and Egyptian precepts, but who copied from whom? That the Hebrew was the original is supported by the strong infusion of Semitic words into Egypt around the time of Amenemope's writing and by the ethical and monotheistic tenor of Amenemope's thought. Along with linguistic influences, so the argument runs, there must have come concepts and ideas. However, Amememope's treatise is based on a long tradition of didactic literature that, as we have seen goes back to the Old Kingdom and that had found a literary form long before the Hebrews emerged as a tribe from the Arabian desert.[2]

Another fact that emerges is when we find the term "El" for the Mountain God was known and worshiped by many ancient Middle Eastern cultures.

> God is One and only, and none other existeth with Him—God is the One, the One who hath made all things—God is a spirit, a hidden spirit, the spirit of spirits, the great spirit of the Egyptians, the divine spirit—God is from the beginning, and He hath been from the beginning. . . . He existed when nothing else existed, and what existeth He created after He had come into being. . . . His name remaineth hidden; His name is a mystery unto His children. His names are innumerable, they are manifold, and none knoweth their number. . . . God is father and mother, the father of fathers and the mother of mothers. He begetteth, but was never begotten; He produceth, but was never produced; He begat Himself and produced Himself. He createth, but was never created. He is the maker of His own form, and the fashioner of His own body.[3]

These quotes from the Book of the Dead were from the Theban Period, dating from 1600 to 1420 B.C.; it was created for Ani, a royal scribe.[4] Many texts in the Book of the Dead contain many hymns to the gods. "The Christian Egyptians, or Copts, used the word 'Amenti' to translate the Greek word 'Hades' to which they attributed all the ideas that their heathen ancestors had associated with the 'Amenta,' of the Book of the Dead."[5] Many other ideas and transmissions of thought come from the Egyptian Book of the Dead as well. Doctrines of the resurrection, the one God, God is a spirit (found in John 4:24) show this Egyptian document had some influence on the writers of the New Testament. Furthermore, a Coptic bishop, who used the Book of the Dead, was present at the Council of Ephesus.[6]

In 1928, the discovery and excavation of the northwest Syrian city of Ugarit and the subsequent finding of clay tablets (*KTU* 1.1–1.25) emerged as a strong witness in attempting to reconstruct Yahweh's position as a supreme god amongst Judaism. It is a scholarly fact that none of Old Testament canon now in use has been dated earlier than 586 B.C.; however, evidence does exist to show that ancient oral traditions, which were employed in the ancient temple liturgies, were later partially canonized and found their way into Israelite worship. In addition, Egypt's sacral kingship formula of ritual coronation also had its widespread use in the Mediterranean world of ancient times.

However, Israel's monotheism did have wonderfully distinct features regarding an addition of ethical behavior as well as a moral compass added for corporate behavior whereas the Semitic gods issued a convenant code sentence of blood oaths, which did not require an ethical response of the deity. Therefore, under a covenantal curse, a righteous decision was not warranted on behalf of the people due to the law of Blessing and Cursing.

> Further, the Semitic god was the owner of the land whereon his people dwelt. All living creatures belonged to him, and all

changes of weather and seasons were attributed to his agency. The Semitic god was not ethical. We find, then, these ideas included in the early heathen conception of God:

1. He was the physical progenitior of his people, and they belonged to him;
2. He was a local god;
3. he owned the land and all living creatures upon it;
4. he was sensuous.

Now, do we recognize similar notions of God among the Israelites? We find a sensuous idea of God which is familiar to all. Feeling and acts are ascribed to God in the language of men. God "*is angry,*" "*is sorry,*" "*repents,*" he "*speaks,*" he "*fights,*" and he "*smells,*" the savory odors of sacrifice. The Jews were inclined to limit the operations of Jehovah to their own people.[7]

As monotheistic theology developed in Israel, the prophets would declare Yahweh as Lord over all nations and the laws of justice and righteousness were truly in his hands to be dispensed according to his divine agency. Israel believed that she possessed a divine role in leading other nations to the sovereignty of God. As the Hebrew nation failed to carry out this commission, she herself was placed under divine judgment. Bernhard Lang expresses the following:

To most contemporary scholars, Keunen's view of monotheism seems out of date, as it clearly over-estimates prophetic creativity. Recently, however, the same view was eloquently advocated by Nikiprowetzky. This author returns to the concept of 'ethical monotheism' and recognises the prophets as the actual creators and promoters of a monotheistic belief, which is one of the 'moral and intellectual basis of modern society'. 'Born of national pride and self-confidence, it grew and gained strength along with it,' Kuenen writes on monotheism. In Nikiprowetzky, we read: 'As intolerant and fanatic champions of Yahweh, the prophets started the religious war in reaction to the Philistine expansionism that led to the conquest of the highlands. The preaching of the prophets represented, on a religious level, calls to battle against the Philistines and to form an Israelite state. Monolatry became symbolic of an imperative duty to Yahweh and to the Hebrew nation'.[8]

Israel's revulsion against polytheistic practices cannot be overemphasized, particularly with the Sh'ma (Deut. 6:4) becoming her national credo affirming the one God tradition. However, many literary forms that run parallel to polytheistic practices of other cultures were not available to scholars until our time. John L. McKenzie explains:

Let us examine this question more closely. The two great myths of Semitic polytheism were the myth of creation and the myth of the death and resurrection of the god of fertility. These were combined into one great myth and ritual of the renewal of the cycle of fertility. Not until modern times has anything been known of this mythology, so obscure and scattered are the allusions to it in the Old Testament, so that, at first glance, Kaufmann's thesis may seem extremely probable in this respect.

Of the myth of the dying and rising god, I think we may say that this was so abhorrent to Hebrew religious sentiment that the Old Testament writers refused even to mention it, although we are now in a position to know some of the reasons why they spoke of the Baal cults with such asperity, why it was called "harlotry." But these are references rather to the external features and practice of the cults, and do not touch precisely the questions raised by Kaufmann. But the Hebrew attitude toward the myth of creation was somewhat different.[9]

One of these distinctions was that Yahweh in the creation motif is responsible for order and chaos. The author of Genesis shows us this by use of the *waw*-consecutive phrase in Genesis 1:2, and the Holy Spirit (*racah kadesh*) vibrated/hovered over the powers of light and darkness[10] rather than a dualistic approach of the "war" between the gods and goddesses/good and evil/light and darkness.

> The *waw*-consecutive is found, as in Hebrew, in prose but not poetry. It is likely that internal passives existed for all the active conjugations of which the *Sahf'el* and *Histaf'el* are noteworthy. The prefix *t*- is often used instead of *y*- in the third person plural masculine.
>
> The use of the prepositions and particles, studies especially by M. J. Dahood and his school, has shed light on possible archaic usages and previously overlooked senses in Biblical Hebrew. The interest of many Hebraists in Ugaritic has helped to establish very clear parallels and points of linguistic, literary, and cultural contact between Ugarit and Israel, resulting in a significant improvement in our understanding of biblical literature in general.[11]

The study of the Semitic family of languages does a great deal to enhance our understanding of many ancient parallel creation accounts, such as the two lights motif, light over darkness, and order over chaos, which are found in various creation stories. As stated earlier in the biblical account, YHWH is responsible for order and chaos, and in Genesis 1:3, the Heavenly Council brings order out of chaos, resulting in light over darkness. Some authors, such as George Pimber and William F. Dankenbring, using the "Gap Theory", have attempted to divide this motif into separate parts, due to the fact that the term "was," *bar'rah,* is capable of being translated "became," indicating this "gap" may have existed for a creative day or an age resulting in the old earth with a later creation of humankind in the historical timeline.[12]

Fragments in other literary traditions, such the Babylonian cuneiform inscriptions, found in the great library at Niniveh, ancient capital of Assyria, indicate these literary units model the *waw*-consecutive—*tohu waw bohu*—as two conjunctive portions of a single literary unit.

This fine fragment is a typical specimen of the style of the whole series, and shows a marked stage in the Creations, the appointment of the heavenly orbs. It parallels the fourth day of Creation in the first chapter of Genesis, where we read; "And God said, Let there be lights in the firmament of the heaven to divide the day from the night; and let them be for lights in the firmament of the heaven to divide the day from the night; and let them be for signs, and for seasons, and for days, and years . . ."[13]

The text of the Septuagint translates *tohu waw bohu,*

Η бε γμ μν αορατοζ και ακατασκευαστοζ, και σκοτοζ But the earth was unsightly and unfurnished, and darkness was over the deep, and the Spirit of God moved over the water (Gen. 1:2–3)[14a,b]

The chaos/order motif is expanded in the early literature of Job contained in the third cycle, which states as follows:

The shadows tremble underneath the earth, the waters and their denizens are afraid. Before his eyes, Sheol is bare, perdition itself is uncovered. He it was who spread the North above the void and poised the earth on nothingness. He fastens up the waters in his clouds, without the clouds giving way under their weight.[15] (Qere in Jer. 43:10 "tent" . . . which, like our verb is a cognate of the Akkadian root *s uparruru* "spread out (a canopy)." Render *stich* a: "His breath spread out the heavens," and cf. Isa. 40:22 and Deut. 33:33b. "the outstretching of the everlasting arms") He covers the face of the full moon, spreading his cloud across it. He has traced a ring on the surface of the waters, at the boundary between light and dark. The pillars of the heavens tremble, awe-struck at this threats. By his power, he has whipped up the Sea, by his skill, he has crushed Rahab.

His breath has made the heavens luminous, his hand transfixed the Fleeing Serpent. This is only a fraction of what he has done and all we catch is the feeblest echo. But who can conceive the thunder of his power? (Job 26:1–14)

Notice the writer of Job also states that Yahweh boasts of the containment of the sea (Heb. Yam) in magnificent cadences, but this imagery of the comparisoning of the infant sea was tailored to Job's comprehension and is poetic rather than contemptuous.[16]

Job also reveals discussions and appearances before the Mighty Council by Satan himself, who acts as the prosecuting attorney for the heavenly court. The writings of Job were transmitted to us via paleo-Hebrew, which may have originated from Moses.

Jewish tradition assigned the authorship to Moses. The rabbinical authorities, the Syrian fathers, the Greek Ecclesiastical writers also, associated the Book of Job with the Pentateuch. According to Deouard Dhorme, "The Syriac Bible places the Book of Job between the Pentateuch and Joshua in such a way as to connect the hero of the narrative with the patriarchial age and Moses." Later the place of Job in the canon was changed to connect it with the other poetical books: Psalms, Proverbs, Song of Solomon, Ecclesiastes.[17]

One reason for placing this document in the canon with other poetical books is in Bildad's second speech, in which he refers to the plight of the wicked and states, "And his lamp shall be put out" (Job 18:6), which corresponds to Proverbs 13:9, with a similar expression: "The light of the righteous rejoiceth, but the lamp of the wicked shall be put out." The writing style of Job is closely related to a musical play, with speeches, strophes, negative confessions, which parallel the Egyptian Book of the Dead (Job 34:5).[18]

Various attempts have been made regarding textual emendations and variations in text readings and translations to determine how much original material was of Job's own composition or whether he borrowed heavily from Near Eastern poetry.

> Thomas J. Meek in an article in *Vetus Testamentum,* January 1956, gives a detailed analysis of one text in Job that troubled commentators who thought it should been emended by the translators. He concludes, however, that the Massoretic Text "is perfectly in order and needs no emendation at all."[19]

These major themes from Job also appear in a genre of Ugaritic literature dealing with the stories of human heroes, which follows the patterns of Job.[20] Among them is the legend of *Keret*:

> It tells of a Job-like, Syrian sovereign who has lost all his family and is heartbroken. We see him retire to his inner chamber, crying with the copious abundance of Mediterranean heroes. . . . El then directs Keret to seek a bride, the fair daughter of powerful King Pabel, at distant Udum (Edom?), who shall bear him children. . . . All goes well with Keret. In due time he brings up fine sons and daughters . . . and toward the end of the story, Keret becomes feeble and, in preordained synchronism, the land and its people decline and become impoverished. The king's own son rises like another Absalom against him and orders him to relinquish his power . . . there was probably still another tablet in which the wrath of the goddess is eventually assuaged and Keret returned to his former vigor, his land to prosperity.[21]

These major themes appear throughout Middle Eastern and Biblical literature and apply to the legends of the human heroes and their struggle with the powers of light and darkness. A similar phenomenon of cultural exchange occurred during the construction of the Hebrew temple when the builders were advised to follow a Canaanite temple blueprint, which was modified by God's inspiration. A literary pattern from the Canaanite traditions was used by the Hebrews and became the framework and the foundation for the Hebrew canon.

> Serious scholars had long regretted our ignorance of the religious concepts, cults, liturgy, and poetry of the Canaanites, which would undoubtedly throw much light on the origin of certain Biblical books, particularly those of a later date, such as Psalms, Job, and some of the Prophets. To what extent have the Hebrews been dependent on Canaanite models?[22]

The extent of the intercultural relationship between the Canaanites and the Hebrew people is not fully known, but, as stated earlier, it appears the Hebrews borrowed Canaanite literary devices as they translated their literary forms into their own native language building from the foundation that they gleaned from the Canaanites.

> The use of the prepositions and particles, studied especially by M. J. Dahood and and his school, has shed light on possible archaic usages and previously overlooked senses in Biblical Hebrew. The interest of many Hebraists in Ugaritic has helped to establish very clear parallels and points of linguistic, literary, and cultural contact between Ugarit and Israel, resulting in a significant improvement in our understanding of biblical literature in general.[23]

Some of these parallels that took place were Yahweh's divine address to the Mighty Council and when the Sons of God shouted for joy (Job 38) during the creation epic, which was later celebrated in the various national temple cults, with the singing of choral groups and in which each culture gave honor to its deities from its original temple cult services. New concepts are introduced in regards to worshiping in the House of the

Lord for the length of days that is continuously without interruption. One's worship life is not simply on Sabbath Days or sacred festivals.[24] The resurrection motif was personalized to state and, *without* literally *from my* flesh I will see God. (Job 19:25–27) corresponds with the Ecstatic Burst of Joy contained in the 16th Psalm.[25]

Ancient Jewish and Christian writers all verify the importance of Job in canonical literature. Origen, Gregory of Nyssa, Olympidorus (deacon of Alexandria about A.D. 600), ancient Jewish commentator R. Assidi Gaon and an Arabic translation with comments contained in Isr. Schwarz: *Tikwath Enosh,* i.e., *Liber Jobi,*[26] all attest to the importance of the development of our understanding regarding Yahweh's address to the Divine Council in dealing with the struggle of good over evil, which was illustrated in chaos motifs of light over darkness, resulting in a celebration motifs in the singing of choral hymns in the temple, not only on Sabbath and sacred festivals but worship that extends all the days of one's life. These theological developments cannot be overemphasized in their role of understanding the Psalter and the temple service from the poetic expressions contained in the literature of Job from which the writers of the Psalter borrowed heavily. This Canaanite/Hebrew structural tradition existed clear up to and including the compilation of the post-exilic psalms.

Regarding the Psalms, Prof. Hans La Rondelle states:

> In the so-called 'nature psalms,' Israel's poets see all of nature in the light of God's action and sustaining power. They do not state, as we do, in gray neutrality, "*it*" rains, "*it*" snows, "*it*" thunders. In Psalm 29, it is the God of glory who thunders and the voice of the Lord that breaks the cedars and strikes with flashes of lightning. And Psalm 104 stresses God's sustaining power and active involvement in the laws of nature. . . . 'You bring darkness, it becomes night, and all the beasts of the forest prowl.' (Ps. 104:20)[27]

John McKenzie is correct in advancing the concept that a dying and resurrected god was not a part of Old Testament belief and practice. However, the sleep of God was certainly lamented in the enthronement psalms found in the Psalter and the questioning of the prophets regarding Yahweh's great sleep and His seeming lack of interest in Israel's current situation. The Psalmist exclaims, "Awake, oh, my God!" (Ps. 7:6 RSV); and once again, the writer states, "Rouse thyself! Why thou sleepist, O Lord?" (Ps. 44:23 RSV, see also Ps. 25:23 and Ps. 59:4–5). This motif does indeed have many parallels in biblical literature, such as the sleep of God or the sleep of a king or the righteous dead rising to life again. It is abundantly clear that New Testament literature incorporated the motif of the death and resurrection of the King into the personification of the Messiah.

As we mentioned earlier, there is evidence to suggest that Middle Eastern oral tribal traditions of early antiquity developed into priestly traditions, then into canonical form. James A. Sanders calls this tradition *From Sacred Story to Sacred Text.* This transition began as independent stories were told and later were embodied into sacred stories and legends. For example, in the Book of Genesis, we find four groups of these stories. The first group includes the beginning of human history (Gen. 1:1–11:9); group two included the Abraham stories (11:10–25:20); and group three, the Abraham cycle and the Jacob stories (25:21–36, 38); group four contains the Joseph stories (37:39–50) and certain universal traditions. The atmosphere and setting are Egyptian. The story of Joseph's temptation embodies elements of an old Egyptian tale of the "Two Brothers."[28] Modern scholarship suggests that the Abramic and Jacob sagas were written in a dramatic cyclical form as they were retold and later codified in Israelitish tradition. Dr. Charles Kent states:

In the introduction to the *Instruction of Ptah-hotep*, the ancient Egyptian sage states that his purpose was to *speak to his son the words of those who hearken to the counsel of the men of olden time.* Ptah-hotep lived nearly fifty centuries ago, yet he spoke repeatedly *of the counsel of the men of olden time.* These allusions indicate that at this early day there was a large body of maxims embodying the experience of the sages of preceding generations. Ptah-hotep's purpose in transmitting the results of his own practical observation and experience in the form of proverbs to his son and disciples is also clearly stated: it was to *instruct the ignorant in the exact knowledge of fairspeaking.* He adds, *If you heed these things that I have said to you, all your plans will progress.* Like Israel's wisdom teachers, he declares that his teachings are *the glory of him who obeys, and shame of him who fails to keep them.*[29]

Ptah-hotep's wise sayings were one of the sources later used in the international wisdom traditions through which wise sayings were later exchanged between sages of the major Mediterranean powers in the Axial Period, circa 600 B.C. This is exemplified in imagery, which is contained in both biblical narrative as well as the re-enactment of these themes in Egyptian literature. Consider the following examples, Utterance 305: *A King climbs to the sky on a ladder*:

A ladder is knotted together by Re before Osiris, a ladder is knotted together by Horus before his father Osiris when he goes to his spirit, one of them being on the side and one of them being on that side, while I am between them.[30] (Gen 37).

Utterance 437: A *'resurrection' text*:

Awake for Horus! Arise against Seth! Raise yourself as Osiris, as a spirit, the son of Geb, his first-born! You arise as Anubis who is on the baldachin, the Ennead tremble at you, the three-day festival is celebrated for you, you are pure for the New

Moon, your appearing is for the monthly festival, the Great Mooring-post calls to you as to Him who stands up and cannot tire, who dwells in Abydos[31] (Psalms 68, 48).

Utterance 481: *A summons to the ferryman*:

I ferry across in order that I may stand on the east side of the sky in its northern region among the Imperishable Stars, who stand at their staffs and sit(?) at their East; I will stand among them, for the Moon is my brother, the Morning Star is my offspring; put your hand on me, that I may live.[32] (Isa. 66:14–23), Ezek. 28, Isa. 14, Isa. 9, Rev. 3).

Utterance 619: *A resurrection text*:

Your face is that of a jackal, your middle is that of the Celestial Serpent, your hinder-parts that a broad hall; a stairway has been set up to the sky that you may ascend and give judgment between the two great gods, (even) you whom the Two Enneads support.[33] (Gen. 3:15, Rev. 13).

Even with a cursory review of the Egyptian and the Hebraic material contained throughout the biblical canon, it is impossible not to notice the common themes that run throughout both cultures. Major themes containing serpents, ladders to the heavens, festivals and new moons, new heavens and new earth[34], death and Hades[35], the east side northern region with the morning star, the sleeping of deity, the departures, hymns of praise,[36] sacred marriages, and a reborn kingship with a new staff, indicate a universal literary tradition in which major enactments were retold within each culture with a localized application.

It is quite possible that the early kings, who were sovereigns over *Kiprat-arbat* or "Four Races," which are called *Arba Lisum* or "Four Tongues," which belonged to the great varieties of human speech, the Hamitic, Semitic, Arian, and Turanian. Is it possible these language groups have preserved the universal themes that began in Eden and passed them down to their own local economies where they would take on a local type character and application?[37]

> It is the simplest and the best interpretation of this passage (Gen. 10-8) to understanding it as asserting that the four races—the Egyptians, Ethiopians, Libyans, and Canaanites—were ethnically connected, being all descended from Ham; and further, that the primitive people of Babylon were a subdivision of one of these races, namely of the Cushites or Ethiopians, connected in some degree with the Canaanites, Egyptians, and Libyans, but still more closely with the people which dwelt anciently upon the Upper Nile.[38]

Various scholars since Rawlingson have attempted to reconstruct the origins of the Genesis account of man contained in the Semitic documents. By the time of Abraham, the four kings are correspondent to a fourfold ethnic division, Cushite, Turanian, Semitic, and Arian. The languages respectively represent the four families of human speech.[39] It is believed by many researchers today, that the Great Semitic Mother Tongue is the basis for transmitting literary information into the Sumar documents and later, to the Ugarit and Akkadian and other Semitic language groups, which would have transferred the information contained in the Genesis account to the Hebrew nation, with other universal traditions applying elements of these traditions to pertain to their own origins.

The Wisdom Schools

Modern scholarship has been divided regarding the question of which one of the wisdom schools came first and influenced all the others. For example, did Egyptian education have a major influence in Israel's literary development or, as many conservative commentators suggest, did Israel later influence Egypt?

> A perhaps even more striking vindication of the possible priority of much Bible material over the sources from which it is supposed to have come is the discovery by Drioton that a famous monument of Egyptian Wisdom literature, which is supposed to have been the source and inspiration of Hebrew Wisdom literature, "is actually an indifferent Egyptian translation from a Semitic–Hebrew original . . . This would be the 'Words of the Wise' on which Proverbs also subsequently drew." The idea that the Babylonians and Egyptians might be dependent on the Hebrews for ideas found in the Bible instead of the other way round is indeed a revolutionary one.
>
> It is interesting that the Hebrew remains, though not scarce, do not have the impact that the foreign materials do. The Lachish Letters, containing eyewitness accounts of the desperate state of things in the land of Jerusalem . . . have excited far less comment that the elephantine Papyri, which show us a Jewish community living far up the Nile, whither they had fled for safety, possibly at the destruction of Jerusalem.[40]

The Lachish Letters provide documentation of early Hebrew settlements far up the Nile in Lower Egypt as far back as 600 B.C. in what we call the Axial Period, when all the great cultural and military powers in the Middle East interacted. Therefore, it is entirely possible that this pollination was shared commonly in both directions between the Egyptians and the Hebrews.

> New light upon the origin of certain biblical proverbs, and especially those in 22:17–24:34, has come from the ruins of ancient Egypt. In 1923 Sir Wallis Budge published in the *Second Series of Egyptian Hieratic Papyri* an Egyptian wisdom book, entitled,

The Teaching of Amenemope, which may be dated about 1000 B.C. It is divided into thirty chapters and consists of popular proverbs. From a writing-tablet preserved in the Turin Museum, we know that it was used as a text-book in the Egyptian schools twenty-five hundred years ago. The most interesting fact, however, is that nine of these proverbs are, as Professor Adolph Erman has pointed out in the May, 1924, report of the Prussian *Academie der Wissenschaft,* almost word for word identical with maxims found in the biblical Book of Proverbs. Seven of these are in the appendices in Proverbs 22:17–24:34, indicating that these later collections were probably made by a Jew living in Egypt during the Greek period, who drew freely from the famous *Wisdom of the Egyptians.*[41]

Charles Foster Kent has produced evidence that shows a possible early Hebraic influence upon Egypt's wisdom traditions and later, during the Greek recensions, of Egyptian literature. Hebrew copyists in Egypt imported this influence back to the Hebraic wisdom traditions.

However, it was Adolf Erman who pointed out precise parallels that could not be accidental. "Almost every verse in Prov. xxii. 17–xxiii.14 finds its fellow in the Egyptian didactic work. Quite a few sentences are essentially the same in the Egyptian treatise and in its Biblical Counterpart. In the opening verse of the corresponding section of Proverbs, the Hebrew text reads: 'Incline thine ear and hear my word,/And apply thine ear to lean [them].' Amenemope reads: 'Give thine ear, hearken to the things I have said,/Give thy heart to understand them.' "

A thorough study of Amenemope even enabled Erman to correct an obscurity in the Bible. A word previously rendered as "excellent things" has always been considered doubtful, the Hebrew alternative offered was "formerly" (*shilshom*) or, as Hebrew scribes have suggested in the margin, "officers" (*shalishim*)—but neither made too much sense. The word, as we now know, is "thirty" (*sheloshim*), a reference to the number of chapters in Amenemope, which are paralleled by the thirty precepts given in the corresponding Hebrew text.[42]

The theme of "thirty" chapters or divisions providing a literary unit is a common structure throughout the Near East.[43] In like fashion, the proverb was an international wisdom saying that was used during the discourse of philosopher kings. The greatest of these philosopher kings was Solomon, who originated more than three thousand of his own wisdom sayings and psalms whose streams of royal, judicial, and literary wisdom encompassed Egyptian parallels contained in the Egyptian tax system as well as twelve administrative districts (1 Kings 3:11). Even his marriage to the Phaoroh's daughter was patterned after an Egyptian marriage ceremony.[44] Later, in the royal Davidic theology around 2100, fragments of royal inscriptions have been found in which we read *Merikare* ascended to the throne and there is little doubt the Davidic court enhanced the establishment of order, justice, and truth by the waving of an olive branch with a final day of retribution on the Day of Judgment.[45]

However, this is far from all of his literary compositions. Plato writes of an encyclopedia, which Solomon originated, which dealt with the history of animals and natural phenomenon. For this knowledge the other philosopher kings, such as Salmon of Greece, sought Solomon's counsel.[45] And in this international wisdom school were types of proverbs similar to the Hebraic genre. A very common type of proverb or wisdom saying is found in Proverbs 14:10, which is the type of proverb that has assertions of value. These proverbs are based on life's experiences, such as "The heart knows its own bitterness." It is crucial to recall that these types of proverbs possess negative and positive values to the topics in this genre. For example, marriage may be viewed as a positive as well as a negative in the same text as a contrast. Therefore, this wisdom saying has its own value system. Such a contrast also exists in the status of women, in which we have the "good" woman, "bad" woman syndrome where the "bad" woman shuns wisdom, leads an immoral life, and corrupts her son and, at the end of this document, the wise woman is held in high esteem by her husband and the wise elders at the gates of the city.[47]

> First of all, the theme of wisdom contrasted with folly continues with great consistency throughout the other discourses in chs. 1 to 9, and in slightly varying form, in chs. 10 to 31. . . . The effect of using one set of imagery serves to intensify the struggle between the way of wisdom and the way of folly. Wisdom like folly is active, aggressive and persistent. Both offer the rewards of happiness and pleasure. Yet one leads to life and one to death.[48]

One of the most common type of proverbs in Middle Eastern literature employs a quadripartite model. "A *valuational topic or its opposite is combined with a second valuational topic or its opposite* in a series of *binary propositions,* until the (four) logical possibilities have been exhausted."[49] These proverbs/wisdom sayings also contained literary cadences for oral readings, with repetitive themes of one, three, and seven, and as the stanza is repeated, the cadence is established for full dramatic effect.

Common Traditions of Literary Development

It was also common for different canons of literature to draw upon a single source. It is commonly believed that the Egyptian wisdom traditions, with the Book of the Dead, drew from the same sources as the Pyramid Text, which was believed to have been a common source from the first dynasty.

From the time of Joseph's governorship in Egypt and the rising of the Hebrew people to national prominence until the time of the expulsion of the Hyksos (the Shepherd Kings) c. 1570 B.C.E. by Ahmose I, it does appear that the Hebrews achieved some influence over the affairs of Egypt. Cyrus Gordon states, "The Hyksos consisted of a mixed multitude, including many Semites along with other Asiatic elements."[50] It would be difficult for any objective researcher to deny that during the reign of the Hyksos/Shepherd Kings over Egypt, who may have been Hebrew and other Semitic peoples, cultural influences would have been interchanged between Joseph and his descendants and the Egyptians they ruled.

To date we have no conclusive documentation to show exactly who the Hyksos/Shepherd Kings actually were. Some scholars believe the Hyksos consisted only of the descendants of the sons of Joseph. They are attempting to show there may have been a point in time when the Hebrew kings ruled over parts of the nation of Egypt. Cyrus Gordon states the Shepherd Kings consisted in part of Semitic peoples possibly including the Hebrews in the Semitic milieu. However, no conclusive evidence has been documented. All that is generally documented regarding the identity of the Shepherd Kings is the document entitled "The War Against the Hyksos,[51]" which identifies a 'miserable Asiatic', a self-proclaimed ruler to whom the letter is addressed. This letter does not identify by name any king or person who would make a definite connection to Joseph and his descendants. However, scholars such as Gaston Maspero and A.H. Sayce do show the literature of Phoenicia and Chaldea did have considerable Semitic influence over the Egyptian literary traditions as well as a major role played by the Assyrian.[52]

Scholars of history are becoming increasingly aware of the fact that many migrations of Greeks and Hebrews occurred as they were accepted as immigrants to help elevate the status of the Egyptian dynasty. Therefore, historically, scholars do see a cultural blend in Egypt whereby the three main cultures would assimilate into a dominant culture in Egypt. Then as that culture, Egypt, impacted surrounding nations, it would carry with it the elements of the cultures they had assimilated.

> The first Ptolemies had a great need for Greek soldiers, officials, inventors, craftsmen and other specialists, so that they favoured immigration. The political freedoms of the *polis,* which had become increasingly more questionable after Alexander, even in the mother country, were replaced by the economic advantages of belonging to a superior class and the possibility of alliance with *politieumata* of fellow-countrymen, in which a Greek way of life could be followed even in barbarian surroundings. On precisely this point, the Jews in the Greek-speaking Diaspora were their apt imitators; they too allied together in *politeumata,* where synagogues took the place of the gymnasium (see ppl. 65ff. below) as the centre of their communal life.[53]

By the third century B.C., during the time of the translation of Septuagint (LXX "seventy"), Alexandrian scribes were gathering Hebraic literature as well as borrowing from all the other known literary traditions, so that Alexandria would have key role as a place of learning as well as to be a place where schoolmen could come and study Classical Greek, the language that they used to translate the Hebraic Old Testament. The library's store of the world's literature was vast.

> "Four hundred thousand books were burned at Alexandria." . . .The conflagration was widespread; . . . and the stores of books; and these books, it is said, in vast numbers and of great value. . . . The words of Ammianus Marcellinus are plain enough; he speaks of Alexandria's priceless libraries, about which ancient writers agree that the 700,000 volumes got together by the unremitting care of the Ptolemies were destroyed by fire.[54]

It is at this juncture in history when the scribes in Alexandria were endeavoring to translate literature from Egyptian as well as Hebrew and other languages into Greek in order to preserve their literary traditions.

> The fact may, however, be regarded as certain, that prior to the year 285 B.C., the Septuagint version had been commenced, and that in the reign of Ptolemy Philadelphus, either the books in general or at least an important part of them had been completed. . . . The basis of truth, which appears to underline this story, seems to be, that it was an Egyptian king who caused the translation to be made, and it was from the Royal Library at Alexandria that the Hellenistic Jews received the copies which they used.[55a,b]

Historically speaking, there has been a larger Egyptian/ Coptic literary tradition that has influenced biblical translations and interpretations from the time of the translation of the Septuagint until and including the interpretations of the Coptic early church fathers. Among the most influential of these church fathers was Origen, to whom Epiphanius, bishop of Salamis, ascribed the authorship of over six thousand books, tracts, and treatises. Some were major in size and influence. Thus Origen's students must have collaborated in his literary traditions:

> One of Origen's principal contributions appeared under the title of *Hexapla* (Greek 'sixfold'). The *Hexapla* comprised the complete text of the Old Testament in both Hebrew and Greek. Origen gathered together the famous four Greek versions of Aquila of Ponus, Symmnachus of Samaria, and the Septuagint in both the original and the revised version of Theodotin. Origen was thoroughly acquainted with all of these second-century works. He arranged them in six parallel columns, probably on papyrus, a perishable organic material, as neither parchment nor paper was yet in use, which accounts for the work's disappearance. Begun at Alexandria in the early decades of the third

century, the unfinished collation of the *Hexapla* was taken by Origen in one of his exiles to Caeserea where he completed his monumental undertaking before the middle of the century. Fragments of it were gleaned by F. Field in his work *Originis Hexaplorum Quae Supersunt* (2 vols., 1867–1875); but the fifth column of the Septuagint survived in toto in a Syriac translation by Paul, Jacobite bishop of Tella in Mesopotamia, in 616–617.[56]

During the days of Origen, Christianity had become the dominant religion in Egypt, thus Coptic Christianity had its own literary traditions, apocraphal/loggia sayings of Jesus as well as apocalyptic traditions. St. Jerome cited the Hesychian Bible Recension that was completed by the Egyptian Bishop Hesychius just a few years prior to the issuing of the Edict of Milan in A.D. 313. The Hesychian recension must have been used by biblical scribes and scholars of the fourth century A.D.[57]

Modern Coptic scholarship is still in its infancy. Hopefully, the future will unveil large volumes of valuable information. Currently, a large library found near the Naghumati site, including a corpus of literature of the Coptic Church Fathers, is being translated. The scholarly implications are that no longer will we need to rely exclusively on the Latin Church Fathers, but future generations of scholars; and researchers will have a much larger volume of literature to compare the entire corpus of Church Fathers' writings from Egyptian sources as well as Latin. Included in the millieu is a growing body of evidence, such as the Lachish Letters that show a Hebraic influence on Egyptian culture and literature.

The Middle Eastern Abraham Traditions

The literary traditions of the Old Testament patriarchs abound as well, as in the Egyptian catacombs, stories regarding

Abraham's journeys and education being completed in Egypt are found. In 1927, Hittite documents were translated to show that Abraham and a large caravan of servants went to Syria (in the Accadian inscriptions Uri, or Accad or Northern Babylonia), later to Haran (a city of Mesopotamia which was the ancient seat of the worship of the moon god, Sin, and whose caravan roads led to Syria and Palestine), and rescued Lot from the nine-nation conflict, which, according to Josephus, was in Assyria.[58] Scholars of the Semitic accounts have had difficulties in harmonizing the origin of Abraham's travels based on the existence of two Babylonian cities, Uru in southern Babylonia and Uri in northern Babylonia, from which he would have had his origins.[59] Other Egyptian traditions suggest that Abraham ascended into the very face of God to receive his calling. Extrabiblical sources contain many larger elements of the traditions of Abraham not recorded in the Genesis account. These sagas are found in pseudipigraphal documents, such as the Testament of Abraham and apocraphyl commentaries, such as the Genesis Apocraphan as well as the Samaritan text.

Another source of Abraham legends is the rabbinical commentary entitled Genesis Rabah from circa 400 A.D., which is also a prominent commentary in the Babylonian Talmud. In this commentary, God is the passionate but tragic hero, always caring about what the people are doing. In this dramatic cycle of redemption brought by Abraham, Isaac, and Jacob and the descendants of Israel, we find a rich and rewarding abundance in a deeply human encounter between God and humanity.

> God's interest, the sages who read Genesis insist, is in finding the good in humanity. Hence God does whatever can be done to give humanity the occasion for gaining God's grace.[60]

These myths tell of Abraham educating the Egyptian court in astronomy (as attested to by Josephus) and the writings and the drama of creation from books such as Enoch and his great-grandfather Shem, who, in Jewish tradition, was claimed to be Melchisidek from whom Abraham received his priestly instruction. These documents also contain sagas of Abraham being thrown into a fiery furnace for his refusal to worship idols, like unto Shadrach, Meshach, and Abednego, as is found in the traditions of Daniel. These traditions tell us Abraham opposed the child-sacrificing rites, which were practiced in Haron and therefore, Nimrod and Terah sought to sacrifice Abraham.

These sagas are based on traditions that originated in Ethiopia, the Mandean texts of Persia, ancient Jewish and Christian documents, the Apocalypse of Abraham from the Dead Sea Scrolls and the Samaritan Pentateuch. All contain different explanations regarding the sacrifice of Isaac not being commanded by Yahweh but by Moloch, the fire god of child sacrifice, due to the fact that Yahweh was always against such practices (Deut. 18).

Regarding the Abraham and Sarah saga, apocryphal literature states that Yahweh, in a dream, revealed to Abraham that he was to state to Pharaoh that Sarah was his sister instead of his wife; otherwise, Abraham would be killed and Sarah taken into the harem. It is interesting to note here that the main elements of this story and the Ugaritc Krt text follow the common ritual pattern of Palestine and Egypt. Aside from the issues of romantic love being one of the special marks of the patriarchal narratives, we have the recurrence of a ritual love triangle, such as the case of Hagar, who sought to supplant Sarah in Abraham's household. The issue is one of authority, for as Josephus puts it, Hagar sought precedence over Sarah; she was told by an angel to return to her "rulers" or else—perish.

Scholars have overlooked the ritual foundation of Abraham's marriage with Keturah, albeit that this marriage may have no historical credibility. The name of Keturah enjoys a prominent place in the Adonis ritual cycles of Phoenicia and Syria.

As Gray points out in his study of Krt, these ritual events could very well have become history when the sacrifices and marriages were repeated at "the accession of each new king" and "at royal weddings." Furthermore, in the seemingly uncomplimentary, if not actually, degrading position of Abraham (and, later, Isaac) in the affairs with Pharaoh and Abimelech, the indispensable element of the year-drama is portrayed: the temporary humiliation of the true king while a rival and substitute displaces him on the throne and in the queen's favor. We see both Abraham and Isaac in the roles of substitute kings or "Suffering Servants."

The humiliation of the rightful king before his return to the throne is a central episode of the great new year rituals throughout the Ancient East. Additionally, the Suffering Servant is the true king during the period of his ritual humiliation, representing his death; at the time his place is taken by a pretender, who is exposed as the *real* substitute when the time for his death arrives. The queen plays quite a different role: she is ageless and immortal, the Mother Earth itself, taking a new spouse at each cycle of renewal and disposing of the old one.[61]

The theme of the Suffering Servant, in which the king is humiliated, was repeated again in the writings of Isaiah's Servant Songs, in which new imagery is employed with metaphors, such as a lamb being led to the slaughter and "he opened not his mouth." This further illustrates the fact that Isaiah was familiar with the imagery of a humiliated king as well as the Opening of the Mouth Rite. These events show that Gray's analysis is correct when the humiliated king in his love triangle is restored to the queen at the royal wedding, thus making the completed ritual an act of history.

Some objections by traditional scholars have been raised at the late dating and true antiquity regarding the origin of these documents and the authenticity of the stories depicted. However, it should be understood that the late origin of these documents corresponds to the dating of much of our biblical corpus of literature and would correlate with its dating. It is well known by Middle Eastern scholars that an oral line of transmission is contained within many apocalyptic books dating from circa 200 B.C. to circa A.D. 100. Interestingly enough, these dates also correspond with the dating of the Dead Sea Scrolls at Qumran. Modern Jewish opinion is shifting from Moses being the father of Jewish nation to the tradition of the fathers, such as Abraham, Isaac, and Jacob actually giving birth to the Jewish nation and faith. Traditionally Abraham has been regarded the father of the nation and Moses the father of the faith.

Let us consider then the nursing father, Moses, who was also educated in the very court of Pharaoh (see Exod. 2:10, Acts 7:22) and later, in the plains of Midian under the direction of Jethro, priest of Midian. Legends of Abraham and Moses are paramount in the Egyptian Hypocephali in which the Egyptian god Ra with the appearance of Osiris are depicted with full and complete faces after their incarnation and with ascension to full deity. In these legends stories abound regarding Moses and Abraham appearing before the great god to be commissioned for their life's calling and destiny. This theme is borrowed in the New Testament from the apocryphal work, The Ascension of Moses and the Book of Enoch, and is cited in the Book of Jude (v. 9).

Much scholarly debate has ensued over this literary borrowing and citation from the Ascension of Moses and the Books of Enoch. Some critics feel this citation proves the apocryphal statements contained in this document are correct and Moses did ascend into heaven at his death while other theologians will say this is an apocryphal addition to Deuteronomy 34 and the writer of Jude may have believed these statements regarding the ascension of Moses, but the statement in John 3:13 would carry the ultimate authority stating, "No man has ascended unto the heaven but the Son of Man which has come down from heaven." This verse would serve as the governing text regarding the origin of the Messiah and the necessity of man to wait for a resurrection to inherit eternal life, but in triangulating both of these points of view, we must conclude that the evidence suggests that early New Testament writers shared both views. It is also interesting to note that verses 14–15 of this same document, Jude, borrows from the Book of Enoch as stated earlier, regarding final judgment and the coming of the servants of the Lord.

As previously indicated, the legends of Abraham and Moses carried a great deal of influence among nations of the Near East. These traditions were also known in the Ethiopian Jewish sect of the Nabatieans, which was a sect of black Jewish converts that existed in Ethiopia. They carried with them the teachings of pre-rabbinic Judaism, and many centuries later, the preaching of Philip to the Ethiopian Eunuch would evangelize many of the descendants of this pre-rabbinnic Jewish sect. In these Ethioptic traditions, the Book of Enoch is most helpful to us in their understanding;

> The Kingdom will last till the close of the tenth-world week, and during it the righteous will enjoy peace and well-being, and see many good days on earth, 91:13–14, 96:8. Then will ensue the final judgment with the destruction of the righteous dead, who have been specially guarded by angels all the hitherto, 100:5, will thereupon be raised, 91:10 92:3, as spirits only, 103:3,4, and the portals of the new heaven will be opened to them, 104:2 and they shall joy as the angels, 104:4, and become companions of the heavenly hosts, 104:6, and shine as the stars for ever, 104:2.[62]

The significance of the numeral 10 in ancient literature is often associated with coming out of tribulation into a perfected state, and by "ten words," a fact was established.[63] The concept of ten words to completion or perfection was known to the writer of the Book of Revelation whereby the Lord cast a church congregation into a sick bed for ten years.

Also, later in rabbinic Judaism, was developed a system that revolved around ten points of Torah, with each point being a teaching or a Torah. Now in the case of the Ten Commandments would be Torah in ten points, a complete summarization regarding the meaning of the whole law. Using the formula of a day/age correlation shows us at the end of the birth pangs during the reign of the Messiah, the creation would finally see its redemption and perfection.

> Here apparently for the first time in Jewish literature appears the equation of each day of Creation week for a thousand years of human history, with its final thousand years of rest. Thus it was both a history of the past and a forecast of the future—a theory which came to play an important role in both early and modern Chiliasm.[64]

Dr. Le Roy Froom explains further in a footnote:

> This six-thousand-year concept for the duration of the world, was not, however, simply Jewish apocalyptic, but was traceable back to paganism. The Zoroastrians in Persia and the Etruscans in Italy believed that the human race was to live six thousand years. Some scholars find evidence of Persian influence in the Jewish apocalyptic and Talmudic writings on this point.[65]

Heavenly Ascent and Platonic Myth

Another concept that was introduced during this time period of Jewish literature was of the prophets ascending into the heavens. Whether or not this term "ascension" applies to the enthronement of a king is highly questionable. But obviously the ideas derived from it were known in the Mediterranean nations of the Near East as a common theme. It is also well understood that today we have only complied a fraction of the text from these ancient documents cited. For example, it was believed the original Book of Enoch may have consisted of at least 366 to 400 chapters. Today the Slavonic Book of Enoch numbers approximately 810 pages from fragments of the Ethioptic text as well as Greek fragments redacted together to form our final text. Some scholarly opinions are:

> In 1960, J. E. H. Thomson could still report that there is still as much disagreement as ever among the experts on the structure of Enoch and the nature and priority of its various parts. C.P. Van Andel reported in 1955 that no overall study of any aspect of the Book of Enoch has ever been undertaken. He gives the Greek Enoch clear priority, since it is intelligible where 1 Enoch is often incomprehensible.[66]

It is also true many of these extra-apocryphal documents are not a part of the deutero-canonical writings and have reached us in fairly modern times, even though they contain a transmission line with stories and tales from much earlier periods of time. Their authenticity is highly questionable. There is also the problem of theological shifts entering the tapestry from this period. Theological modifications took place regarding the state of the dead (Slavonic Enoch 65:9, 10) as well as the eschatological realization of the kingdom of God (8:3–6, 65:9), predestination (23:4–5), the cosmic struggle of good and evil (Persian Zoarastrianism, Slavonic Enoch 42:1 col. b), and the doctrine of eternal punishment (Slavonic Enoch 10:1–6). We have contrasting views regarding these theological subjects in the Syraic Apocalypse of Baruch, death, sleep and resurrection (chapter 21:24; 23:4,5; 54:15), eschatological view of the last things (chapters 24–27, 29) and sleep of the righteous dead until Messiah's return (chapter 30).[67]

Further theological shifts occurred between 3 and 4 Esdras regarding the state of the righteous dead.[68]

> Thus the soul was not distinguished from the body. In biblical Hebrew, *neshamah* and *ru'ah* both mean "breath" and *ne'phesh* to the person or even the body (cf. Num. 6:6).[69a,b]

Neither Hebraic nor Greek cultures originally considered the notion that life could be separate from the body and continue forever, *athanasia,* because all inherited life was the exclusive property of the gods (in Greek culture). In Hebraic tradition, it was the Lord alone who is everlasting (Ps. 90:2) because "all flesh is grass" (Isa. 40:6). Both cultures believed to go to the underworld was to enter the realm of death. Later in subsequent revisions of this doctrine, beginning with Plato (Phaedo 107D–114), death would be seen as a separation of the soul from the body and could exist in paradise or the underworld where it would undergo reward or punishment, separate from the person's existence.[70]

These shifts continued in the writings of the Dead Sea Scrolls in the document of the final battle between the sons of light and the sons of darkness and on into amalgamations of Neoplatonic, Jewish, and Christian theology. Another literary shift was already in progress between the former Wisdom traditions and the increasing use of apocalyptic literature, which was employed by the prophets with an eschatological focus, such as the servant songs of Isaiah, which do show this point of transition. As apocalyptic traditions developed, authors such as Daniel, Enoch, and 4 Ezra developed a style by which a warning and a last days setting before the Lord's intervention would sift the sons of darkness from the sons of light during the time that we call the "Day of the Lord."

> In 4 Esdras 7:50 (cf. 8:1) we read: "The Most High has made not one age, but two"—a basic principle of apocalyptic thinking.

Of these two ages, people know and experience only *this* age, the present, the old, the visible course of the world. It is full of trouble and woe, filled with perils and distresses. It is marked by sorrows and tears. Death rules in it. Discord and injustice fill it. It is called the "age of woes".[71]

A common theme that runs through apocalyptic literature is that mankind is on a downward spiral and cannot be stopped without the Lord's intervention and only an exposition of the knowledge contained in these documents can prevent God's covenant lawsuit from being issued, as in Daniel 12:4" . . . the knowledge; *la connaissance*; RSV: (and) knowledge; NEB; (and) punishment; TOB: (*mais*) *la connaissance*; L: (*und grosse*) *Erkenntnis*"[72]. This linguistic evidence shows us the knowledge referred to in this passage is not worldwide secular knowledge beginning to be discovered in the last days, but rather a bringing forth of the wisdom internally contained in this document, with an apocalyptic warning. Jesus used a similar technique recorded in Matthew's gospel where He makes known the application of the Daniel material in the form of realized eschatalogy to his own generation.

Modern critics of apocalyptic traditions are now including the Olivet discourse in this tradition, as well as the Book of Revelation. This due to the heavy use of the Daniel material found in Matthew's account of the Olivet discourse. Dispensationalists and fundamentalists alike have overstated the apocalyptic relationship between Daniel and Revelation. First, the 404 verses of the Book of Revelation contain citations that are lifted from the entire Old Testament rather than just the corpus of literature found in the Daniel tradition, such as the Bell and the Dragon and other small editions to Daniel. Second, as previously indicated, the olivet discourse stands between the two documents within the apocalyptic tradition.

The Son of Man and the suffering servant themes appear in Daniel's courtroom judgment scene where the Son of Man appears (Dan. 7) as well as the Servant Songs, which are found in Isaiah 53 and show a humiliated Messiah. Dr. Hansen explains:

> It is my tentative judgment that wisdom was wedded to the tradition of apocalyptic eschatology as a part of efforts being made by visionary circles to establish their credentials in the third and second centuries B.C. at a time when prophetic figures were being regarded with a great deal of skepticism and even animosity by many religious leaders. This search for credentials led to pseudonyms borrowed from figures of hoary antiquity, like Enoch and Moses and the construction of history resumes from earliest times down to the eschaton. . . .[73]

In the eschatological process, Abraham was to be an heir over the world. However, in the pseudepigraphal tradition, Abraham is given flight over the nations as he completes his journey into heaven, which has come from Egyptian tradition. This is not supported in the biblical text due to the fact Abraham died at the age of 127 and the Book of Hebrews states, "these all died having not received the promises" (Heb. 11:13). But the pseudepigraphical and biblical text are in agreement in that Abraham saw the city, "which hath foundations, whose builder and maker is God" (Heb. 11:109).

> Thus says the Lord your God, who led you into the promised land, who blessed you more than *than the sand of the sea* and *the star of heaven*. . . . But to you I did not send Death. I did not allow a fatal disease to befall you. I did not permit the sickle of Death to come upon you. I did not allow the nets of Hades to entwine you. . . . And the archangel Michael went down and took Abraham on a chariot of cherubim and lifted him up into the air of heaven and led him onto the cloud, as well as sixty angels. And on the carriage Abraham soared over the entire inhabited world.[74]

There has been much debate regarding the clouds in the earth's atmosphere, meaning to translate or relocate Abraham on the earth to a new location. In a similar fashion do we find the account of Elijah being taken up in a whirlwind. Some theologians argue that the text he should not see death regarding Enoch would imply that there was no death entry into the chronological record as in the case of Melchisedik, "without father, without mother," not being entered into the genealogical table by the scribes being at least a possible explanation. Is it possible that the unknown writer of Hebrews is attempting to demythologize the legends of Abraham by reinterpreting them in the light of historical fact and biblical theology, taking out of this process Abraham and Moses ascending into the heavens similar to the last rite of the assession of a king but leaving that rite for the Messiah, the King of Kings?

Dr. L. E. Froom asserts the following:

> The Apocrypha separate from Scripture, was a unique admixture of fact, fancy and fiction. Truth and error were intermingled. The component books included not only historical and literary treatises but a collection of apocalyptic missives brought forth by mystics and seers, and left on record for the centuries. Some of Jews accepted them as canonical, others rejected them as noncanonical and apocryphal. But they were neither forbidden nor suppressed.[75]

Some scholars suggest that the Egyptian god called "Aten," one of the gods among the Nabatieans of Syria, opens the way to understand the divine name of Exodus 6:3, which Dr. C. J. Wenham defended positively in 1980. His contemporary, J. A. Motyer, states that the divine name was one that denoted character. Both views advance the concept of the divine name predating Moses.[76] Another group similar in belief and custom to the Nabatieans were the Falasha.[77] With the divine name of the mountain god predating Moses and the monotheistic belief of Imhotep of Egypt, it's not surprising to note that other biblical figures appear in Egyptian literature. Hugh Nibley observes the following:

> In the Egyptian version of the 'lion-couch' drama, the resurrection motif was paramount. The sacrifices of Isaac and Abraham, apart from typifying the Atonement, were also foreshadowings of the Resurrections. There are persistent traditions in each case that the victim actually was put to death, only to be resurrected on the spot. We have seen in the Abraham stories, how, when no knife cut his throat, he was catapulted into the fire, which thereupon was transformed into a blooming bower of delicious flowers and fruits amid which Abraham sat enjoying himself in angelic company. This at once calls to mind the image found in numerous (and very early) Oriental seals and murals of the revived or resurrected king sitting beneath an arbor amid the delights of the feast of the New Year. St. Jerome cites a Jewish belief that Abraham's rescue from the altar was the equivalent of a rebirth or resurrection. It is Abraham who leads out in the resurrection: "After the things," says the Testament of Judah (25:1), "shall Abraham and Isaac and Jacob arise unto life, and I (Judah) and my brethren shall be chiefs of the tribes of Israel."[78]

For decades commentators have debated who was the angel who visited Abraham and wrestled with Jacob. Was it Yahweh Himself or was it His mediator? Much confusion is due to the fact that in the post-exilic period one group in Israel had accepted the fusion of El Elyon and Yahweh. When Yahweh had become El Elyon, his roles were filled by other angels. Many scholars refer to this process as the retirement of the gods. During this time, Yahweh was seen as very distant and angels were being overtaken by pagan deities, along with the triumph of monotheism, whereby the local gods were defeated in war (along with the local kingdom) and the victorious god became the ruling deity. The defeated gods were relegated to the stature of lower angels or demons or were extinguished altogether, their powers and characteristics being absorbed into the victorious god.

> Several crucial texts in the Hebrew Bible which mention angels have become obscure; at other places the Greek, which was thought to have introduced newly fashionable angels into the text, has been shown to have kept an earlier Hebrew now recovered at Qumran. The problem now is to account for the disappearance of the angels, not for their appearance. It seems that their demise was one of the results of the development of monotheism.[79]

The Divine Agency of the Exalted Patriarchs

As we become familiar with Middle Eastern deities and their relationships to their watchers and messengers and prophets, it is easy to ascertain a divine relationship that originates from the prophet or messenger following the divine prescription. This makes the messenger a divine instrument or agent and thus, as an angel or watcher or messenger may be a part of the Divine Council that surrounds the ultimate deity,

> In Hebrew, Phoenician, and Canaanite sources, "The council of the gods met to decree the fate of both gods and humans." It was not only a royal court, but a judicial court or quasi-legislative assembly. Thus in 1 Kings 22:17–23, the Lord, speaking before the council, decrees the death of Ahab. In Isaiah 6, surrounded by angelic hosts, the Lord calls the prophet Isaiah and declares the impending doom of Judah. And Isaiah's experience has a clear parallel in Ugaritic or Canaanite mythology: "Keret seems to have participated in the divine assembly, much as the prophet Isaiah in his inaugural oracle saw the proceedings in Yahweh's

> cosmic temple and took part in its actions." In Judges 5:23, we read the condemnation of Meroz, delivered by an angel, for his failure to send an army to the aid of Israel. In Zechariah 3:1–10, an angel of Yahweh, as messenger of the council, proclaims the high priest Joshua free of iniquity. Job 1:6–12 and 2:1–6 record the decision made by Yahweh before the council to allow the testing of Job.[80]

In many other instances, Yahweh addresses the council in the royal court in dealing with the creation of man, and later confounding man's languages as well as testing His servant, Job and on other occasions, Yahweh issues a royal proclamation to His divine council when he calls them "sons of God."

> In both Ugaritic and biblical literature, the use of the first person plural is characteristic of address in the divine council. The familiar "we" of Gen. 1:26, "Let us make man in our image. . . ." Gen. 3:22, "Behold the man is become as one of us . . .," and Gen. 11:7, "Come let us go down and let us confound their language . . .," has long been recognized as the plural address used by Yahweh in his council.[81]

In Near Eastern literature, the term "sons of God" may apply to the heavenly or messengers or, indeed, humans, as in son of the king or a descendant from a divine ruler who executes judgment as a divine right.

> "Divine being" rendered literally would be "a son of a god," that is, in Semitic idiom, a member of the class "gods." Such a polytheistic designation is quite appropriate on the lips of Nebuchadnezzar. They . . . are in any case well known in the Hebrew Bible—for example, Genesis 6; Ps. 29:1; cf. Psalm 82; Deut. 32:8. This designation is obviously rooted in New Eastern polytheistic mythology. In Jewish and Christian tradition, the "sons of God" are treated as angels; thus Dan. 3:28 attributes

> the deliverance of the youths to an angel, and the Greek version describes the descent of an angel into the furnace.[82]

This would explain the fact why the word *bene eloim* is so universally applied to God as well as His divine council. In the case of Psalm 82:6, some scholars suggest the plural usage denotes judges while other scholars such as Mitchell Dahood suggest the plurality applies to pagan deities.

> The psalmist had been under the impression that the pagan deities were of some importance, but now realizes that they are nothing, because they are quite incapable of defending the poor and rescuing the downtrodden. . . . *Yet you shall die.* Because of their unconcern for the less privileged, the gods of the surrounding nations have been stripped by God of their immortality.[83]

Notice the phrase *you shall die like men,* which is often used by conservative theologians to suggest that these were divine judges, but the text says *die like men,* not that these divine messengers from the divine council were men. This further exemplifies the "retirement of the gods" concept. But the designation *son of God* would apply to all of God's children.

> The New Jerusalem Bible say that "We are all his children." . . . Likewise, the 1990 Arabic New Testament say of God that we are his *Ana* ("children"). The Modern Hebrew New Testament, using a word derived from the root meaning "to beget," also says that we are God's "children" (*yeladim*). . . . The 1950 Arabic Catholic New Testament, published in Beirut, says that we are God's *dhurriyya,* which means that we are his "progeny," "descendants," children, or "offspring." The 1972 Turkish Bible uses precisely the same word (in its Turkicized form [*zurriyef*]), with precisely the same meaning. Western versions have used analogous language. Deploying a word obviously cognate

with the term *genos*, the 1556 Latin translation, prepared by the Calvinist Theodore Beza, says that we are the *progenies* of God. We are also *progenie di Dio,* or "God's progeny," according to the 1914 Italian Bible. This is the same word that the University of Chicago's Constantine Trypanis chooses to translate *genos* in the original passage of Aratus's astronomical poem *Phaenonmena,* from which Paul was quoting.

The 1991 Hebrew translation of the Bible Society in Israel says that we are God's *se'sa'im,* using the common modern Hebrew word for "descendants." The popular-language German translation of the New Testament entitled *Die Gute Nachricht satsm "Von ihm stammen auch wir ab"* ("We also descend from him"). The roughly equivalent modern-language Spanish New Testament entitled *Dios Liega al Hombre,* straightforwardly indicated "*Somos familia de Dios*" ("We are the family of God").

Martin Luther's historic German Bible renders Acts 17:28 as "*Wir sind seines Geschlects*" ("We are of his race"). . . . Konstantin Rosch's early twentieth-century Catholic New Testament concurs with Luther, explaining that "*Wir sind von seinem Geschlect*" (i.e., again, "We are of his race"), "*von Gottes Geschlect*" ("Of God's race"), as does the 1958 translation by Rupert Storr ("*Sind wir doch seines Gesschechtes*"), which proceeds, like Luther's to speak of our "divine race" ("*Sind wir nun so hottlichen Geschlechtes*"). . . . The relatively recent *Einheitsubersetzung,* which takes its name from the fact that it represents a collaborative effort on the part of the Roman Catholics and the major Protestant denominations of Germany, Austria and Switzerland, renders the passage even more strikingly; "*Wir sind von seiner Art,*" it says, which means, "We are of his type," or "We are of his kind.". . . "*Car nous sommes aussi de sa race,*" says the original Jerusalem Bible, as produced by the Ecole Biblique, which reads in the following verse that we are "*de la race de Dieu*": "We are of his race . . . of the race of God."[84]

With this overwhelming evidence just presented, is it any wonder why Peter stated "we are offspring of God" (2 Pet. 1:4) as well as Our Lord Jesus Christ in John 10:22, when he exclaimed "ye are gods," for you are "children of the Most High." In light of present-day research, it is shown that some Jewish thinkers and other cultures believed man was directly descended from his Maker in heaven and special rights and priestly blessings were passed through a sacradotal system.[85] Although the name *Yahweh* is a causitive Hebrew verb, which is translated, "He caused to be" denotes in a few instances sons of God to be born either as offspring or by the New Covenant method of adoption.[86]

> These are terms which indicate familial or blood relationships, such as father and brother—the name Abijah means—"YHWH is my father" (1 Kings 14:11) and Ahijah means "YHWH is my brother," (1 Kings 11:29)—but they are not Israel's primary way of referring to the deity.[87]

The primary methodology used in Israel's relationship to Yahwah was through the initiation of blood covenants, which brought the Israelite or the Gentile into a patriarchial and familial relationship with God. The literal offspring concept was one of general Semitic acceptance.

Later in salvation history, the father to son patriarchial blessings were broadened to include all the holy people whom God has consecrated for His purposes. Over the centuries this theology has been weakened in the West by modern evangelicals. Paul's uses the term "adoption" to show that we are adopted into the family of God as Sons of God,[88] due to the re-establishment of our citizenship (Phil. 3:20, πολιτευμα the *condition, or life, of a citizen*),[89] rather than simply being Gentiles converted into the House of Faith. Many theologians believe that Genesis 5:3 teaches that man lost his original image and sonship and the only hope of restoration that mankind has is in Christ with His plan of redemption. In Orthodox Christianity it is believed that on the human side of glorification, the saints can receive a deification (*theosis*)[90] through the Holy Spirit due to the change in our aberrant nature, a position that originated with the Greek Fathers.[91]

Church historian Philo believes Moses is deified in the sense that Moses was blessed with a special measure of divine qualities. Dr. Larry Hurtado explains:

> Moses is the supreme example of the highest kind of attunement to God-Philo draws upon Deut. 5:31 and other Old Testament passages to make his point. Philo takes Deut. 5:31 to mean that God makes 'worthy the man (*ho spoudaios*) sharer of His own Nature (*tes heautou physeos*), which is repose (*eremias*)' (Sac. 28). A similar point is made in *Gig. 49*, also by reference to Deut. 5:31. Clearly Deut. 5:31 was a favorite text of Philo's both for exalting and presenting his view of spirituality.[92]

Notice Philo's use of the deification of a patriarch as he grows in the nature of Yahweh. This was an ancient expression, grammatically showing one object becoming another by adopting its attributes. In Isaiah, we see Yahweh as a bird or man becoming god while he runs without fainting or a man flying as an eagle, which is a zoopromorphism. In other cases, Yahweh is referred to as a mother hen hovering over waters, or Jesus states he would have gathered Jerusalem as a hen gathers her chicks. Anthropomorphic expressions, in which God is given the temperament and characteristics of men, are as follows; in the Psalms, God sleeps, He refuses to hear the cry of His people, He journeys, He is jealous or angry. This is the opposite of man rising to the level of God.

The Semitic hierarchies of gods and goddesses have always a male deity at the top of the pyramid.

> According to the belief, El-or, as we shall most often refer to him in the paper, El—was the creator-god. (Evidence strongly

suggests that he was the original chief god of the Semites generally.) As creator, however, he also stood at the head of the pantheon as the "father of the gods" or the "father of the sons of God" (*abu bani ili*) and was called the "ancient one," the "patriarch," and the "eternal one." Consequently, the gods, as his sons, were designated collectively as "the sons of El." El was also called "the Father of Man" (*'abu 'adami*). A Phoenician incantation from the seventh century B.C., found at Arslan Tash in Upper Syria, depicts the father-god sitting, as it were, with his divine consort and their children:

> The Eternal One has made a convenant oath with us,
> Asherah has made (a pact) with us.
> And the sons of El,
> And the great council of all the Holy Ones.[93]

The Sumarian documents and king list reveal genealogical lists from the "deep waters of the flood" back to *Adamu's* war with the Semitic god *Shutu* in the land of *Edin* where *Adamu* warred against the god, *Shutu,* who had created him. After this conflict, *Adamu* was tried before *Shutu* for a heinous offense and sin of a casting down and maiming of a divinity.[94] Biblical genealogies along with Semitic king lists must have been available during the compilation of the Book of Genesis due to the fact that colophons were summaries taken from existing tablets and condensed into a single statement by the biblical writer or priestly redactors.[95]

The biblical writers understood Yahweh's conquering His opposition as He stood alone as the only true deity worthy of worship. This information could have been drawn from literary traditions of the great Semitic mother tongue that was transferred through the literature of Sumaria and then adopted by the Semitic family of languages and literary traditions. Later, Canaanite religion and temple practices employed these earlier legends and applied them to the cult of Baal worship, which included the death and resurrection of deity based on the agricultural vegetation sabbatical cycle. As concluded by Leo Dueul, "Familiarity with Canaanite texts would possibly reveal borrowings at least as extensive as those made by the Hebrews from Egyptian and Mesopotamian literature."[96]

Today modern scholars, such as Alter and Kermode, are strengthening the link between the Canaanite literature regarding the assembly of the gods and the worship of El in Israel's holy mountain;

> The assembly of the gods is a well-known institution in ancient Near Eastern religion. It is in the assembly of the gods that the decision is taken to punish tumultuous mankind by means of the flood, and in the Babylonian creation epic, it is the assembly that commissions Marduk to defeat Tiamat the sea goddess and her chaotic henchmen; Marduk is elevated to head of the assembly, a sort of *primus inter pares,* after accomplishing this feat. El is described as presiding over the assembly, with Ba'al waiting upon him. The assembly takes place in El's holy mountain, which is not to be confused with Ba'al's Mount Sapunu or *mons Casius*; it was called *m'd*, Hebrew *mo'ed,* "assembly." Even after Ba'al becomes head of the gods, the assembly remains the domain of El. The assembly is mirrored in various forms in the biblical corpus, the most obvious reference being Psalms 82:1, where the gods are described as assembled in the congregation of El. The mountain of the assembly (*har mo'ed*) is also mentioned in Isaiah 14:13, with further reminiscences in Psalms 89:5–8 and 29:1–2, 1 Kings 22:19, and Isaiah 6-1–8. It is before the assembly of the gods that the dramatic scene of Daniel 7:9–14 takes place. The "tent of the assembly," *'ohel mo'ed,* originally partook of this meaning, since this was the place where God was to meet with the children of Israel.[97]

In Semitic tradition, the "El" or "God of the mountain" is found in both Sumerian and Canaanite, as well as Israelite traditions. This male god presided over the other deities of the assembly. Once the people reached the temple on holy ground at the top of the mountain or "great *duku*" to celebrate a cultic meal, this was the location where the *Anunnaki* would present themselves to the people in regards to their decisions.

> The important points to be noted here are that (1) Shamash (the sun-god) was the god of judgment and therefore presided over the divine court; (2) the *duku* is called "a great mountain"; and (3) even the other gods are subjected to judgment there.[98]

Just as at Sinai where seventy elders ate and drank with the God of Israel to show His right to judge the nation, the god who was above all other gods, the same correlation is made with the male mountain god ruling over the divine council and He, alone, having the right to judge the people.

Today many feminist expositors are advancing the notion that prior to 1250 B.C. a pantheon of goddesses existed under the direction of a female god and later, the male-centered warlike Yahweh dethroned her and claimed the worship given her. However, Tikva Frymer-Kensky, a Semitic scholar, states:

> Israel could not pit one god against another, or ask one god to intercede with another, for the core idea of ancient Israel is the exclusive worship of one God. According to the Bible's understanding, Israel owes all its loyalty and worship to the god who brought the people out of Egypt. Until the eighth or seventh century B.C.E., biblical writers did not categorically deny the existence of other gods, But these deities belonged to other nations; for Israel, there is only one YHWH. As we would expect, YHWH, Israel's God, took the supreme position over the pantheon that the young male gods, Baal and Marduk, held in polytheism. Moreover, in the monotheist leap, "He also absorbed all the character and functions of the female goddesses. As a result, the dynamic interaction between the polytheistic gods disappeared into the unity of One.[99]

Expressions of the belief in this monotheistic god with male and female qualities or the one who balances the *Ying* and the *Yang*, or *mercy* and *justice*, or *muthos* and *pathos* is found in most ancient cultures. In the Shang Dynasty, circa 1776–1300 B.C., we find evidence of a belief in a supreme deity.

> The fusion of the *Ti* and *T'ien* traditions evidently occurred during Chou times, as the Lord-on-High, also called Heaven, became recognized by all as a supreme deity, lord of other gods, spirits and deified ancestors called upon in prayer, for blessings and approvals. The character of divine transcendence came into sharper focus. The *personal* character of God was safeguarded, however, in the frequent accounts of prayers addressed to God—either as Lord-on-High or Heaven, or sometimes as both. The *ethical* implications of the belief in God were especially emphasized. God is the source and principle of the moral order, the judge of good and evil. To this Lord, the royal ancestors of the Chou house were clearly subordinate.[100]

As in most traditions, the original doctrines on many subjects become obscured by the later traditions, which replace the earlier teachings. Such is the case with early monotheism, which gave way to animism, forms of reincarnation and ancestor worship. The monotheistic deity and Israelite traditions had a great deal of difficulty defining its monotheistic credos in the midst of polytheistic paganism because of the similar liturgical cycles and new year's coronation rituals, which ran parallel to their pagan neighbors.

The Semitic God and Creation Temple Liturgy

The religion of the Semitic god is one that comes with a cosmic temple ritual signifying creation and cosmic signs of deity dealing with His creation. Ancient temple liturgies show us that accounts of creation were read at the beginning of the sacred new year. The most notable amongst these, and possibly the oldest Egyptian text, is the Shabako Story of creation that may have been a script of a drama wherein certain key scenes were presented by actors as the story was recited and explained to the temple audience by a lecturer/priest. Some have suggested that the creation account of Genesis 1:1–2:4 was used in the temple liturgy of Israel at the New Year's festival before the Babylonian exile. The text of Genesis 1:1 to Genesis 2:4 was read in toto on *Simhat Torah,* the final day of the Feast of Tabernacles by the priest and in part each Friday night to welcome the Sabbath rest, twice during the service and once at *kiddush* to honor the Lord of Creation.[101]

The origin of creation stories and the Sabbath of Genesis have long been a matter of much scholarly debate. It is commonly believed the kingship coronation ceremonies originated in Egypt while the Sabbath has its origin with Yahweh's divine rest given to His people as a divine mandate. The Jewish nation was not the only nation to undertake a form of Sabbath resting. In fact, since the 1880s, scholars have found evidence of other nations resting on their own solemn Sabbath days at their own appointed times. For example, an Egyptian pyramid text reads as follows as the king takes part in the regular festivals " . . . for the festal meal of the sixth day of the month is my breakfast, the festal meal of the seventh day is for my supper."[102] Some Babylonian menologies revealed regularly recurring evil taboo (*ume lemnuti*), which occurred on the 7th, 14th, 19th, 21st, and 28th day of the month.

> But if references to the Fall are few and obscure, there can be no doubt that the Sabbath was an Accadian institution, intimately connected with the worship of the seven planets. The astronomical tablets have shown the seven-day week was of Accadian origin, each day of it being dedicated to the sun, moon, and five

planets, and the word Sabbath itself, under the form of *Sabbattu*, was known to the Assyrians, and explained by them as "a day of rest for the heart." A calendar of Saint's days for the month of the intercalary Elul makes the 7th, 14th, 19th, 21st, and 28th days of the lunar month Sabbaths on which no work was allowed to be done. The Accadian words by which the idea of Sabbath is denoted, literally mean, "a day on which work is unlawful," and are interpreted in the bilingual tablets as signifying "a day of peace" or "completion of labours."[103]

Other Babylonian texts identify the Akkadian term *sab/pattu* with the monthly full moon day. Only during a later period did it develop into a weekly day of rest. Another theory some scholars have advanced is the Kenite theory. This was the teaching that the Israelites simply adopted the Sabbath from Kenite smiths at the time of Moses. Another agricultural thesis suggests the Sabbath was developed on the basis of the *hamultum,* a Babylonian unit of "fifty," constituting a period of time made up of seven weeks plus one day from which a pentecontad calendar was reconstructed. Some scholars have attempted to show this pentecontad calendar was the basis for the general background of early Semitic calendar constructions. However, no definitive proof of any of these theories has ever surfaced to convince the majority of scholars. Some studies have advanced the notion of the origin of the Sabbath in correlation with the number seven in Mesopotamian and Ugaritic text due to the number seven of the recurring week.[104]

Another example of early Sabbath recognition is in the land of Egypt where it is suggested during the reign of the Shepherd Kings called Hyksos who ruled in lower Egypt. From the pyramid writings of the fourth dynasty, we find a great deal of Sabbath information contained in the Queen's chamber.[105] This Sabbath information also calls the Lord, the Creator of all creation. The Jewish Sabbath represents a creation motif, as well as the Lord leading His people by redemption into the new creation (see Isa. 66:22–23) when a new rest will be given in the creation of the new world.

The picture of this new rest is found in the Sabbath Songs of the Dead Sea Scrolls that are a foreshadowing of the Hallelujah Chorus in Revelation 19:1–10 when a new song is sung in a heavenly liturgy to give praise to God for bringing His righteousness and rule into the sacred marriage. This represented in the Hebrew mindset, the act of creation and the rejoicing at the giving of the Torah, and in New Testament theology, the church would rejoice at the giving of the Spirit at the birth of the New Testament Church. As Genesis 1:2 deals with light over darkness, other creation ritual accounts have a pattern of nature prevailing over chaos. Stephen T. Ricks, Dead Sea Scrolls specialist, observes the following:

> Among the documents recovered from this late period are priestly liturgical commentaries, 'order of service' manuals prepared to guide the priest in the proper performance of the lengthy and complex rituals of the *akitu* festival, which lasted through the first twelve days of Nisan, the first month of the Babylonian calendar. On the fourth of Nisan, in the temple of Marduk (the temple serving as a symbol of the ordered cosmos in the ancient Near East), the priest was instructed to read the *Enuma Elish*, the Babylonian creation myth, which recounts the victory of Marduk over the powers of chaos personalized in Apsu and Tiamat and his creation of the world, and concludes with a hymn extolling the kingship of Marduk. In the later states of the festival, the victory of Marduk over Tiamat was ritually reenacted.[106]

Notice the term "ritually reenacted." It has long been held by scholars of liturgical forms that narrated time, which is closely related to liturgical time, is found in the creation liturgical drama, rather than a linear time line of historical events placed in chronological order. The liturgy reenacts the divine drama and liturgical events in with a narrative plot and dramatic action, which condenses the time lines to fit each part of the novella as the acts in the drama are played out. Such is the case with the creation liturgical drama in which the acts of creation are dramatically expressed in acts in each of the seven days of the creation. It has also been assumed that *in the beginning* from the Greek phrase *ex nihilo* implies a sudden creation from nonpre-existence of matter.

However, this view did not enter Orthodox Christianity until the third century A.D. In the ancient mindset, it was commonly understood that deity was the "Great Architect" and the "Master Potter," who crafted His creation in stages until final creation was completed. This fact is also demonstrated by Plato seeing no contradiction between the Genesis account and his treatise *Timaeus,* in which the notion of creation was an organizing of pre-existent matter.[107] This same correlation exists between the Genesis account and the *Qu'ran.*

> The root *bara'a* cognate with the verb *bara'* of Genesis 1:1, occurs almost solely (in the contexts which concern us) in the neutral meanings of 'creator' (Q 2:54; 59:24) or 'creature' (Q 98:6–7). The one exception to this is Q 57:22, which speaks of misfortunes in this life, whether earthquakes or diseases or war, are 'brought about' out of preexisting matter or circumstances. Thus, again, nothing in the Qur'anic use of *bara's* compels one to assume *ex nihilo* creation—as we have seen, its biblical cognate *bara'* was taken for centuries to mean an organisation of preexistent matter—and, indeed, what evidence the book does furnish would seem to militate against such an assumption.[108]

In order to balance our understanding regarding the exegesis of the Greek term *ex nihilo* from the Septuagint of Genesis 1:1–2, we need to understand the component of revelation that Yahweh has revealed to man. We have already established that our present understanding of the *ex nihilo* concept in terms of our modern thinking may, at best, be exaggerated regarding the methodology deity used in bringing His creation into full bloom, namely, special creation without process. If we get beyond the Protestant Reformational view that has held sway in Western Christian thought, we become increasingly aware of the fact that *ex nihilo* is referring to deity being the ultimate creator and the seven-day creation pattern is what was revealed in the Book of Genesis.

> As a matter of fact, the Sabbath embraces the whole creative activity and thereby points to the *ex nihilo* concept. It is significant in this sense that the section of Sabbath echoes the introduction of the creation pericope as everything belonged still to the "not yet," and the same token refers ultimately to the only one who was then present, namely, the Creator. The creation perhaps is here also conceived as more than a human maturation along the centuries; it is brought up as a Revelation from the Creator himself. Here is the "necessity" aspect of the Revelation, which is pointed out; what required the Revelation.[109]

Based on the seven-day creation pattern, Hebrew liturgy just before the Sabbath would occur, would reenact the creation scene. This gave rise to later Rabbinic interpretation and applications of this text. In the tradition of the Greek Septuagint, knowledge of the invisible world was paramount while the Hebraic model of God being a master potter was very naturalistic in its interpretation as well as God's active part in bringing about his creation.

The sacred stories of creation that found their way into the liturgies of the Near Eastern cultures do serve as a model for the creation of a king and his rebirth as well. These creation accounts are narrative in structure, and they were orally transmitted so the creation drama, or the creation of a new king could be preserved and orally transmitted to succeeding generations. In this transmission we find patternisms that were borrowed from surrounding cultures and couched within a new context whereby Yahweh's divine instruction was revealed through the forms of these stories that became our sacred text.

> There are also similarities in religious observances, liturgy, and institutions. Canaanite Ugarit had its High Priest and its Holy of Holies. The Jewish Pentecost had a Canaanite model. And a close parallel can be seen in the Hebrew sacrificial system and purification ceremonies. Festival and holy days such as the New Year, the Day of Atonement, and harvest feasts, with their agricultural connections (including the eating of unleavened bread), and have precedents in the Canaanite traditions.[110]

It is once again quite clear that more than one culture in the Mediterranean employed an annual spring renewal festival for the cleansing of the nation, such as the "unleavening" process typified by the eating of unleavened bread followed the singing of the hymn Song of Sea, found in Exodus 15:14, in which Israel celebrates her victory over the Philistines.

> We must posit two New Year's festivals in the early cult of Israel, convenant-renewal festivals. The autumn festival, falling on the New Year common to Canaan and Egypt, in Israel became the first feast of the era of kingship, both in Jerusalem and Beth'el. The spring New Year, with its ultimately Mesopotamian connections, appears to have been the time of the major festival at the old league sanctuaries of Gilgal and Shiloh, a covenant festival, which virtually disappeared during the monarch as a national pilgrimage feast, until the archaizing reforms of Josiah (2 Kings 23; 23; cf. 2 Chron. 30:1–16). The associations of the Gilgal rites with the spring, with the covenant, and with the sea crossing and the "ritual conquest" seem very clear indeed.[111]

The patternism used to build Solomon's temple was both by the direction of the Spirit *ruah* and the pattern *tamnit* was borrowed from the Canaanites. John Bright states as follows:

> It is, of course, likely that features of Israel's royal ideology were borrowed. The Israelite monarchy was, after all, an innovation for which no native precedents existed. A state that absorbed thousands of Canaanites, that patterned much of its bureaucracy on foreign models, and whose national shrine was constructed on a Canaanite pattern, doubtless borrowed features of its cult—and of its ideal of kingship—as well. But whatever was borrowed was brought into harmony, at least in official circles, with normative Yahwism. Some scholars believe that Israel celebrated a feast of Yahweh's enthronement at the new year, comparable to that in Babylon, save that the struggle reenacted was not with mythical powers of chaos but with Israel's—and Yahweh's—historical foes.[112]

Arnold Wallenkampf, adds:

> If we had only the archaeological remains of the Jerusalem temple without the Bible, we might conclude that it was a typical ancient New Eastern temple. Such temples and their furnishings, along with other types of temples, did lie in Israel's environment. According to certain ancient texts, some of them were even built by divine command and according to divine plan. But while the Jerusalem temple fits into a definite cultural context, at the same time there are significant and crucial differences that made Solomon's temple unique. Perhaps the most important distinction was in the way the temple functioned in Israelite theology; it was not God's palace where His human servants supplied His physical needs, but it was the bearer of His name, and thus the focus of religious attention to which prayer was directed. The Jerusalem temple was an accommodation for the needs of His people. God guided its builders (1 Chron. 28:11–12, et al), not in a cultural vacuum, but among the current

> options, to choose an arrangement that already had some meaning but one which could be modified to teach Israel how and why she was different from her neighbors.[113]

Based on the evidence just presented, it becomes apparent that patternisms were employed in natural cultural context as a blueprint for operations, as Yahweh accommodates the natural gifts of mankind by using the agency of His Holy Spirit to illuminate and inspire His human servants. This also shows us that Yahweh's spirit flows in the normal operation and accompanies His people as they are directed to do the Lord's work. Therefore our model of inspiration has an accommodation factor, but does not do violence to Yahweh's divine agency to accomplish His will through human agency. It has also been shown that cross-cultural patternisms and literary borrowing do not diminish from Yahweh's ability in maintaining His revelation to His community.

> For such believers in continuous revelation, rejected opinions still may be used for leverage in situations in which the previously established law is no longer realizable.
>
> In contrast to both of these views, one may adopt the position that revelation was indeed a single, unique event, endowed with unique power and authority. The Torah of Sinai is the product of this revelation; and the Torah as canonized by Ezra, we have said, is not only the closest possible approximation of this original Torah, after centuries of idolatry, but it is also the canon as endorsed by prophetic authority. This Torah serves as the basis and the inspiration for all subsequent decisions of law, and disputes arise, not because of continuous revelation of any kind, but because of the imperfection of human understanding and lacunae of tradition.
>
> If we do not accept continuous revelation, and do not see the later decisions of *poskim* (halakic commentators) as endowed with revelatory power, then such decisions have primarily pragmatic value—they foster unified behavior among various constituents. By themselves, these decisions add no new divine

dimension to the views they expound. Deciding in favor of one view over another does not affect the revelatory composition, whose source and validation lie solely in the Sinaitice revelation of the Torah (written and oral) and in the interpretation of this revelation. No human act can aspire to that status.[114]

Many historical commentators have assumed through the process of verbal inspiration that the inspired writer was moved by the Holy Spirit in an inerrant fashion and, under this inspiration, Yahweh would never allow the inspired writer to use his own prejudices or assumptions.

Yet there is evidence to confirm this was not actually the case; the first of which was the two reports regarding the death of Saul and the second case is in the writings of the New Testament, Dr. Luke in the Book of Acts reports Paul having been in Jerusalem contrasted by Galatians first person report where Paul denies ever being in Jerusalem at the time of Luke's report. These and many other reports throughout the pages of Scripture may only give us partial accounts, the whole of which may no longer be a part of our rescinded text, thereby making it difficult to triangulate all the events that actually took place.

Nevertheless, biblical inspiration does in fact lead us along the historical path so we can find the direction of the divine voice as Yahweh's will is revealed by our trial and error. Thus the pattern of inspiration does lead the people of God and is suitable for its purpose. Jeremiah lamented greatly in the temple when the reversal came from on high to capitulate to the Babylonians after former prophets had told the Jews never to surrender to this invading power. But we must realize the circumstances of impending doom had indeed changed, and so the revelation of God had to adapt to the changing situation. This inspiration model also works in the area of temple patternisms whereby we see the pattern of man integrated with the patternisms that God laid down for the construction of the temple, which was based on the heavenly reality.

Sacral Kingship and the Coronation Marriage Ceremony

When comparing the ancient coronation rites, we see many striking parallels to the biblical view of salvation history. While not all of these rites and rituals are directly used in biblical revelation, there does remain a ptolemic reference by many biblical writers as they reveal Yahweh's position in salvation history regarding these rites. However, these sacral kingship rites do reveal the ancient patternisms found in salvation history, which were definitely understood in all rituals and ancient temple liturgies of the near east. These liturgies were dedicated to each nation's tyrannical god as those deities were worshiped in their national shrines. Let us examine a brief overview of these coronation ceremonies.

Features of the Coronation Ceremony

1. Austerities. Previous to their coronation, some kings prepared themselves for the ceremony through fasting, remaining in solitude, or some other act of discipline.
2. Secrecy. The coronation ceremony, which often contained religious secrets known only to initiated, was frequently guarded in order to prevent the entrance of the uninitiated.
3. Reverence. During the coronation ceremony itself, those who were allowed to attend were expected to maintain a discreet silence.
4. Humiliation. During certain ceremonies, the king became the butt of practical jokes, sneers, derision, and 'grotesque and fantastic puns' and was sometimes even the object of a severe beating.
5. Promises. In another important constituent of the coronation ceremony, "the king is adominished to rule justly and promises to do so."

6. Gods. A feature particularly evident in ancient coronation ceremonies, but found less often in modern ones, is the impersonation of the gods by priests or other officials.
7. Ablution. During this part of the coronation rite, the king was ceremonially washed.
8. Anointing. A feature of the ceremony that generally followed the ablution was an anointing of the king with oil.
9. Sacrifices. Animal sacrifice frequently attended the installation rituals of the king. Human sacrifice is also attested, but only rarely.
10. Jubilation. Numerous coronations and with ritual rejoicing that was frequently accompanied by acclamations, such as "Long live the king!"
11. New Names. During the course of the coronation ceremonies, the king generally acquired a new name, often either a title or the name of a predecessor.
12. Rebirth. During many coronation rituals, some act suggesting the rebirth process was performed: acting as one who is new to the world, going through a burying ceremony, being ritually reawakened, or acting like a newborn babe.
13. Creation. The coronation ceremony was thought of as a time of new creation, a day like the day on which the world was created. This intimmate association of coronation and creation was often ritually expressed by the ceremonial repetition of the creation account.
14. Combat. This is often a ritual combat of 'sham fight,' a fight or battle enacted in a ritual in order to illustrate a battle told of in myth. The result of this battle is the (temporary) destruction of the cosmic order or of the life of the community.

15. Marriage. A 'sacred marriage' between the king and his consort frequently accompanies the other rituals associated with the coronation, and in some rituals it is the final act.
16. Procession. The coronation ceremony generally included a tribunal procession, either around the sacred site of the king's enthronement or through his realms, in order that the king might receive homage from his people.
17. Garment. In the course of the enthronement ceremony, the king was generally clothed with a garment endowed with special powers.
18. Crown. During the coronation rite, the king was frequently given a crown, cap, or some other head covering with sacred associations.
19. Shoes. In many coronations, the king puts on shoes or other footwear as part of the rites.
20. Regalia. During the installation rites, the king receives various symbols of his regal power; a sword, a scepter, or a ring.
21. Throne. The ritual enthronement of a king during the coronation ceremony is enacted more frequently than the bestowal of the crown or the receipt of other regalia.
22. Masks. The use of masks by priests impersonating gods is evident in certain ancient royal rites.
23. Communion. In a number of coronation rites, the king received food or drink of a ceremonial or sacramental nature.
24. Feast. In the course of most coronation rites, a feast was given for the king and all others attending the ceremony.
25. Dominion. In a number of cultures, the new king performed a rite, such as taking a set number of ceremonial steps, touring the kingdom, or shooting an arrow.

26. Officials. In many cultures, officials were consecrated either in the course of the coronation ceremony or shortly thereafter.
27. Progression. In most of the coronation ceremonies under study, the king was permitted to be consecrated several times, progressing each time in the scale of kingship.[115]

Even a cursory reading of these rituals show us many familiar patternisms that emerge and are correlated within the narrative of the death, burial, and resurrection motifs, which are contained in synoptic traditions. These themes will be evaluated and examined when we compare the liturgical order of these rituals with a salvation history commentary.

During the age of the patriarchs, there was a great connection between marriage and kingship.

> These stories illustrate the relationship between marriage and patrilineal descent. The emphasis on inheritance, both of lineage and of property, allows us to infer that marriages are formed to keep inheritance of land within certain kinship boundaries.[116]

Both possessed land and inheritance and the divine right of kingship did express itself in a sacred marriage contract between the king and his people. This idea is expanded and enlarged in the New Covenant marriage supper (see Jer. 31 and Rev. 5:10), where we shall be kings and priests and shall reign on the earth. Some sacred marriage ceremonies would included water rites (see Gen. 21:25–34) where also in New Testament literature, Jesus is given the deed to the earth to heal the nations with divine waters.

1. R. H. Moye ("In the Beginning: Myth and History in Genesis and Exodus," *JBL* 109 [1990] 577–98) argues that the relationship between myth and history, and the structural pattern connecting genealogy with narrative in Genesis and Exodus, reveal

that "the story of the Pentateuch as a whole is preeminently the story of the fall, or the exile, of humanity from the harmony of paradise and the perfect balance and order of God's creation into the disordered realm of human history and the subsequent desire for a reunion with the divine, a reunion that is accomplished not by a return to a mythical Eden but by the manifestation of the divine on earth and within history and by the return to a human and historical version of Eden, the promised land given to the chosen people by God." (598) On the theological unity of Genesis, see T. W. Mann, "All the Families of the Earth," *Int.* (1991) 341–53.[117]

The subject of divine kingship and the Son of Man traditions have long been a source of scholarly debate. These concepts also are linked to both sides of lineage of the heir of the inheritance. The term "Son of Man" means "Son of the King" who gives him an inheritance from that kingship and royal family.

Until the 1920s, scholars such as Moewinkle have been linking Israel's enthronement psalms to festival-day readings and enthronement coronations. It cannot be overemphasized that the king going through the enthronement ritual is Yahweh Himself. It should also be noted there is a leading tendency of modern scholarship to link the beginning of the development of the Psalter to Canaanite hymnity due to the fact that oral traditions seem to come from ancient sources and form the hymnity, which was eventually gathered together and developed into Israel's temple hymnbook. Arthur Weiser states:

"In the liturgy of Ps. 81.3 ff. the *traditional obligation* to celebrate the feast of Yahweh regularly every year is stated even more distinctly and with historical accuracy: 'on our feast day [sic], for it is a statute for Israel, an ordinance of the God of Jacob. He made it a decree in Joseph, when he went out over the land of Egypt.' The tradition of the feast of Yahweh dates back to the time of the wilderness, and the tribes of Joseph were the first to give support to this tradition. That the feast mentioned in the liturgy of Ps. 81.3 ff. is that of the renewal of the Covenant is proved by the reference to the self-revelation of Yahweh, his name and his commandments in v v. 9 f., to his saving acts in v v. 6 f., and to the judgment pronounced on those who are disobedient in v v. 11 ff. Ps. 11.9, reading: 'he has commanded them to keep his convenant for ever,' also refers to the tradition of the Covenant Festival at which the divine saving acts were recited (Ps. 111.6), a tradition which was meant to be permanently kept alive, and so does Ps. 78.5 ff: "He established a testimony in Jacob, and appointed a law in Israel, which he commanded our fathers to teach to their children . . . so that they should not forget the works of God, but keep his commandments."[118]

Worship in ancient temples considered of national identity, as represented by a territorial deity. Feasts days were often regarded as sacrificial days. The emphasis of the worship was spiritual and temporal, but in Israel's case, Yahweh's saving acts were also celebrated, as He would bring victory for his people and overcome Israel's foes. This same model exists in the law gospel tension of the New Testament. God's mighty saving acts are a precursor for the New Testament gospel when the church is victorious based on Christ's victory over his foes at the end of the age and Christ's throne will be firmly established in the eschaton. It is also evident that Jewish sect of the New Testament church kept the same liturgical pattern as established in the Torah and in the writings (John 7, Acts 20, 1 Cor. 5,7,8) the new Passover imagery is employed.

2 The Psalter: Jewish Temple Hymnody

In the New Testament corpus of literature, Isaiah is the most quoted of the major prophets, followed by the Psalms. This literary borrowing, as we shall discover, is not by accident but by design. A theme of deep theological constructs lies between the Testaments and is conveyed in the New Testament corpus of literature. It is now to the enthronement Psalms that we turn our attention.

Due to the influence of Hermann Gunkel, many attempts have been made to study the Psalms according to their various literary types, clauses and strophe (*Gattungen*) and their correspondences to life situations. The most significant genre in application to our study is obviously the enthronement psalm and certain liturgical psalms. Psalms 47, 93, and 96 through 99 were sung at an annual enthronement of Yahweh. This is very similar to the Babylonian god Marduk, who was enthroned each year at the Spring festival.

As of this date of this writing, no conclusive proof exists to show that Israel celebrated Yahweh's yearly enthronement. However, Prof. Warner Eichrodt maintains one of the strongest scholarly positions regarding the cultic practices found in the Ugaritic text and their links to the Babylonian New Year Festival and the Egyptian Enthronement Festivals, which have a direct literary link to the Enthronement Psalms.[1] In the enthronement psalms, God's reign over His people was celebrated. It is also quite clear from the Ugaritic literature of the fifteenth century

B.C., in which were discovered the ancient roots of Hebrew poetry, that this literature had quite an influence upon the structure of Israel's royal psalms.[2]

Ancient temple hymnity of the Near East reveal many striking patternisms and common use of symbols and liturgical scenes. There was much competition between the pantheons in temple worship, as choruses dedicated to singing the praises of each god would attempt to out-sing or out-chant the others during the temple service (which is strikingly similar to the "show down" at Mount Carmel between Baal and Yahweh during the ministry of Elijah). Such a practice was also employed by the Gnostics and was developed in the center of Judaism from 722 B.C. and maintained up until the time of the early church in the temple cult.[3]

Since the 1920s, scholars such as Mowinckel and others believed they saw a relationship in Psalm 132 between the annual Babylonian feast and Israel's enthronement of Yahweh. But not all scholars are convinced that the enthronement psalms and other related genre, such as royal and other processional psalms, were borrowed from the enthronement of other deities. They claim Israel's monotheistic theocracy would have known of these ritual enthronements used in other literature. They maintain that Israel's monotheistic belief was strong enough to stand independent of the influence of other surrounding cultures. One of the scholars who maintains this position is Douglas A. Knight in his classic dissertation entitled *Rediscovering the Traditions of Israel:*

> A decisive, if not final, response to these issues, primarily to that of divine kingship, has been given in NOTH's extraordinarily perceptive article; '*Gott, Konig Volk im Alten Testament.*' In this tightly argued treatise, NOTH concedes the presence of the divine-kingship ideology in ancient Egypt, in Mesopotamia, and probably also in the Syro-Palestinian world of the 14th century

B.C., although its actual extent and character is somewhat nebulous. NOTH doubts that premonarchial Israel knew of this ideology, but admits that "the possibility of Israel having taken over elements of an 'agricultural' ideology bound up with the establishment of the monarch cannot *a priori* be ruled out. We merely need to prove the existence of one such adoption." But, asserts NOTH, this evidence has not been produced convincingly enough by the Scandinavians. Especially the tendency of these scholars to be so historically and temporally indiscriminate in their search for Old Testament and Oriental evidence arouses suspicion.

NOTH's final conclusion turns the tables on the proponents of the divine-kingship hypothesis: 'The fact that we appear to have deviations from conceptions of a divine king ideology, applied in the Old Testament to the Jerusalem monarch, is stronger evidence that its ideology itself was not accepted on the basis of the Old Testament belief. The minimum consequence of this total rebuttal by NOTH is that the thesis of divine or sacral kingship in the ancient Near East and in Israel in particular can no longer be treated as a self-evident presupposition in the interpretation of Old Testament texts.[4]

The idea that Israel's monotheism demands the type of preeminence that leads to the historical belief of the supremacy of Israel's monotheism presupposes that this type of purism existed in Israel's belief system. If this indeed were the case, number one, why is the retirement of the gods a dominant theme in Israel's writings that gave way to monotheism as the gods competed giving way to Yahweh's superiority?

Two, why do the prophets constantly warn Israel not to surrender her worship to these pagan deities if she had knowledge of their deification and temple cult practices?

Third, it is not reasonable to assume that Israel's traditions of literary borrowing existed in a vacuum from the nations that surrounded her.

It is a major fallacy to teach that monotheism belonged only to Israel in a historical context. Her uniqueness in her relationship to Yahweh is in her position as a monotheistic nation and in her corporate identity. It is untenable to assume that Israel had no position in the development of either receiving or sharing in the literary traditions of other nations.

Four, in premonarchial Israel, the assumption is made that she had no knowledge of divine kingship, but they did believe in the divine right of kings to speak for Yahweh, and they did apply the ascension and descension narratives in part to Yahweh and His mighty acts as the Divine King. Due to this fact, it is highly unlikely that Israel would have not had knowledge of divine kingship in order to claim that only Yahweh had this right.

The various camps of scholarship have long debated the extent of the enthronement practices and number of rituals from the enthronement theology, which were adapted into Israel's festival liturgy and temple practices. The division is over the covenant renewal ceremony, for in Hebrew tradition Yahweh was honored as "King of Kings" and "Lord of Lords." In pagan liturgies the covenant renewal was based on the death and the rising of the deity, whereas in the Jerusalem temple cult, the covenant renewal would apply to the Holy Wars of Joshua in 24:1–15 where Yahweh establishes the religion of the people as well as the conquest of Canaan, being reacted in recitation in Psalms 105.[5] The new birth imagery would apply to the healing of the nation and Yahweh's reign in the hearts of his people resulting in the rebirth of the covenant.

> The festival then passed into a mood of rejoicing as the people, newly pledged to the covenant, welcomed the LORD as king. This was not an enthronement ritual in the strict sense of the word, since, unlike the dying-and-rising gods of paganism, the LORD had never relinquished his rule. It was rather the nation's

recognition of the kingly majesty of God and acknowledgement of his rule over Israel. At this point in the ceremonial, the ark of the covenant, the symbolic throne of the LORD, was carried in procession up the slope of Mt. Zion to its resting place in the temple, the glad crowds singing the praise of God the King, mighty ruler of the universe and of human history.[6]

In the royal Davidic theology, there does seem to be a fusion of the concepts regarding the reign of the king as a righteous ruler due to the fact this royal emmissary is to act righteously as God's ambassador bringing justice and a new birth deliverance to his people. It is out of this theological development that the Messianic kingship qualities of the coming Messiah would be born and would also replicate a life, death, and resurrection motif as saving acts of God established in God's plan of salvation history for the redemption of mankind.

This theoretical description of the Israelite new year festival combines motifs of the premonarchial covenant renewal ceremony, with themes similar to those of the Babylonian and Canaanite new year feasts. Where would such a fusion take place? The most reasonable answer is, in Jerusalem. The city was not conquered until the reign of David, but soon after, it was added to his possessions, it became the religious center of his realm, a change in status signalized by the bringing to it of the ark.[7]

In contrast to the pagan notion that a divine king would pass through initiation rites and a new birth process, in a convenant renewal ceremony to achieve god-like status as a sinless ruler providing justice to his people, this Egyptian formula of justice was reinterpreted by the Psalmist to say only the God who never dies could supply this type of righteous rule. It is interesting to note how the Messiah in New Testament theology of the new covenant would become sin for us by taking the guilty verdict of our sins upon his own head so that we would not have to face our own verdict in the last judgment and that we might become the righteousness of God through the new birth process of the saving acts of God.

> From the [Messianic] Psalms already examined, we learn to know the Messiah as a *divine and glorious King*, whom all the nations of the earth shall obey, and also as a *Priest* of a far higher and more illustrious order than the priests of the first covenant; who was, consequently, to make an atonement for the sins of his people; for this was the peculiar due to the sacerdotal order. But the Psalms we have hitherto considered, are silent both concerning the method, by which, as a *king*, he should gain his widely extended dominion, and, as a *priest*, accomplish the work of expiation.[8]

The biblical data reveals biblical coronation ceremonies that were performed during each Sukkot at the beginning of a new year. The first coronation is found in 1 Samuel 10 where we read of Saul's ascension to the throne of Israel. As with Saul's coronation, the same ritual cycle was applied to the reigns of David, Solomon, and through the reigns of the divided kingdoms of Israel and Judah. With every new ascension year, the kingdom was to be cleansed for a year of renewal. A peace offering was made to Yahweh on behalf of the nation, with purification and other ceremonies and the anointing of the ritually reborn righteous king. Feasting, sacrifices, and rejoicing followed in celebration of the renewed convenant.[9]

In modern times, conservative scholars continue to advance the opinion that Israel's monotheistic theology had always been anti-syncretic due to the fact that Israel was called to be a separate nation. This writer is suggesting that Israel was never a purely syncretic nation. In fact, clear from Moses' last sermon, this theme runs through the major prophets, namely, not to forsake Yahweh for the worship of other gods and the pursuit of justice. Therefore, Israel's prophets called for religious syncratism, but its highly questionable if Israel ever achieved it.

Later, after the priestly reign of the sons of Zadak, a religious purism grew up in Israel and was in full bloom after the exile and the rebuilding of the temple c. 457–445 B.C. Out of these puristic movements sprang the Pharisee and Saducee religious sects. At a later period, other communities, such as Qumran and Masada, would react against the temple abuses in Jerusalem, claiming these sects had the hidden key to Jewish puristic religious practices. It should be fully realized that part of Israel's anti-syncretic view was due to the fact that a divine king was expected to unite many diverse cultures, religions, governments, and languages into one homogenized nation. Oftentimes, the only practice the subjects had in common was the assessment and payment of taxes.

> Conquered or vassal states that submitted to an overlord were, as often as not, of different language and culture backgrounds. They might have had little or nothing in common with a king's people except the taxes they paid and the person of the king. Ultimately, the only common denominator which divine kings had to offer to unite their various subjects was their royal and divine persons. It was in the king that fusion could occur, and through him that syncretism took place.[10]

In the ancient world, it was quite common for the religious leaders/wise men (sages, et al) to be in search for the perfect king who would complete the creation of man from his perfect character. Such a concept exists in the Hindu Vedas, through which their quest was for the appearance of the perfect man, a messiah figure.[11] However, at the birth of Jesus, this revelation was not accepted by the Hindu sages as fulfillment of the quest for the perfect man, so forthcoming generations of Hindus were open to the doctrines of Karma and reincarnation as taught by the Bhramas. In Jewish apocalyptic tradition, the prophet Daniel speaks of a "divine" man/messiah figure (Dan. 7:7) and throughout the centuries, debates in Jewish and Christian traditions have ensued over the exact nature of Daniel's man. Would this messiah be a conquering king who would elevate Jerusalem to the top of the nations or would the messiah be a personification of Yahweh Himself? In this case Daniel is perplexed.

The vision of the heavenly court judgment scene shows that judgment is being dispensed in a latter time and, as we have previously indicated, the heavenly view of reality was the ultimate cosmic fulfillment of what is truly real. Therefore, the verdict of judgment is apocalyptic and would be first rendered in heaven by the heavenly king and then received by the heavenly king's earthly subjects. As apocalyptic tradition reveals, the opening of a sealed room is symbolic of opening the prophecies contained in Daniel's vision that are sealed on earth until the completion of those things contained in the vision.

An often misunderstood prophetic verse in this fulfillment is Daniel 12:1–4, "in the latter times, knowledge would increase . . . " is often cited by futurist expositors to mean a knowledge explosion just before the end of this age. However, as Aramaic scholars know, this is an "aramaism" that suggests it is the opening up of the seals of Daniel so that the internal content of his relegation is understood and is what fulfills the 1335 days and the rest of his seven prophecies. At the completion of the revealing of the prophecies that are contained in the apocalyptic Book of Daniel is the great appearing of the Son of Man. And in the Son of Man traditions, this Son of Man, whose origin is heaven, returns to this earth and dispenses true justice and righteousness. According to the apocalyptic Son of Man traditions, this heavenly king is the only personage who can lead the world in truly sincere worship.

Israel's prophetic picture of the Messiah was that in the later times all nations would come to worship the Eternal Lord of Hosts, and there would be one world religion and economy, under the leadership of His reign during the Messianic Age. The Messianic Reign in Jewish thinking was to elevate Israel to the top of all nations and would teach these nations Yahweh's laws of love and justice. This is the reason why Yahweh's rule in Psalm 132 and other enthronement psalms is so important to our understanding regarding the development of a balanced perspective concerning religious syncretism in ancient Israel.

Most commentators believe Psalm 132 was used during the festival of shelters in the fall when Yahweh's seventy years as king of his people was celebrated while others believe this psalm was sung during Yahweh's enthronement as the Ark of the Covenant was being carried into the temple.[12] In some aspects this Psalm resembles the royal psalms Ps. 2, 28, 20 and 21 as well as songs of praise Ps. 46, 48, 76 and 87.[13] Elmer Leslie states:

> In a truly remarkable manner, this unique psalm intertwines these distinctive themes. Mowinckel, with fine sensitiveness to the drama in Judson worship, rightly views it as "the dramatic processional liturgy of a festival which repeats the first entry of the ark of the Lord into Zion." Thus is part of the annually celebrated ceremony of the enthronement of the Lord, which took place on New Year's Day. But it is probable that, as was the case in Babylon, an annual ceremony of the official enthronement of the Judson king took place also on New Year's Day, the date of his reign being reckoned from the first New Year's Day after the death of his predecessor.[14]

It is interesting to note the last initiation rite of the ascension of Yahweh to His throne takes place at the sounding of a trumpet. Dr. Gerhard S. Gerstenberger provides the following insights on Psalm 47:

In fact, v. 6 ('God went/goes up with noise; Yahweh at the blast of the trumpet') easily falls into the category of such an expansion, for it expresses exactly the theme of vv. 3 and 8, and the perfect *'ih,'* 'to ascent,' corresponds to the prefects of v. 9. V. 6 then, depicts the very moment of enthronement, that is, the central event of all the enthronement psalms (Pss. 93:1; 96:10; 97:1, 9; 99:1; and, outside the genre, Pss. 22:29 [RSV 28]; 79:6; 82:8; 113:4–6). This verse most unmistakably mentions Yahweh's taking his place on the throne"[15]

The Psalter was indeed the temple's hymnbook, consisting of many genres and parallelistic structures, as recorded in 1 Chronicles 24 and was later set in liturgical order during David's reign and redacted under Josiah and Ezra. The book was used in the royal court by the priests for liturgies during sacred times and festivals. The structure of the royal court consisted of such subjects as described below:

Upon further reflection we might picture the occupants of the throne room as well. The royal court in the ancient Near East, often included magicians and astrologers (Exod. 7:11; Dan. 2:2, see Magic), servants and waiters (I Kings 10:5), a "cupbearer (Neh. 2:1–5) and wise men who could act as counselors (Dan. 1:3–5). Other officials, such as military generals, the high priest, district leaders and royal secretaries were also present (2 Sam. 9:15–18, 20:23–26; I Kings 4:1–7). The recognition that all these people—servants and officials alike—were part of the royal court enhances our mental picture further, suggesting that a royal court is a place of harmonious and orderly service."[16]

A key function of the royal court was to issue edicts for what the king said in the royal court was law. These edicts also established the parameters of the duties of sacral kingship and followed an Egyptian liturgical order royal protocol in the coronation of a sacred king.

Israelite kingship is frequently seen as governed or restrained by covenantal obligations. Von Rad (1966) identified the problematic *edut* of the coronation ceremony (2 Kgs. 11:12) with the Egyptian royal protocol containing throne names and the rights and duties of kingship. The term *hoq* (Ps. 2:7) and *edut* are frequently understood as some form of document or inscription containing the rights of kingship or the terms of the Davidic convenant. This is often compared with the *mispat* of the kingdom (1 Sam. 10:25; cf. 8:11) and the so-called law of the king (Deut. 17:14–20) as evidence for a constitutional understanding of Israelite kingship. Halpern (1981) provides an extensive treatment of the various aspects of this problem. He concludes that Judean and Israelite monarchies were determined by legal constraints.[17]

A second function of the royal court was to render legal decisions that were binding upon the king's subjects. In biblical theology, we see a definite connection between the royal temple and sanctuary and Yahweh's heavenly temple and sanctuary where His royal edicts and judgments are rendered to His subjects on earth and the earthly temple and sanctuary were indeed a foreshadowing of the ultimate cosmic reality of God's righteousness that would fill the universe.

It is also clear besides the Psalms being used in temple hymnity, they were also used as competitive hymns between different choirs within the temple cult. For example Choir "A" on the left side might be praising God over David slaying a thousand Philistines and Choir "B" on the right side of the temple might reply that David slew ten thousand Philistines, the literary connection being that the Lord fulfilled His promises to David no matter how small or great the number the need might be to slay the enemies of Israel. Until the finding of the Dead Sea Scrolls, many biblical students assumed the 150 Psalms contained in the Old Testament canon comprised the complete collection.

> The date and composition of the principal non-Biblical scrolls, the work of unnamed writers, determined by the aforementioned evidences, may be assigned to the late second and first centuries B.C., and the first century A.D. Therefore they fall largely within the inter-testament period. They are evidently from the headquarters library of what would appear to be a quasi-ascetic Essene brotherhood at Qumran. And most of them were obviously hidden in the caves for safekeeping when destruction of the center by the Romans under Vespasian was imminent.[18]

However, a new addition to these psalms from the Dead Sea Scrolls is under current investigation. They consist of the following categories: *Col.* XXIV (*Psalm* 155) 3 YHWH, *Col.* XXVI (*Hymn to the Creator*), *Col.* XXVII (*Composition of David 2 Sam.* 23:7), *Col.* XXVIII (Psalm 151) 11QPsalms (11Q6[11QPs]), 4QNon-Canonical Psalms A (4Q380), 4QNon-Canonical Psalms B (4Q381).

The new collection of psalms deals with purification rites, with compositions from David borrowed from 2 Samuel 23:7, dealing with the perfect path before God and Yahweh giving a wise and enlightened spirit.

Other texts include hymns to Judah, admonishing her to observe the Lord's feast and to fulfill her vows (11Q5[11QPS]).[19] Certainly these psalms do contain enthronement language regarding the purification of one's being, providing one stays on the path of God, and we might add that images from these rites of passage may have been borrowed from Egypt to show the Lord's purification through our rites of passage as we grow in His nature and maturity.

3 Sacred Temples of the Ancient World

Every nation in the Middle East erected temples dedicated to their gods as well as planets. As far as modern research is concerned, Israel was the only nation that would attempt to build a tabernacle where Yahweh would eschatologically dwell and righteousness would prevail over all nations. This was cosmic reality that was pictured in the sanctuary service during the Feast of Tabernacles, whereas the Egyptian view of eschatology involved the great appearing of Osiris to make his final cosmic appearance in the eschaton.

The Edenic narratives of Genesis 1, 2, and 3 have within them powerful symbols that represent archetypal descriptions of Israel's temple system. This was a prototype pattern that was later used in Israelite temples. The Garden of Eden was not an edifice, but was the heavenly prototype of the temple. The Book of Jubilees, chapter 3:19, adds: "The Garden of Eden is the Holy of Holies, and the dwelling of the Lord." Ancient temples in Israel employed eleven prototypical aspects. They are:

1. The tree of life was located both in the garden and in the temple.

   The menorah was a stylized tree of life whose description is found in Exodus 25:31–40.
2. Both the garden and the temple were associated with sacred waters.

   The waters of Eden represent the quintessential

sacred waters and are located opposite the throne of glory (3 Enoch 18:19) (Num. 20, God gave them water)

3. Eastward orientations played a role in the garden story and in subsequent Israelite temples.

   The eastward orientation of the garden parallels the mosaic tabernacle and Jerusalem temples both having entrances in the east, and Adam and Eve were barred from reentering the garden by the cherubim at the "east of the garden" (Gen., 3:24).

4. The cosmic mountain was symbolically affiliated with the garden and temple.

   Ezekial 28:11–16 delineates Eden as having a mountain in the "Garden of God."

5. The account of the earth's creation is closely connected with the Garden of Eden pericope and the temple.

   The liturgy of the temple is a celebration of the creation of cosmos and the erection of the tabernacle.

6. Cherubim, or heavenly beings, function as guardians of the garden and the temple.

   The cherubim's role was to protect the tree of life so that man in his fallen state could not reenter the garden at the east gate.

7. Revelation was an essential part of the garden and the temple.

   Divine conversation occurred between man and God as they walked together in the garden.

8. Sacrifice existed in the garden and in subsequent temple systems.

   Adam and Eve wore garments made from animal skins.

9. Similar religious language existed in both the garden and the temple.

God "walked" with man in the garden and was "with" him in the temple.

10. Adam and Eve in Genesis 3:7 wore a garment of skins and an apron of fig leaves and the priests wore sacred vestments following the instructions of Exodus 28:29.
11. Abundance was associated with the garden and the temple.

    "Eden" means luxury and delight and therefore connotes a paradise of abundance, a ceremonial clean prerequisite for Israelites temples as well as a blessing for prosperity and fruitfulness (see Isa. 51:3, Ezek. 36:35, Joel 2:3).[1]

The rabbis used parallel tracts of the theological development in teaching the similarities between Genesis cosmic account of the creation of Eden as a prototype of the sanctuary where the creation story was told in liturgical form. For centuries scholars have seen the creation/fall/redemption cycle, in what we call the protoevangelium, denote a coming Messiah figure and His struggle with the serpent. However, scholars have not often looked at the role that this passage has played out in the ancient sanctuary services to picture ultimate cosmic reality. The work of the Aaronic priest at every Yom Kippur liturgically pictures this redemption cycle by his priestly acts.

After the west entrance of the tabernacle, after passing the fire of the altar of sacrifice, the waters of purification, and the ritual cleansing in the bronze laver, he entered into the Holy of Holies to sprinkle the blood of the atoning sacrifice on the mercy seat of the Ark of the Covenant. After offering prayers of atonement for the sins of the people, he exited by Holy of Holies through the east entrance. This was a foreshadowing of mankind's creation in Eden, expulsion after the fall through the eastern gate, where man positionally in salvation history remains until the Messiah leads us back to Eden when paradise lost will be paradise found.

Therefore this temple liturgy of creation/fall/redemption cycle will eschatalogically lead God's people back to Eden and restore God's presence with His people once again in the sanctuary. To explain this process more thoroughly, which is accomplished through "curse reversal," we find in the temple liturgical reality, two liturgies. One is called the Elements of the First Sukkot/found in Exodus 24; then forty years later, as the Israelites were preparing to enter into the land of Canaan, we have the liturgy of the Feast of Tabernacles, which was developed from priestly traditions. John A. Tvedtnes states as follows:

> The Book of Deuteronomy was evidently used anciently as the basis of the liturgy of the Feast of Tabernacles, as we shall see below.
>
> The gathering together of the people at the Feast of Tabernacles provides the backdrop for several special ceremonies in ancient Israel, including (a) thanksgivings for the fall harvest, (b) prayers for rain to begin the new agricultural year, (c) a rehearsal of the law of God and a public commitment to obey his commandments, (d) coronation of a new king or a renewal of the kingship, (e) celebration of the end of the season of war (due to rainy weather) and the establishment of peace, and (f) dedication of the temple. In the third year, tithes of farm produce were collected for the Levites and the poor (Deuteronomy 14:27–29; 26:11–14; Amos 4:4), with a call for special help to the poor during the seventh year (Deuteronomy 15:7–11).[2]

At the beginning of every new year, with the renewal of the kingship, a new chronical of the king's history was undertaken, as the renewal of the convenant was enacted. This included a special call for the liberation of the poor, with the cancellation of previous debts as well as a rejoicing in the Torah with expectations that Yahweh Himself would someday dwell with His people.

We've already established the fact that Israel did indeed borrow Canaanite patterns for the design of Solomon's temple, while the sanctuary and its worship of Yahweh alone would be unique to the Hebrew. The enthronement Psalm 132:5b indicates that David was erecting a home for Yahweh to inhabit, from where He would rule Israel with peace and justice. In Jewish and Arab concepts, the House of Yahweh's was where He dwelt in a great cosmic tent where ultimate reality was enacted in the heavenly temple as the community of the elect would act out their cosmic roles here on earth. Such an example is found in Isaiah 54:2 where a formula is used in the form of a love letter (*billidu*) commanding Israel to, "Widen the space of your tent, extend the curtains of your home, do not hold back!" (New Jerusalem).

This Hebraic love letter also implies a two-fold message that Israel is to employ. First, enlarging Israel's tent through bearing offspring in the midst of the Sinai Desert was considered to be a great act of faith in fulfilling our Lord's command to multiply and subdue the earth. Second, the tent would someday grow large enough to bring blessings to all mankind whereby the God of Israel would also dwell. This concept is given with greater dimension in the New Testament where in the prologue of the Gospel of John, he states in chapter 1:14, "and the word was made flesh and *dealt among us,*" literally, *tabernacled; pitched a tent.* And in the final reality God will ultimately make the earth His tabernacle and He will pitch a tent with men (Rev. 21:1-4). Ultimate reality is treated most effectively by Dr. John M. Lundquist:

> One sees this clearly in connection with Mount Kailash in Tibet, the holy mountain *par excellence*, thought to be the site of the sacred mountain of the Hindu and Buddhist traditions, anciently

know as Mount Meru. The impetus to build sacred mountains, to erect structures that resemble holy mountains (the Old Testament Mount Zion if Jerusalem becomes likened to the mountain of God in the wilderness), will result in similar architectonic arrangements, imitating the topography of the mountain—this is so clear in the Hindu tradition of temple building—as well as the types of physical movement necessary to negotiate it: circumambulation, walking upward (the threshold of each successive section of any Egyptian temple rises in absolute level as one approaches the rear of the building), and walking into the building toward the rear of the most holy place.[3]

It is also evident that both Egyptian and Israelite temples did employ a central passage hidden from public view by a series of portholes that ran along the entrance through a pylon back to a "great place," as the Egyptians called it. These early shrines were a microcosm of the world and the realm of the god.[4] In addition, Psalm 104 has striking similarities to an old Egyptian hymn dedicated to the sun god Aten from the 14th century B.C. The fundamental difference between the two poems is that one is dedicated to the sun, the creation, and the other is for worshiping the Creator.[5]

The reality of developing a relationship with a supreme deity has always been the ultimate quest for man as long as salvation history has been unfolding. However, this writer cannot overemphasize the fact that even through literary borrowing techniques that transmit universal cultural beliefs, which are retold in a localized cultural context from a transcendent universal formula, the original message in many cultures was lost to the nature worship and animisms and worship of the pantheon, in addition to the planetary adoration. This derailed the pagan cultures from finding that ultimate reality, Yahweh. The major prophets, such as Isaiah 22, often spoke of the road back to Zion where Yahweh will dwell in the aeon to come and in this present aeon. We must try to walk down the road to Zion by truly discovering the realities of biblical rites of passage and the divine liturgy that will assist in preparing us, as we celebrate the Lord's presence with us today.

From the time of Moses' last sermon until the ministries of the major prophets, God appeals to Israel again and again to take the highest path of righteousness and for the priesthood to declare the temple scrolls from the highest spiritual reading possible. Israel's captives, widows, orphans, and all oppressed peoples would lead the world through Yahweh's victory in peace and prosperity. It is in this realm of thinking that Psalm 104 is so important to this study because Israel is praising the future victory of the God of Creation. This creation motif is given greater detail in the article *Return to the Temple,* by Dr. Hugh Nibley, a scholar of classical literature:

> According to the eminent N. A. Dahl, 'most important has been the discovery of the importance of the worship of the temple, especially the great festivals [i.e., the rites in which all participate] as a common point of departure and coincidence. In the common worship, the *creation* was commemorated and *re-enacted*, and the future renewal for which Israel hoped, was prefigured.' M. Dahood sees the closest association between the name and the creation motif in the earliest temples, in such names as 'the Voice has Created'—Creation by the Word.
>
> Where did the creation begin? The answer for the Jews was in the temple: 'The first thing which emerged from the primordial waters was the temple,' from which point creation spread in all directions, specifically this earthly creation, for the temple was actually transplanted from a preexistent world created long before. The ancient temple drama begins with the council in heaven when the creation is being planned. [6]

There is considerable theological debate over how much reality that preexistence covers. Theological views range from all things preexisting in a prematerial state during the plans of the Creator until they changed via the material creation to the traditional view that only the Savior and the Redeemer of this world had a preexistence, to the view that all things, including the Savior, preexisted in the mind of the Creator. This is why the stoic hymn, renarrated in the *logos* doctrine with a Christological application, states in the beginning, the Great Architect generated or brought forth the *logos,* meaning reason, who created all things. This commentator believes the reality of the Greek concept of the *logos* doctrine should be understood in the light of the preeminence of Jesus alone.

As witnessed in the preceding quotes, we deal with the tension of Aten over creations that are very similar to the light over darkness or chaos motifs in which Aten is in opposition with nature. In Yahweh's case, He works with and controls the forces of nature for His own purposes. The second point of tension between Yahweh and the Egyptian theodicy was that only Yahweh could dispense true justice through His servants.

It is apparent that Israel was quite critical of the lack of justice being dispensed in Egypt because the psalter would lament and cry for Yahweh to act with justice and righteousness. In defense of Israel's rejection of the Egyptian deities, Walter Brueggermann states as follows:

> It may be concluded that the entire arrangement, theological as well as social, is to be rejected, because the legitimating God is in collusion with the human exploiters, and the collusion is so deep and unjust that the whole system must be rejected. Seen in the radical way, the exodus-conquest tradition is a protest against an established Egyptian theodicy. Israel rejects not only Egyptian civil authority, but also the Egyptian gods. The Egyptian gods are seen to be so enmeshed with the unjust social system that it must all be rejected; and in rejecting the entire social system, Israel introduced a new social system (*torah*) and a new God (cf. Josh. 24:14–15; Judg. 5:8). That is, Israel adopted an entirely different *scheme of theodicy*, erected a new *nomos*

> in the form of torah, and the entire movement was marked by egalitarianism.[7]

One of the many conditions for Israel inheriting the land of Canaan was that justice would be pursued by the ruling authorities and would pertain to all forms of Israelite society. Yahweh's original goal was for Israel to have laws and codices that would grant protection to all men, women, and children as well as animals used for agriculture (Deut. 16:20).

> A concern with enforcing standards of justice likewise is behind the ordinance 'Magistrates and officers [*shotrim,* the word for officers, means "police" in modern Hebrew] shall you appoint in all your cities' (Deuteronomy 16:18). In biblical times, three, twenty-three, or seventy-one judges, depending on a case's severity, adjudicated both disputes and criminal violations.[8]

The obvious objection that Israel had with her counterpart Egypt also dealt with the divine right of kings to exercise or enact any type of decree, judgment, or legislation they deemed necessary.

As the evidence indicates, Israel rejected Egypt's inequality over its subjects. However, in the larger literary frame, there is no doubt that Israel's literature has many Egyptian counterparts. The reason why many commentators feel the Hebrews borrowed literary structures from other Near Eastern cultures is that many of them predate Israel. For example:

> Hermann (1961), Killian (1966), Notter (1974) and Ultvedt (1980) have argued that closer parallels are to be found in Egyptian literature. Notter notes many motifs in a wide variety of Egyptian texts, which resemble features in Gen. 1 and 2, e.g., the creation of chaos as the first step, the concept of a firmament, the making of man in God's image, man being made from clay and then inspired by God, the symbolism of sevens. Notter

is not claiming that any of Egyptian material he cites served as direct source of Gen. 1, simply that the writer was quite familiar with Egyptian ideas of creation.[9]

In the next chapter, we shall examine some examples from the major prophets.

4 The Art of Literary Borrowing and Cultural Interchange

By the twentieth century, lexicographers began to develop more dynamic renderings of words as archaeology and studies of social and religious history began to make their impact upon the lexical forms of the words rendered.

> An author who undertakes a New Testament Lexicon at the present day, without sketching in each article the history and statistics of words and meanings, is tearing the word-apostle from his word and the gospel from history, shooting off the New Testament from the light of research, and taking up his own position far behind Thayer and Grimm, even behind Cremer, along with Stellhorn and Schirlitz, *i.e.*, outside the pale of scientific lexicography altogether.[1]

By the 1970s, a new literary criticism of the biblical text began to emerge. Literary critics such as Robert Alter began to tie literary analysis to the nuances of biblical lexical meanings. In current biblical studies, we concern ourselves with far more than the literal lexical rendering of any word or phrase. We now employ within the word usage such renderings as vernacular speech usage with religious expressions based on the religious/liturgical practices of a culture. Also employed is the wider view of the culture's sociology where scholars endeavor to reconstruct the entire sociological functions of that society and its impact upon the lexical meaning and usage. Therefore, Bible scholars now present a dynamic rendering of the text rather than a static version to be universally applied to all cultures and times. Alter states:

> . . . the advances in biblical philology over the past several decades have been a necessary precondition for the development of the new literary criticism of the Bible that began to emerge in the 1970s. There are words and phrases and verses that will remain dark spots on the map, whether for philological or textual reason, but by and large the Hebrew text is now more accessible to understanding than it has been for the past two thousand years.[2]

We've seen thus far a correlation between Israel's temple and the pattern of Canaanite temple construction. We have also established familiar literary forms being borrowed and reassembled in the enthronement and royal psalms, as we as have examined the Abraham, Isaac, and Jacob cycles and their relation to the Egyptian lion couch drama. It should be noted that the Book of Genesis draws literally from Babylonian accounts of creation in its use of chaos motifs dealing with the universal theme of light winning over darkness, with the use of the WAW consecutive in Genesis 1:2. Consider the Anu, who appeared in two forms of Lakhmu and Lakhamu, which probably corresponded to the Greek forms Dache and Dachus.[3] George Smith further enlarges, "These forms are said to have sprung out of the original chaos, and they are followed by the two forms Sar and Kisar (the Kissare and Assorus of the Greeks). Sar means the upper hosts or expanse, Kisar the lower hosts or expanse; these are also forms or manifestations of Anu and his wife."[4] These motifs are also used in the Book of Isaiah as well as Psalms and are echoed again in the Book of Job.

As seen thus far, the conflict of deity with other gods as well as battling sea monsters and nature was one of the most universal motifs to cross cultural boundaries. These combat epics would later find themselves expressed in the temple liturgies, such as the combat ritual as well as the apocalyptic genre of literature.

> This same myth of the conflict between God and the monster of chaos appears in different guises in several other apocalyptic passages. It is no doubt reflected in Ezekiel's reference to 'Gog of the land of Magog' (chs. 38–39) and in the so-called "antichrist legend" which plays a significant part in both Jewish and Christian apocalyptic writings. Sometimes the monster is identified with an historical person or persons. In the *Zadakite Document*, for example, 'the kings of the nations' are described as 'the Serpents' (VIII.10) and in the Psalms of Solomon, 'the pride of the dragon' (2.29) alludes to the Roman general Pompey, no doubt under the influence of Jer. 51.34 where Nebuchadnezzar of Babylon is referred to in similar terms. In the Book of Revelation, the dragon appears as Satan, and the enemy of the Messiah and his saints, who will at last be bound and cast into the abyss (12.9; 20.2); other beasts, associated with this dragon, are in the end also destroyed by the Messiah who appears under the figure of a 'Lamb' (13.1ff; 14.1ff).[5]

Similar themes and literary forms run continuously through apocalyptic literature, such as Daniel, the Bel and the Snake, Ezekiel, Isaiah, Enoch, Moses, Ezra, and throughout the Book of Revelation, oftentimes with a suspension or time gap in the middle of the drama to postpone the events until the wisdom of the book has been fully declared.[6]

> Their books are said to have remained hidden for a long time, in accordance with God's decree, sealed up from the eyes of the earlier generations. But now they are revealed, since the fulfillment of what was once written down in them by way of revelation is approaching and the generation has come for which they were written:

For you Paradise is opened, the tree of life is planted;
The future age made ready, blessedness prepared;
The city built, a resting-place appointed;
Good works created, wisdom prepared;
The [evil] roots sealed off from you, illness eradicated before you;
Death hidden, Hades put to flight;
Corruption forgotten, sorrow passed away;
But the treasures of immortality are revealed to you in the end.[7]
(see also 4 Esdras 8:52–54; cf. 14; 45–47; Ethiopic Enoch 42; 82; 1)

These themes and motifs, which commonly found apocalyptic literature that deal with light over darkness, order over chaos, ritual combat, courtroom scenes and judgment speeches that occur with the opening of the seals, which reveal the hidden meaning of the document at a time of cataclysmic events are changing the powers of chaos into a new creation of order. It is hard to imagine that the writers in the apocalyptic tradition wouldn't have had a complete working knowledge of the Canaanite and Babylonian combat ritual initiation rites when even major prophets, such as Isaac, employed elements from these rites, as did John in the Book of Revelation, as they reinterpreted the rituals and applied their liturgical order to a new eschatological pattern. Isaiah was one of the most influential apocalyptic writers ever. He is quoted more times in our New Testament corpus of literature than any other single author. His words are a literary masterpiece, as he employs large literary units with smaller structures contained therein.

It is interesting to note that Isaiah's typical style of Hebrew was very cryptic in nature. Various attempts since the 1890s have ensued to development a dual or a trio authorship for the Book of Isaiah. These attempts have succeeded in showing three major divisions within Isaiah literary structures, but have failed to firmly establish the reasons for these divisions, as well as they have failed to absolutely prove two or three redactors that may have existed in the schools of the prophets attempting to preserve the Isaiah traditions.

> The first section of the book reaches a climax in deliverance from the armies of Assyria under Sennacherib. In the last section, prophetic vision looks forward to deliverance from Babylonian captivity. A similar transition occurs in the Book of Ezekiel, with the fall of Jerusalem in 586 B.C., from anticipation messages borne by Isaiah during youth. The latter chapters of the book reflect a maturity of prophetic insight and literary style characteristic of age, and as a result constitute a masterpiece surpassing in depth of thought and majesty of expression even the fine passages of the earlier part of the book.[8]

Paul D. Hanson adds:

> The scholars who accept this division in turn fall into two groups, those accepting Duhm's view of unity of authorship in Third Isaiah, and those feeling that Isaiah 56–66 represents material from a number of authors.
>
> Karl Elliger has advanced the most vigorous argument in favor of seeing Isaiah 56–66 as the work of a single author—a disciple of Second Isaiah of the first generation after the return, who also edited the work of his master leaving his imprint on the material. . . . That Elliger's study demonstrates that certain similarities on these levels do tie the bulk of Isaiah 56–66 together can be granted, but, . . . this is best considered as evidence that the material all belongs of a common tradition rather than as proof that it all derives from a single hand. This view has the added advantage of accounting for both the similarities and the differences existing between Second and Third Isaiah.[9]

However, conservative scholarship has also fallen short of fully explaining Isaiah's literary shifts and the changes in his grammatical styles and literary genres. Isaiah even employs smaller structures within larger structures, which overlap in their common usage. Conservative scholars uphold the single authorship of Isaiah based the dating of his life and their traditions, which surrounding his death where it is claimed he was sawed in half by his persecutors. Today, modern evangelical scholarship asserts the changes in Isaiah's literary shift are due to his maturing process because he was called at such a young age and later he would use prophetic/oracles/judgment motifs. Then as he matured into his old age, he employed the *bfid* structures and the servant songs.

To date, according to Kermode and Alters, it is asserted that 85 percent of modern scholarship upholds the trito thesis in some form due to the unquestionable three main literary divisions that exist in Isaiah's literary structure. However, as modern scholarship is beginning to discover, the Egyptians, Israel, and other nations employed in their vassal treaties a three-part structure, which Isaiah may have used.

Isaiah is also one of the prophets along with Moses and Job, who uses the creation to chaos motif. At the time of the writing of the first part, Isaiah was at the time of decline of Assyria in which several vassal treaties were entered into by Israel and other nations against the will of the Lord for which Israel was to suffer convenantal curses and convenant lawsuit. Avraham Gileadi affirms Isaiah's use of chaos and creation:

> A chiastic pattern of alternating chaos and creation motifs in Isa. 40–46 confirms that the three Isaianic figures in the second unit variously manifest a single ideal vassal. Within that chaos/creation pattern, the three figures identify with one another parallelistically as powers of creation. Both of the chaos/carion patterns—in Isa. 1–12 and 40–46—define the Lord's new creation in terms of Israel's redemption. The new Creation proceeds upon the Lord's intervention: the Lord raises up an ideal

again of punishment and deliverance in order to render Israel's enemies extinct of ineffectual.

The metaphorical terms *hand, light,* and *righteousness,* which appear in both units, express attributes the Lord's ideal vassal exemplifies.[10]

A central theme that runs through the theology of Isaiah dates back prior to 1400 B.C. and was modeled after the Near Eastern suzerain-vassal treaties, such as the Vassal-Treaties of Esarhaddon.[11] The terms of the treaty had a six-part literary formula based on Middle Eastern treaties, which included lists of blessings and cursings, i.e., w. 419–669. (Deut. 28), all of which were duly sworn to by all parties concerned (see Josh. i.e., v. 283). The servant incurs legal prosecution, and the covenant curses upon his failure to keep the covenant, i.e., v397. The sender of this treaty was in a most difficult position. He was dealing with a superior force acting as a vassal, witness and as an enforcer of this treaty. During the period of the Late Bronze Age, when these suzerainty treaties were in use, an appeal was made by the vassal to the gods for his own protection in order to prevent him from breaking the contact. The oath that he entered is as follows,

> As far as the form of the statement is concerned, at first glance it may seem to be an oath formula. Compare the very frequent *'a udu bi'lliah* in Islamic literature, and the discussion in Lane, s.v., *'ada*: "One says also *ma'ada 'llah 'an 'af ala kada for min 'am 'af ala kada.* 'I seek preservation by God from doing such a thing,' as though meaning 'May God preserve me from doing such a thing.' *Qur'* and XII 79, and some reckon *ma'ada 'llah* among the forms of oaths." A very closely related phrase is found in Isaiah 8:10; *w'yiss'reni milleket b'derek ha'am hazzeh,* "And may he correct me from walking in the way of this people."[12]

(See also Isaiah 53:10, which is expressed as a servant song).

Once again we see Isaiah's use of the term "servant," which might be an allusion to the humiliated Messiah with a ritual humiliation of a divinely placed king. It may be employed in a similar fashion in the Book of Psalms, showing that not only David but the major prophets would have had such knowledge of ritual decension of kings. The enthronement psalms show a procession to the throne and the suffering servant of Isaiah shows a procession from the throne to humiliation.

Aubrey R. Johnson concludes:

> The Davidic king is the Servant of Yahweh; but . . . at the New Year Festival, he is the suffering Servant. He is the Messiah of Yahweh; but on this occasion he is the humiliated Messiah. The fact is that we are here dealing with a ritual humiliation of the Davidic king which in principle is not unlike that suffered by Babylonian king in the analogous New Year Festival.[13]

The entire vocabulary of Isaiah's convenant theology included the relationship of father/son, master/servant. If the servant abides by the terms of the covenant, he no longer regarded as a "rebel." The term "love" defines the relationship as well if the servant "loves" the suzerain, the suzerain will extend mercy and compassion and create peace. It is important to notice a particular literary form that Isaiah employs in own use of structures, which was the curse reversal. This form was not employed by other Near Eastern writers, but was unique only to Israel. As a legal act of grace could be invoked by Yahweh or his servants, a convenantal curse could be reversed and therefore God's convenantal curse would be avoided, thus allowing the son's of light to have victory over the powers of darkness and chaos.[14]

Dr. Nyman is quite correct is stating that only the Jewish writers allowed a curse reversal. This was due to their belief that Yahweh could extend His loving arm into human history and reverse the consequences of that which would naturally occur. Few biblical students seem to recognize that the cursings of Deuteronomy 28:30 as well the Mosaic curses "unto the tenth generation" were removed in the Book of Ezekiel, starting in chapter 30 and ending in chapter 36 due to the new birth of Israel as a nation. However, in other Near Eastern cultures, due to the divine right of kings, neither Persian nor Assyrian law would permit such an action as in the case of Esther where the King of Persia, Artaxerxes, does not rescind his edict, but he amends it by allowing the Jews to take up arms and defend themselves. The curses were forever. An example of this exists in v. 377 of the Vassal Treaties of Esarhaddon:

> If you try to reverse the curse, to avert the consequences of the oath, think up and carry out *stratagems* in order to reverse the *curse,* to avert the consequences of the oath, you and your sons who will live in the future will be *adjured* by this oath on behalf of the crown prince designate Ashurbanipal, son of your lord, Esarhaddon, which will stay (in vigor) from today until after this treaty.[15]

In Hebraic curses, where the word "*olam*" is used, meaning "throughout your generations" implies this curse, unless lifted by the hand of Yahweh, exists as long the conditions are in force for a radification of the curses to be invoked. As we become familiar with the curse of the law in biblical theology, it becomes very apparent from Middle Eastern thinking why the new birth by resurrection to divine kingship was so important in creating a sinless, righteous king on behalf of his subjects. This is how the new birth in the *bfid* structures of Isaiah would apply to the nation of Israel, as the curse reversal was employed and once again righteousness would prevail.

31 1. In the ancient Near Eastern context, *sdq* related to the loyalty a king or priest owned as servant to his god or suzerain.

> It may indeed have actually been the name of a deity, "Sedeq"; cf. Gen. 14:18, the theophorous name of a king, Melchizedek, *Malki-sedeq,* perhaps "(the god) Sedeq is my king"; and Josh. 10:1; "Adonizedek king of Jerusalem." In Egyptian religion Maat, daughter of Re, was a goddess of justice and righteousness but was also connected with world order; the Pharaoh ruled with Maat (Ps. 89:15 could reflect this background—"righteousness and justice are the foundation" of Yahweh's throne; the king's throne "is established by righteousness," Prov. 16:12).[16]

God's covenant lawsuit, as expressed by the prophets, would also be reversed and the people once again had the opportunity to receive the new convenant (see Jer. 31:33). Professor James A. Sanders declares, in the covenant lawsuit tradition, the major prophetic writers employed seven principal categories within three main groupings. There are as follows:

1. Reference of Authority

A. The Prophet's story: The Court Officers:

1a Autobiographic material	The prophet's call and
1b Biographic material	credentials

B. Israel's Story: The Accused

2a Epic traditions	Israel's call
2b Other history	and credentials

II. The Mercy of the Court

A. Hope in Reformation: The Prophet as Mediator

3a Pleas to people to repent

3b Pleas to God to relent

III. Judgment and Salvation

A. Judgment: The Prophet as Messenger

4 Indictments	Reasons for judgment
5 Sentences	Judgment

B. Hope in Transformation: The Prophet as Evangel

6 Transformation	Purpose for judgment
7 Restoration	Israel's new call and credentials[17]

It is important to remember that in covenant lawsuit tradition, in Israel's courtroom scenes, God is both the judge and the redeemer. Once the plea has been entered into the record of the court, after the credentials of the prophet and Israel are established, a judgment of the court is issued, which may result in curse reversal and restoration of righteousness. Once the convental curse has been suspended, Israel is seen in Yahweh's eyes as a Holy Nation.[18]

In much broader terms, the Dead Sea Scrolls and the Pauline corpus of literature contained in the New Testament deal with curse reversals via the doctrine of justification. First, in the Essene community, one would be given grace and righteous mercy if one were a member of that community (1QH 4:37; 7:29–31; 9:34, 11:29–31; 16.9). Thus the Rule of the Community 11, a text that equates divine righteousness and mercy with God's selection of the members of Qumran community beginning with the teacher of righteousness. A similar combination of righteousness, mercy, and election occurs in the Rule of Community 4:2–8 (1QS 11:5–7, 11–12),

. . . and if I fall in the sin of the flesh in the justice of God, which endures eternally, shall my judgment be. (1QS 11:5–7, 11–12)[19]

In the Dead Sea Scrolls, themes such as corporate election and predestination occur quite frequently. Such concepts were known to the New Testament writers as well. The Apostle Paul, for example, believed in the reversal of Deuteronomic blessings and cursings from the Palestinian covenant, the sacrifice of Jesus having accomplished said reversal. (See Gal. 3:10–14; Rom. 1:16, 3:31, 5–8, 9:30, 10:8, Phil. 3.)[20]

Isaiah also uses motifs that show a return to chaos in chapters 1-5 where gloom and darkness prevail over the land once again, see chapter 8:7–8. Then Isaiah speaks of a new creation, the dawning of a bright light that dispels the darkness (9:2). The chaos creation pattern once again links diverse prophetic material as well as successive units of the *bfid* structure.[21] The *bfid* structure demonstrates the wicked who break covenantal law will experience ruin while the righteous (those who comply with the terms of the Lord's convenants) will experience rebirth. Such intervention takes the form of agents or chosen individuals who carry out the Lord's punishment or deliverance.[22]

It should also be noted that Isaiah and Ezekiel, in chapter 36 (see also Ezekiel 30-33), talk about the rebirth of Zion as well as the rebirth of God's agents. There is also an alternate textual reading of Ezekiel 34:14–16, containing a reference to a divine cow who did not give birth reported by Ephanius and in an earlier pseudepigrahic text, *The Acts of Peter,* 24 and in Tertullian (A.D. 145–220). This prophecy contained in the variant textual reading of Ezekiel 34:14–16 was rejected at the Council of Yabneh in A.D. 90. Neither is it found in any of the Dead Sea Scrolls from Cave 4 that contain many sources from Ezekiel of fragmentory remains.[23]

However, the biblical writers were well aware of the ancient, such as the new birth of not only cows, but goats as well.

So this imagery is being reapplied to the rebirth of a nation and later narrowed to the individual. It can be clearly established that John's use of the *aorist* tense in John 3:3–11 with the Greek word *gennao—γενναω*—shows that Nicodemus, as a teacher of Israel, was supposed to have knowledge of the birth and the ruin and the rebirth of Israel.

> γενναω, 1 aor. pass.
> 1. beget—a. *to become the father of* (Gen. 4:18); Mt. 1:3,d 5f. Pass. *be begotten:* γκ τηζ παιδισκηζ κατα οαρα w. *the slave-woman, according to the flesh* Gal. 4:23. σ κατα σαρκα γευυηθειζ he that was begotten in natural fashion (opp. σ κατα πυενμα) v. 29 το ευ αντη γεννθεν εκ πωευατοζ εστιν *that which is conceived in her is of the Spirit.*[24a,b]

The Latin equivalent of this term is *generatio,* the aorist tense in Latin being *generatiuus,* meaning having begetting power. The lexical definition of *generatio* is as follows:

> (*of divine persons, esp. of the relation between God the Father and Christ*) reproduction; (also *spiritual*) birth (of *men*); birth (of *Christ*); origin; (*with personification, allegory*); element re-generation; a generation; extent of a man's *life from birth to death;* all future life, eternity; class (*of men, according to their piety or impiety*); race; whole human race (GAVEDENT. serm. 8, 35: CASSIOD. in psalm. 15.8); (*of soul, thought, desires*) origin; (*of earth animals*) product, offspring (*also fig.*); class, species.[25]

Jesus is taking the concepts of the called agents and applying it to the assembly of the called-out ones who were the individuals who experienced the rebirth of the spirit as well as a new citizenship in the new community and the new Jerusalem. It was also common knowledge in the Jewish frame of thinking that in daily Jewish life they considered the activities of the day beginning at morning to be a type of resurrection to a new life, a type of ascension. Then at the retirement of evening, a sleep at the end of the day, which would picture death and a type of descension to the grave: one's life was in the hands of the Creator while one slept due to the lack of the awareness of the passing of time during sleep. *L'hiahim* or life in the Jewish mindset was facing daily activity of life in regards to how we conducted our lives.

Paul also adds to this concept in regard to his human nature by stating "I die daily" (to his old self or lower nature), nevertheless in Christ he received a newness of life. That's why the experience of the new birth on a higher spiritual plane fits the Jewish model. We walk in newness of life as a new creation. Therefore the evidence of conversion would be in the change of how one conducts his life.

All these concepts must have been in the thoughts of Jesus during his dialogue with the teacher of Israel, Nicodemus. It is possible that in a wider grammatical and cultural linguistic concept, the word *ganneo* could possibly imply the entire *bfid* structure of from ruin to rebirth, not just for Israel, but for God's called agents as well? The use of the *aorist* implies the conversion of God's called agents at this time with the final redemption of the body, soul, and spirit as experienced as new birth in the resurrection. Notice the striking patternism between Jesus's new birth by the water and the spirit into the kingdom of God and the allusion to the ancient enthronement and coronation rituals in sacred kingship as well as the rebirth of the pagan deities.

Until the 1950s, various attempts were made to isolate Isaiah's servant songs from the rest of the three divisions of his writings. The exegesis that resulted from this effort neither broke new ground nor appeared to resolve any perennial problems. "For a short while, Engnell's attempt to interpret the songs within a mythical pattern of the death and rebirth of a divine king evoked much debate, but soon the alleged ancient Near Eastern parallels dissolved under close scrutiny."[26]

Scholars are divided regarding just how deep of an impact the literary borrowing of the motif of death, burial, and resurrection of divine made upon Israel's theology. Exegites in both the Psalms as well as the servant songs of Isaiah are in real conflict over this matter. It appears Israel used similar literary and liturgical forms to reveal Yahweh's dwelling amongst His people and the *bfid* structures of the death and rebirth applies to the nation of Israel itself.

As far as the servant songs are concerned, they are Messianic in scope where the Messiah shall suffer humiliation and mocking, and the death, burial, and resurrection motifs are found in New Testament literature. It was the exegesis of Isaiah 53:3 regarding the rejection of the Messiah that was crucial to our understanding. The Hebrew sages have regarded this text to apply to Israel as the suffering servant while Christian tradition interprets this passage to represent the church's messiah suffering on behalf of the sins of His people.

The Ascension of the Reborn King

Scholars such as Samuel A. B. Mercer held that the "ritual act of ablutions—washing and sprinkling—symbolized new birth"[27] This ritualistic ceremony was possibly adopted by Israelite kings as they ascended back to the throne completely cleansed of all wrongdoing, whose sins were buried in the past of the previous year. This indicates some similarity between the ritual cleansing and the forgiveness of the sins of the nation offered through the high priest every Yom Kippur.

> There may be an intimation of the nation of rebirth in the accounts of the ancient Israelite kings. It is recounted of Saul that

the Spirit of the Lord came upon Saul following his anointing whereupon he became a new man (see 1 Samuel 10:6, 10). Similarly, the Spirit of the Lord came upon David immediately following his anointing to be king (see 1 Samuel 16:13). In later Jewish tradition, the association of coronation with rebirth became explicit: in the Talmud it is said that the king becomes on the day of his coronation 'like a one year old babe who has not known the taste of sin.'[28]

As biblical students and scholars, we should never forget this liturgical reenactment is not always recorded in the biblical chronological record with the same beginning of the ascension year versus a non-ascension year. The ignorance on the part of a few researchers has caused fatal errors in the attempt to harmonize the chronological orders found in the list of Israel and Judah as well the tables of the surrounding nations.

The years reckoned in Ptolemy's canon are Egyptian years of 365 days each, with no leap years. For this reason the 907 years of the canon are 226 3/4 days shorter than 907 Julian years, and the year of the canon was thus a wandering year, beginning with 26 February 747 B.C. and commencing one day earlier every four years. By A.D. 160, the Egyptian New year's Day had moved back to 14 July. In the Babylonian and Persian sections, the canon reckons each reign from 1 Thoth, the Egyptian New Year's Day, after the king came to the throne.

For the Greek and Roman rulers, the canon reckons each reign from 1 Thoth preceding the ruler's accession. It will be noticed that this method employed by Ptolemy is equivalent to the use of the accession-year system for Babylon and Persia and the nonaccession-year system for Greece, Egypt and Rome—the very systems used by the rulers of those lands at those times. A king whose reign was less than a year (which did not embrace the New Year's Day) would not be mentioned in the list. No fractions of years are counted, these being taken care of by throwing the beginning of a ruler's reign forward to the New

Year's Day following or back to the New Year's Day preceding his actual accession as above mentioned. For a good discussion of this and other related phases of this problem, see Josel Honthein *'Die Chronologie des 3. and 4. Buches der Konige' Zeitshrift fur katholische Theologie* 42 (1918): 4632–82, 687–718.[29]

The data supplied by Thiele demonstrates that we are dealing with a cross-cultural liturgical cycle of temple reenactment, at least as far as the order of most of events are concerned. Therefore, biblical chronologists since the 1920s have been increasingly aware of the fact that these liturgical New Year's celebrations can't always be measured with one standard calendar.

The death and rebirth liturgical cycle was also understood to apply to the life-giving waters provided by the Nile River. "The flood represented a 'renewal' or even a 'rebirth' of the river; as early as the Old Kingdom, its waters were called 'the new water.' "[30] Allen J. Christenson adds,

> The annual rising of the Nile in Egypt was believed to recapitulate the Great Flood at the dawn of time. The feast commemorating the Nile inundation was called the Feast of Intoxication in honor of the miraculous changing of the floodwaters to wine. All Egyptians drank heavily during the feast, believing that the sweetness of the wine and their own drunkenness would ritually cause the gods to forget men's faults and limit the floodwaters from destroying them again.[31]

Modern scholarship suggests many ancient parallels are common amongst all Near Eastern temple motifs in the fact that they have a creation drama with fall and redemption cycles reenacted in temple drama. Chaos motifs of light and darkness were also employed to show that in the great eschatan, light would rule over darkness. We also find the death/burial/resurrections cycles in the ascension of the Egyptian king, who was given a coronation name that often marked the Pharoah's burial sites. This was symbolic of the new nature and the new righteousness, which would proceed through the king's just rule due to the fact his divine right of kingship would have come from the deity who provided his resurrection and anointed him to reign with divine authority over his subjects. Alongside of these rituals, we have the mysteries of Dionysus and Aristaeus, who derive their resurrection cycles from the mystery of the bee and honey and the royal jelly as well as the wedding feast, which symbolizes pollination and rebirth,

> "the Righteous Aristeaus," the only one of all his brethren to escape the great destruction of the human race. In the beginning he traveled through the earth bringing the civilizing blessings of horticulture, and especially the bee culture, to a benighted humanity. . . . Arriving in Africa, Aristaeus bestowed there his gifts of honey and olive oil; he also celebrated a super drinking bout with Dionysus, a contest in which the god of wine was the victor. And there at the end of his journey, he founded a city and a dynasty; the land was named Cyrene after his mother, and the dynasty was that of the Battids, the original possessors, H. R. Hall would believe, of the *bat* or *bi.t* titles of the rulers of Egypt.[32]

The Greeks shared in this death/burial/resurrection motif recorded in the myth of Dionysus:

> The Greek god of wine was Dionysus. In Dionysian tradition, water was also a symbol of death, whereas wine was the instrument of new life. Soon after birth, the infant Dionysus was hacked to pieces and submerged in boiling water. He miraculously achieved rebirth to immortality by means of a sacred grape vine.[33]

Another cycle that was quite common in ancient cultures was the water to wine motif. Water is the symbol of destruction and wine is the symbol of redemption. However, Israelite culture viewed water as a symbol of cleansing or purification and wine the symbol of life in the community through the convenant. Jesus uses this by way of analogy in his first miracle during the wedding feast at Canaan where He turned approximately 120 gallons of water into pure wine. And at this particular wedding feast, many were getting drunk. In the Johnine epistle, we see the terms "water/wine" stated in water theology through the work of the vine as his theme where he records Christ's high priestly prayer couched in temple motifs borrowed from Ezekiel.[34] He includes Christ's miracles at marriages, including the work of baptism and the new birth.

Even the Savior Himself in John 4:10, cites living waters flowing out of the belly, *mayim hayyim,* quoting the Old Testament (Num. 19:17) translated as "running water."[35] Oftentimes New Testament literature refers to the new birth, with phrases like "being born of the water and the spirit" (John 3:5–6) as well as being "washed by the water of the word." In addition to the statement in Romans 6, dealing with baptism being the symbol of a watery grave as the New Covenant member is involved in becoming a convert to the biblical community of faith. Even in John 7, during the Feast of Tabernacles, Our Lord once again uses this liturgical cycle. "On the last day, the great day of the festival, Jesus stood and cried out: 'Let anyone who is thirsty come to me! Let anyone who believes in me come and drink!' As scripture says, 'From his heart shall flow streams of living water.' " (John 7:37–39a)

A concept that is found in the writings of Isaiah (25:8) shows us overcoming death by the power of living water that stems from temple imagery and is restated in the Book of Revelation where God shall wipe away all tears from their eyes (Rev. 22:1–2). The concept is employed to show the tree of life and the *new* waters from the Messiah's holy city completing the ritual cycle that began with the Messiah like a lamb, opening not his mouth (Isa. 53:7). This text indicates the lamb didn't open his mouth and go through the "Opening-of-the-Mouth" Egyptian rite, but it is an allusion to it and the writer was obviously familiar with it,[36] such as is found in the papyrus of Ani,

> Thy mouth was closed, but I have set in order for thee thy mouth and thy teeth. I open for thee thy mouth, I open for thee thy two eyes. I have opened for thee thy mouth with the instrument of Anubis. I have opened thy mouth with the instrument of Anubis, with the iron tool with which the mouth of the gods were opened.[37]

We find a similar pattern in Isaiah 6:6–7, which resembles the Egyptian rite of the Opening-of-the-Mouth ritual, which was the first enthronement ceremonial rite. Once again Avraham Gileadi explains:

> The seraph formalizes Isaiah's expiation of sins by the symbolic act of cleansing the lips with an ember that he takes with tongs from the altar of atonement (6:6–7). That performance resembles the Egyptian rite of the Opening-of-the-Mouth with an adze or meteoric iron, which, in the older Egyptian temple literature, represents an initiatory phase in the king's ritual ascent to deification. The restoring of the eyes to see, the ears to hear, and the legs to walk accompanies the Egyptian rite of the Opening-of-the-Mouth.
>
> "Isaiah's identifying himself with his people by means of the imagery of unclean lips takes on another aspect when we consider that this represents a premeditated account. At the Opening-of-the-Mouth rite, Isaiah seems to be expressing a desire to do for this people as has been done for him. Isaiah does not anticipate that his mission will be to bear evil tidings when he so willingly accepts his call (6:8). He learns the magnitude of his people's rebellion against the Lord only when the Lord commissions him as a hardener of the heart: 'Go, and say to

these people, Go on hearing, but not understanding; go on seeing, but not perceiving!' (6:9).[38]

Just as Isaiah stated to Israel, Yahweh's own people would "hear and not understand," our Savior, though the authorship of Matthew, which Matthew related to his own community, was as follows: "The reason I talk to them in parables is that they look without seeing and listen without hearing or understanding. So in their case what was spoken by the prophet Isaiah is being fulfilled" (Matt. 13:13–14). Dr. Daniel H. Ludlow makes the following observation:

> 13:9 This verse could also have been translated 'Let him that has ears listen.' Other translations are 'The man who has ears to hear should use them' and 'Listen, anyone who has ears.' . . . 13:13 This verse could also have been translated 'This is why I speak to them by the use of illustrations, because, looking, they look in vain, and hearing, they hear in vain, neither do they get the sense of it.' The basic meaning of the Greek term is that the people listen but they do not hear nor understand.[39]

The Greek term "to listen" is one of three zones of function that relate to the eye's heart, (Matt 6:19, 7:6); the second relates to mouth-ears, (Matt. 7:7–11); and the last group refers to the hands-feet found in Matthew 7:13–72. However, in Matthew's description of the generation that hears and does not understand, is not functioning corporately with mouth-ears, eyes-heart, hands-feet connections of all three zones. The corporate personality is dysfunctional. The hands-feet zone is an allusion to the Spirit of God, which literally means "to blow." It is only by this power are we able to hear (mouth-ears) so we can do (hands-feet) the will of the Father as revealed to us. The symbology of eyes, arms, legs, mouth, of a linen-clothed man, flaming arms and legs, voice sounding of many waters, mouth issued two-edged sword, face like the sun shining in full strength (Rev.

1:14–16) illustrates the complete functionality of personhood. The apocalyptic vision is one of complete personhood pictured in the Son of Man.[40]

Hebrew Parallelisms and Apocalyptic Literature

One of the methods used in interpreting Old Testament literature is through a study of Hebrew parallelism that was later adopted by Greek poets and is used sparingly in the New Testament. In modern times this common pattern in Hebrew poetry had ceased to be used until Bishop Robert Lowth of the Anglican Church rediscovered this poetic style in 1753. This was 2000 years after Hebrew had ceased to be a common spoken language.[41] Some examples and types of parallelisms are:

1. Synonymous parallelism: a theme of the first line repeats itself in the second line, but in slightly different words:

    a. A fool's mouth is his ruin, and
    b. His lips are the name of his soul (Prov. 18:7).

    a. An ox knows his owner, and
    b. An ass his master's crib (Isa. 1:3).

2. Antithetic parallelism: a thought of the second part of a couplet contrasts with an opposite theme in the first:

    a. When pride comes, then comes disgrace,
    b. But with the humble is wisdom (Prov. 11:2).

a. If you are willing and obedient, you will eat the good things of the earth;
b. But if you refuse and disobey, you will be devoured by the sword (Isa. 1:19–20).

3. Emblematic parallelism; the ideas of two lines are compared by means of a simile or metaphor:

a. Like clouds and wind without rain
b. Is the man who boasts of a gift he does not give (Prov. 25:14).

a. Though your sins be [red] as scarlet,
b. They shall be white as snow
c. Though they be red as dyed wool,
d. They shall be [white] as fleece (Isa. 1:18).

4. Synthetic parallelism: the second line *completes* or *complements* the thought of the first in a variety of possible combinations (question-answer, proposition-conclusion, situation-consequence, protasisapodosis, etc.) An idea is introduced in the first line, which is incomplete or generates questions about that idea. The second line then completes the idea, or answers a question raised by the first line.

a. Yes, though I walk through the valley of the shadow of death, I will fear no evil;
b. For thou art with me; thy rod and thy staff they comfort me (Ps. 23:4).

a. I [the Lord] have nourished and brought up children,

b. And they have rebelled against me (Isa. 1:2).

5. Composite parallelism: three or more phrases develop a theme by amplifying a concept or defining a term:

Blessed is the man
a. Who walks not in the counsel of the ungodly,
b. Nor stands in the way of sinners,
c. Nor sits in the seat of the scornful (Ps. 1:1).

a. A nation of sin!
b. A people laden with iniquity!
c. A brood of evildoers:
d. Children that are corrupters:
They have forsaken the Lord (Isa. 1:4).

6. Climactic parallelism: part of one line (a word or phrase) is repeated in the second or other lines until a theme is developed, which then *culminates* in a main idea or statement:

a. Ascribe to the Lord heavenly beings
b. Ascribe to the Lord Glory and strength
c. Ascribe to the Lord glory of his name
Worship the Lord in holy array (Ps. 29:1–2).

a. Your country is desolate
b. Your cities are burnt down
c. Your land is devoured by strangers before your eyes
It is desolate; as overthrown by strangers (Isa.a 1:7).

Sometimes the statement is given first and then followed by the repeated term (a phrase or word) with its attached phrases:

The daughter of Zion is left
a. Like a booth in a vineyard
b. Like a hut in a cucumber field
c. Like a city beleaguered (Isa. 1:8).

7. Introverted parallelism: a pattern of words or ideas is stated and then repeated, but in a reverse order. This parallelism is also called chiasmus:

a. We *have escaped* as a bird
b. From *the snare of the fowlers*
b. *The snare is broken,*
a. *And we have escaped*! (Ps. 124:7).

a. Ephriam shall not envy
b. Judah
b. And Judah
c. shall not harass Ephraim (Isa. 11:13).

The poet can develop and then introvert as many ideas as he desires:

a. Make the *heart* of this people fat,
b. And make their *ears* heavy,
c. And shut their *eyes*,
c. Lest they see with their *eyes*,
d. And hear with their *ears*,
a. And understand with their *heart*,

And convert [return], and be healed [heal themselves]. (Isa. 6:10).

(abc) Come to the house of the *God of Jacob*, . . .and *we will walk in his paths*

d. And he shall judge among the *nations*, . . .
ef. And they shall beat their *swords into plowshares*,
e'f. And their *spears into pruninghooks*:
d. *Nation* shall not lift up sword against *nation*, . . .
(a'b'c') *O house of Jacob*, . . . *let us walk* in the light of the Lord (Isa. 2:3–5).[42]

Introverted parallelisms are bound frequently in literature and are used by the prophet in the inspired prophetic voice to inspire future readers of the text. This writer has already stated the rabbinic use that Our Lord employed with in-house teaching from Isaiah 6:10 and reapplied it to his disciples in Matthew 13:13. It is interesting to note that Our Lord reinterpreted an introverted parallelism in which he lifted Isaiah out of its own context and applied to his own generation using ears, eyes, and heart metaphors to show the people's spiritual condition was the same as that in Isaiah's day.

Isaiah also makes use of this prophetic voice when he employs the prophetic past tense as illustrated in Isaiah 42:9. That is, he would write about the future as though the event had already happened. The Apostle John also makes use of this form in the Book of Revelation where he makes the statement regarding the beast and the false prophet already being cast into the lake of fire. Another use of parallelism in the prophetic voice is the composite parallelism employed by the prophet Daniel in which he refers to the existing kingdoms in his own day and uses the third amplification to expound on the Kingdom of God (Dan. 2:44).

It should be clear to biblical scholars that it is essential for us to understand the use of poetic parallelisms employed by the Old and New Testament authors if we are to fully comprehend the application of the writer's message. Parallelisms also help us in our understanding regarding the New Testament writers' reinterpretations of the prophetic voice and the foundation that Our Lord and other New Testament writers used to develop their theological themes. These forms also existed in the Dead Sea Scrolls and in other intertestamental literature, showing that these parallelisms and literary structures were widely used in the Near East before the existence of the New Testament church and the completion of its canon.

Ezra, Scribe and Editor

The 400-year period between the testaments, commonly called the intertestamental period, has been considered to be a time when a famine of God's revelation allegedly took place, ostensibly, after the closing of the canon.

> The time period of the writing of the Apocrypha covers roughly the last two centuries prior to the Christian Era and the First Century A.D. . . . The names of former Jewish prophets and leaders were also invoked in support of various of these apocryphal productions. Although the activity of the Hebrew prophets had ended and the Old Testament canon was closed, these apocalyptic writings were frequently sent forth under the name of some ancient Hebrew worthy in order to add greater weight to these new predictions of things to come—such as *The Book of Enoch, The Testaments of the Twelve Patriarchs, The Wisdom of Solomon, The Assumption of Moses,* et cetera.[43]

During the days of Ezra, many traditional scholars claim there existed a great Jewish Synagogue where the *Soferim*, the

Great Assembly, edited the Torah, Haftorah, and the writings, which resulted in the closing of the Old Testament canon.

> Undoubtedly, such instructions and supplements have existed from the very time of the giving of the Law, and they were included in the Mosaic Oral Law. The subsequent ages also added interpretations, which helped to clarity the Law. As interpretations in ages previous to that of the *Soferim.*[44]

Modern scholarship maintains that Ezra only served as a general editor of the Old Testament and there was no closure placed upon the canon, therefore the writings of the Pseudepigrapha and the Apocrypha and the Dead Sea Scrolls may not have been as far from normative Judaism as previously thought. This could possibly explain why diaspora Judaism accepted them as canonical while the School of the Poor at Jerusalem did not. This was the tradition of the ruling at Jamnia, from which western historical Christianity derives its canonical authority for the Old Testament. It was possibly out of these extra-biblical writings from which Josephus derived his sources for the history of the Jews.

As previously indicated, some form critics have questioned the validity of the closing of Old Testament canonical literature by asserting that Ezra served as the general redactor due to the fact that the Old Testament corpus had not been canonized, but was considered a sacred story, even in the Qumran text as late as 50 B.C. and the tradition of Moses, which contained much larger bodies of material that had been transmitted through oral tradition, with different reporting techniques one of Ezra 10 and another for Nehemiah 10, showing a different emphasis between the two leaders, who served in different functions in their community. This was edited in the day of Ezra from various traditions into a smaller redacted body of literature.[45]

Ezra arrived in Jerusalem with two important documents in his hand. One was the "*torah* of Moses," and the other was a letter from the Persian emperor, Artaxerxes, giving him authority in Judah. The emperor's authorization empowered Ezra to teach and to enforce "the law of your God, which is in your hand." The enforcement powers included included fines, imprisonment, and the death penalty.

What was this "*torah* of Moses," this "law of your God which is in your hand"? References to it in the biblical books of Ezra and Nehemiah include material from JE, D, and P. It is therefore likely that the book that Ezra brought from Babylon to Judah was the full Torah—the Five Books of Moses—as we know it.[46]

The major questions between historical and redactive critics are how much redaction took place amongst the scribes under Ezra's leadership. One of the few anchor points that form critics have is in the validity of the traditions, which may contain sources of earlier oral transmission lines of priestly authority, which became the historical accounts.

But where a tradition has been established on the basis of a historical event, and where the historical event is also accorded permanent significance, the norm of a possible criticism of tradition must be primarily only the "return to the source," the investigation of what was originally experienced, done and meant.[47]

The reactions of historical and form critics regarding the documentary hypothesis are still radically different. However, moderate schools of thought are now emerging, attempting to avoid the pitfalls of either extreme. This moderate approach recognizes the unity and the diversity of sources that comprise the church's canon.

5 The Cultural Influence of Hebraic Literary Traditions

As stated earlier, during the reign of the Egyptian Hyksos, the Hebrew people had settlements all the way up the Nile. This influence grew steadily with several migrations up to and including Nebuchadnezzar's campaign, when the prophet Jeremiah, in one of his letters to Babylon, issued a prophecy that was fulfilled in 568 B.C.

> Vv1-14. Jeremiah makes a last appeal to the apostate people. Not all Jews had settled at Tahpanhes (ch. 43:7–8). There was a colony at Migdol, a city near the northeastern boundary of Egypt, about twelve miles south of Pelusium. Others had gone farther south, to Noph, Memphis, about 125 miles south of the Mediterranean Sea; still others had gone as far as Pathros, the Egyptian Pa-ta-ris, "Land of the South," Southern, or Upper Egypt, extending southward from ancient Memphis.[1]

Nebuchadnezzar defeated Egypt and campaigned as far south as Syene, whose modern name is Assuan. Josephus records that this campaign occurred earlier when all the Jews in Egypt were then deported to Babylon after the murder of Gedeliah. While in Babylon during the seventy-year exile, the Jews would prosper as well as develop their Talmudic literary traditions. After the seventy years were completed, during the decree of Cyrus, the Medio-Persian monarch (see Ezra 1:3–4, 6:1–12) migrations back to Jerusalem and Egypt would keep Judaism's influence alive in those regions. Later, great temples would be erected in both Elaphantine and Suza in Egypt circa 250 B.C., while the resettlements of the Hebrew people along the Nile would allow for a Semitic Greek literary tradition to be compiled. Meanwhile, under the leadership of Ezra and Nehemiah, Israel's literary traditions would once again be reestablished.[2]

In the Fourth centuries B.C., when Classical Greek became the international language during the campaigns of Alexander the Great, a Semitic Greek dialect was used for literary purposes. Although this dialect was never spoken to an international audience, it was employed in that local economy when dealing with those Hebrew settlements.

> "Moreover, it remains to be considered how far the quasi-Semitic colloquialisms of the papyri are themselves due to the influence of the large Greek-speaking Jewish population of the Delta" (Swete, *The Apocalypse of St. John,* 1906 p. cxx). Thackery (*Gr. of the O. T. in Gk,* vol. 1, p. 20) uses the small number of Coptic words in the Greek papyri against the notion of Hebrew-influence on the κοιυη in Egypt. However, Thackeray (p. 27) notes that the papyri so far discovered tell us little of the private life of the Jews of Egypt and of the Greek used by them specifically. The marshes of the Delta were not favourable for the preservation of the papyri. The κοιυη received other foreign influences we know. The Jews of the Dispersion spoke the vernacular κοιυη everywhere, but they read the LXX, "a written Semitic Greek which no one ever spoke, far less used for literary purposes, either before or after." And yet the Hellenistic Jews all over the world could not read continually the LXX and not to some extent feel the influence of its peculiar style.[3]

For decades scholars of the classical languages have noted forms of speech used by the priestly class versus the language of the common people. This was true in Semitic cultures as well as Greek and Egyptian. From the development of the sacred writings, which were oftentimes borrowed from the oral traditions of the priests, we see a form of Egyptian dating from the Thinite Dynasties called Hieratic, written cursively from right to left, while the Hieroglyphic or "sacred writings" was written in columns from either direction. From the time of the First Intermediate Period through the Middle Kingdom into the New Kingdom, when the Pyramid and Coffin texts were compelled, the Hieratic and Hieroglyphic traditions were in constant use as "sacred writings" until the Persian period in circa 500 B.C. when the Demotic form of Egyptian was in full use by the common people. During this period, the Book of the Dead and the Hypocephali transmission lines would extend through the Ptolomaic Period until their final compilation.[4] As previously stated, the tongue of the common people was shared in the Greek-speaking Jewish centers of Egypt as well as larger national use of the Demotic Egyptian for the rest of the Egyptian general populace.

The Exportation of Middle Eastern Culture to North America

It has long been assumed that Middle Eastern empires such as the Hittites, Phoenicians, Babylonians, and Egyptians only affected the Mediterranean geographical area. This has been challenged since the 1920s and revisited in the '60s and '70s by scholars such as Cyrus Gordon, Frank C. Heibben, and Barry Fell, and by archaeological discoveries in the Americas showing that worldwide trade may have existed with both the American continents and these empires as far back as 800 B.C. Certainly map makers such as Peleg were known to North American explorers in early times if we follow the witnesses of early Greek historians, such as Homer, Heroditus, and Diodorus (5:19; 1–5). Some have suggested that even the Celts possibly migrated from Assyria in c. 400 B.C. to Spain and Portugal via ships of Tarshish to the Americas, and later to Ireland, Lister, and Iona in the fourth century A.D. The Celts also brought their Ogam language to the Americas,

> First of the foreign alphabets is one that the scribe calls Egyptian, and in this he certainly correct, for it matches very well the tables of Egyptian Aramaic forms compiled by Professor Robert H. Pjeiffer from Egyptian papyri of the period around 400 B.C. and published in his work *Ancient Alphabets* (1947). These tables had already been completed in 1936, in which year they were exhibited as a part of the special celebrations of the tercentenary of Harvard University. Thus, as we now see from the comparative tables given in this chapter, the medieval Irish monk who wrote the Ogam Tract was already in possession of information that was only regained by modern students of Semitic epigraphy after years of excavation and research in the Egyptian desert. But all the modern students of Irish could find to say about this important correlation was that "the Egyptian alphabet, so called, is a very corrupt form of the Hebrew alphabet."[5]

Further research indicates that there were three main migrations of the Celts from Assyria to Mesopotamia, from the Iberian peninsula into the British Isles, as well as to the Americas. Their influence was felt as far north as Scandinavian, where Odin would later settle from his origins in Circassia, an area lying between the Black and Caspian Seas, the home of the Goths. (The Saxon kings traced themselves back to Odin, who was traced back in his descent from David, as may be seen in a very ancient manuscript in the Herald's College of London.)[6] The document just referenced from Heralds' College in London described Odin's ancestry dating back to Jerusalem during a period of polytheistic worship. It is believed that during Odin's migrations from the land of the Goths to northwestern Europe, he brought with him various pagan forms of polytheism. And from the migrations of the Iberian peninsula, came the Celts bringing with them ancient practices dedicated to the god of fire of the Canaanites, Moloch as well as the Egyptian concept of sun worship.

From 400 B.C. to the fourth century A.D., these trade/migration routes of ancient peoples included those of the Celts, the ships of Tarshish, and the Phoenicians as contained in II Esdras 13:40–47, which describes the movements of the Celts across the Euphrates into Mesopotamia, passing near to the village of Pastash before their western migrations would take place. With this migration came sun worship through Phoenicia, with origins in Egypt, which practices were adopted by the Celts in their new homeland in the Americas. In the later wave of Celtic migrations to Lister and Iona, Jewish Christianity would flourish and continue the same rivalry against sun god worship as had been in the ancient lands.[7]

> These calender matters, linked with Celtic religion and hence reflected in the physical orientation of their religious buildings, are undoubtedly to be traced back to an ancient cult of sun worship, and certain symbols widely distributed across the Old World at sites where the sun was worshipped occur also on the walls or lintels of some of the Celtic temples in New England. There are also found at some other sites linked with various tribes of North American Indians, and there can be no doubt that the Indian shamans acquired these symbols from contact with ancient colonists in America such as the Celts.
>
> The sun, as the giver of warmth that promotes the growth of all vegetation, both the forest foliage and the edible crops, and whose annual return after the winter months ushers in spring and the birth of the young of many wild animals, came to be regarded as the *Giver-of-Life,* a phrase that appears in the ancient Semitic Creation Hymn preserved by the Pima people of Arizona and Mexico.[8]

Furthermore, Egyptian, Phoenician, and Hebraic artifacts and inscriptions found in the Americas do seem to have a close resemblance to their counterparts in the Near East. Not all scholars are convinced that these findings produce as concrete an example of a linguistic connection between the Old and New Worlds as scholars like Gordon and Fell. But when we assemble all of the known data together, the evidence at this time seems very compelling.

> In Telezinco Nahuatl, *wa* means "and" as in Semitic. For reasons of internal Egypto-Semitic linguistics, we know that an earlier form was *iwa.* Again quite independent of Nahuatl evidence, final: *n* is sometimes suffixed, so that a complete form in Egypto-Semitic would be *iwan* identical with regular Nahuatl *iwan* "and" (often spelled in Spanish fashion, *ihuan*). Sooner or later Old World philosophy will have to reckon with linguistic phenomena from the New World.
>
> The Indo-European impact on Middle American is evident even at the grammatical level. Thus an initial vowel (called "augment" by Indo-Europeanists) appears in Nahuatl. Sometimes it is hard to tell which Indo-European language is responsible for loans in Nahuatl. For example *teo-tl,* "god," could have been introduced from Greek *theo-s* or Latin *deu-s.*[9]

The correlation between the Middle Eastern creation accounts and the creation accounts discovered in the Americas may linguistically show a common source, which may have contained an equivilant to the Hebrew *waw* consecutive. This may have been derived from the great Semitic Mother Tongue and was translated into the Semitic creation accounts. Then, as the settlements in the Americas developed, so did their own localized usage of the chaos/order and light/darkness motifs.

> Before Creation "there was only immobility and silence in the darkness, in the night. Only the Creator, the Maker, Tepeu,

Gucumatz, the Forefathers were in the water surrounded by light" (P. V., p. 81). Thus darkness existed prior to Creation, as in Genesis 1:1–2, which means: "When God set about creating Heaven and Earth, the Earth was chaotic, with darkness over the surface of the Deep, and the Spirit of God flying over the surface of the water." Moreover, water is preexistent in both P. V. and Genesis.[10]

Another universal theme, which runs continuously through the creation accounts, is the number seven, which starts with the Western tradition of Genesis 1 and is also found in transatlantic cultural borrowing as well as the sabbatical cycle, which even appears in the Mayan calender.

> This preoccupation with "seven" also pervades the records and institutions of Mesopotamia, Egypt, Ugarit, Greece, tcs. A good Mayan example is P.V. pp. 219–220: "for seven days he [Gucumatz] mounted to the skies and for seven days he went to Xibalba. . . . "[11]

Could it be possible that this preoccupation with "seven" originated from creation as the record of Genesis 2:2–3 affirms?

Other Hebraic stories abound as well, such as the North American counterpart to the Joseph saga, which is contained in the legend about Eototo, a Moses figure.

> Eototo became the leader of his people and escaped the land. Aholoi was cut off from the Exodus. These two were to meet again in the distant future "in the guise of other men." A similar story is told of Joseph in Egypt (the young brother of the House of Israel), who died before the Exodus, and whose descendents were separated from the main body . . . and Moses (a descendent of Levi, the elder brother of Joseph), who led the Israelites out of Egypt but never entered the promised land with them.[12]

In this legend a Semitic type of blessing was received by Eototo and Aholi, with Eototo being the elder, receiving the right-hand blessing and Aholi, the younger, receiving the left-hand blessing, such as Ephraim and Manasseh.[13] The main difference between the Semitic and the North American Hopi blessings is that the Semitic was a patriarchial blessing and the Hopi was a matriarchial blessing.

Just as right- and left-hand blessings were employed on both sides of the Atlantic, another interesting parallel practice occurred, which was entitled the prayer circle, which resulted in a chant and Davidic dance as practiced in the Jewish synagogue, later continued in the early New Testament church, and is still existent in Orthodox Christianity today.

> When a prayer circle is formed in a kiva ceremony, it is to be free of all impurities. "They sing a purifying song. Anybody who has a guilty conscience or some bad thoughts that are bothering him, he is supposed to put it out of his mind, wipe it out of his heart." (The same ambiance was required in ancient Syriac prayer circles. A man at the altar tells the circle, "If anyone has any ill feelings against his neighbor, let him be reconciled. If any feels himself unworthy, let him withdraw, for God is witness of these ordinances, and the Son and the Angels.")[14]

This same practice of ritual purification followed by reconciliation is a common theme that runs through biblical literature as well as the philosophies of the three great monotheistic religions. This three witness formula, of "God, the Son and the Angels," was used to consummate a covenant, and through this consummation, forgiveness and righteousness were established as examplified by baptism in the name of the Father, Son, and Holy Spirit (ουομα ιου Παιροζ χαι ιον Υιον χαι τον αγιον πνευματοζ) found in Matthew 28:19, from the authority of the Father, through the Son, and consummated by the Holy Spirit.

It is more coincidental that in both the Inca and Mayan calendars, as well as the Hopi of Arizona, there is possibly contained an Egyptian influence of sun/god worship with a New Year's festival to begin the sacred New Year, followed by an eight-day celebration, which corresponded to the Jewish Feast of Tabernacles.

> I followed the pattern performed in Hopi ceremonies and at a place pointed out by "the people." And it happened on the very day and for the very purpose that Jews celebrated *Rosh ha-Shanah,* the Day of Judgement, of Remembrance, scriptually called "a day of blowing the trumpets", Num. 29:1, "a memorial [proclaimed with the] blowing of trumpets." Lev. 23:24.[15]

Also from these practices, a similar universal ritual pattern emerges, which was closely related to the death/burial/resurrection/birth of the gods motif employed by Middle Eastern cultures.

> The mating of the gods with women is quite widespread. In Homeric epic it is routine. And although our officially purified theology tends to shut our eyes to it, the Bible reflects it too. Genesis 6:2–4 states quite plainly that only the deities mated with the fair daughters of men to sire the ancient heroes. The most important example in history is also Biblical, for Mary conceived Jesus from the Holy Spirit. The P. V., pp. 119–126, relates that a girl names Xquic, impregnated by divine juice, gave birth to the twin gods Hunahpu and Xbalanque, who "were really gods" (p. 94). The birth of a pair of gods (Shabar "Dawn" and Shalem "Dusk") by womankind impregnated by the great god El is incorporated into Ugaritic text #52.[16]

The mating of gods was an erotic Greek concept, a kenotic form whereby the gods became men, but in the Egyptian rebirth cycle, the men became gods. Both Greek and Egyptian concepts were employed in the ritual cycles of the Americas. These concepts were expanded to include the incarnation of the rulers or kings. It was common for the kings of the Mayans, for example, to have a ritual death, burial, and resurrection to deity in the spring fertility ceremony, in which both the king and queen would be "buried" in the temple, their "blood" would be shed (usually by self-piercing), and they would be "reborn" into deity and perfection at the end of the ritual. Due to our lack of knowledge of many of the archaeological and textual ruins left behind, it is very plausible that we have underestimated the greatness and the effect of these world empires.

The Philosophical Schools and the Development of the Dead Sea Scrolls

Across the Atlantic, another development during this period was the establishment of philosophical schools regarding the methodology of interpretation in key centers, such as Alexandria and Athens. Alexandria held the seat of two parallel schools. The first school majored in the Greek philosophers as the philosophy began to flourish in Rome. This Platonic school of thinking was championed by such Roman philosophers as Cicero, who taught Platonic doctrine. The other school was influenced by the Alexandrian wing of the Jewish synagogue, particularly from Philo.

> Though they shared a common language, the Greek and Jewish cultures could not have been more divergent at the time of Christ. Except among the elite in Jerusalem and the Hellenized Jews of Alexandria, the practice of Greek rhetoric and oratory were largely eschewed by the Jews. The complexities of unreal reality accepted by the Greek philosophers in their metaphysical machinations were entirely foreign to those raised on the absolutes taught by Moses and the prophets. This condition reflected

the general attitude of the Jews toward the Gentiles, and posed a major problem for the Church when the Gospel was eventually opened to all nations.[17]

Later, at the beginning of the Christian Era, a new school progressed, founded in Alexandria, Egypt, called the Eclectic school, majoring in Neoplatonic philosophy. In this revamped academic environment, there was marriage of the two philosophies, Hellenism and Platoism, into Neoplatoism, which would heavily influence Christian doctrine. The Mandeans in Persia also established, at this time, religious practices based on the nine steps of Zoroastrian rites.

> The ancient society, remnants of which still survive, traces its origin back to Jerusalem, whence they are said to have migrated first into the desert of Judaea, where they flourished as a typical "baptist" sect for a while (they always display special devotion to John the Baptist). After that they migrated to Harrana and then to southern Mesopotamia, where a handful of them still practice rites, especially baptism, and teach secret doctrines that are at once Jewish and Christian, with a rich Iranian mixture. Their departure from Judaea has been placed in the time of Isaiah. . . . Inevitably their teachings were "sucked into the Gnostic whirlpool" and became exceedingly hard to disentangle, since they "reflect theosophic theories held by certain gnostic groups scattered throughout the Middle East." It is typical of the Mandaeans that though "entirely independent of Christian influence, they kept Sunday as a holy day." Their practices look so very Christian that Alfred Loisy could write that Mandaeism cannot be understood without reference to Christianity.[18]

No doubt this Persian/Gnostic/Jewish/Christian matrix amalgamated many divergent religious practices, which originated in their home country to give way to a new early Christian interpretation of these rites as well as influencing their interpretations of both Jewish and Gnostic texts. Some even suggest the doctrine of the Marcionites of baptism for the dead was practiced by this group.[19] This rite has caused many conservative commentators to doubt the Christian orthodoxy of this group. However, they did retain many Early Orthodox Christian practices, such as the lifting of the hands in praise and worship.

> The Mandaeans, who claim to be descendants of the disciples of John the Baptist, also spread their hands in prayer, *Mandaean Canonical Prayer-book* 35 contains the words, "I address to thee . . . for this congregation of people who have bent their noses to the ground and stretched forth their hands to the intermediate and upper (*worlds*)."
>
> In the Armenian *History of Abel and Cain, the Sons of Adam* 11, we read that when Abel offered his firstborn lamb, it was "with outstretched hands [that] he prayed to the Lord." In one Ethiopic document, Abraham stretches out his hands while offering prayer, while in another Joseph does the same before he dies. In the pseudepigraphic *Gospel of Bartholomew* 2:6–13, Mary stands with the apostles in prayer, spreads out her hands to heaven, and prays. The *History of the Virgin* 156a also has Mary spreading out her hands to pray for the apostles, who were then preaching in various nations. In *Acts of the Holy Apostle* and Evangelist John the Theologian. John "stretched forth his hands, and prayed.[20]

The Mandaean practices contain a hybrid of Gnostic, and early church practices. Coptic influence can also be seen there, with a heavy emphasis on baptism and Sunday resurrection celebrations. The Zoroastrian concept of good and evil was also a part of this matrix. This would have great influence on early patristic Christian theologians in their opinions regarding good and evil.

> The influence of Zoroastrianism, and indeed of the whole Perso-Babylonian culture, is amply illustrated in the writings of the

Jewish apocalyptists of this period and even, though to a lesser extent, in the works of Phariasic Judaism. It is evident too, in the writings of the Qumran Convenantors where there appears, for example, a form of dualism in many ways similar to that of Zoroastrianism, which cannot be explained simply by reference to Old Testament religion. An acquaintance with Zoroastrian eschatology (i.e., doctrine of 'the last things') is indicated in the Old Testament itself; but the Jewish apocalyptists, including the writer of the Book of Daniel, are much more strongly influenced by it. Their whole outlook is governed by the belief that this present evil age was fast drawing to a close and that the new age would speedily be ushered in. This dualistic view of the universe coloured their beliefs concerning the messianic hope, for example, which in the course of time assumed transcendant characteristics and also their conception of the life after death. In this latter case Zoroastrian influence is evident in such matters as the separation of the soul from the body at death, the lot of the departed between death and resurrection, the doctrine of resurrection and their teaching concerning the Last Judgment. Another realm in which the influence was deeply felt is in the greatly developed doctrine of angels and demons and in particular the personalization of evil spirits for which there is no parallel in the Old Testament.[21]

Also in this intertestamental period, the Qumran convenantors were reacting to the temple oblations, claiming they had the correct convenantal understanding as the divinites of light regarding the new convenant established in the writings of Jeremiah because the new covenant was supposed to reestablish the Levitical holiness codes, which were no longer extant at the Jerusalem temple. This group of Essenes located at Qumran also canonized extra psalms not contained in the Masoratic Hebrew Text. These psalms contained praises given to the Lord who is over all divinities, as well as songs of Sabbath sacrifice (4Q404—4QShirShabb). These scrolls also contain seven psalms of magnification where seven wonderful words of thanksgiving will bless the powers of the "divinities" and all those who have hope in the Merciful King and who seek for a return of merciful compassion given to all those who will praise His glorious kingship.

> [And may he bless all the holy ones] who bless him [and proclaim him just in the name of his glory. And he will bless those permanently blessed. *blank*] 12 [Of the Instructor. Song of sacri]f[ice of the seventh sabbath, of the sixteen]th of the mon[th, Praise the God of the exalted heights.] 13 [you exalted ones among the divinities of knowledge. May the holy ones of Go]d [magnify] the Ki[ng of glory. . . .] (4Q405)[22]

The major difference of understanding kingship and deification between the Qumran community and the Jerusalem temple cult were, at Qumran, the "holy ones" made Qumran covenantors divinities of light and by this illumination process, a type of deification was entered into, while, at Jerusalem, in the temple cult, their doctrine of true holiness was that only God could provide divine holiness from His divine kingship, which would bring justice to the entire earth, which is the divine king's possession (see Is. 6:3), which is liturgically reenacted as the king was under the sovereignty of Yahweh.[23] Their positions on latter-day events were similar to Egyptian apocalyptic genre as well as some apocalyptic traditions within Judaism.

Babylonian, Egyptian and Greek Influence on the Biblical Text

All these schools of thought became the matrix supporting the writings and the canonicity of the early New Testament church as well as the beliefs, practices, and methodology of interpreting Scripture, which were employed by the early church fathers.

Another crucial point that many theologians overlook is the Hebrew language, which formulated the Jewish Old Testament, is a verb-oriented as well as conversational in its approach in revealing God's actions with the prophets, i.e., God walking with Adam/God conversing with Abraham/God showing himself to Moses. Even the Hebraic concept of grace is verb-oriented in its definition and application while the Christian Greek New Testament is very noun-defined and emphasizes a state of being, i.e., *being* in God's grace as well as God Himself empowering the *Logos* from outside the solar system making Him a divine mystery. Therefore the focus of the Hebrew Old Testament is naturalistic in concept while the Christian Greek New Testament is very transcendent in its theological conceptions. Various attempts were made to militate a marriage between the two systems.

> The earliest methods of Christian exegesis were continuations of the methods which were common at the time to both Greek and Graeco-Judeaen writers. There employed on the same subject-matter. Just as the Greek philosophers had found their philosophy in Homer, so Christian writers found in him Christian theology. When he represents Odysseus as saying, "The rule of many is not good: let there be one ruler," he means to indicate that there should be but one God; and his whole poem is designed to show the mischief that comes of having many gods. When he tells us that Hephaestus represented on the shield of Achilles "the earth, the heaven, the sea, the sun that rests not, and moon full-orbed," he is teaching us the divine order of creation which he learned in Egypt from the books of Moses. So Clement of Alexandria interprets the withdrawal of Oceanus and Tethys from each other to mean the separation of land and sea; and he holds that Homer, when he makes Apollo ask Achilles, "Why fruitlessly pursue him, a god," meant to show that the divinity cannot be apprehended by the bodily powers.

> Some of the philosophical schools which hung upon the skirts of Christianity mingled such interpretations of Greek mythology with similar interpretations of the Old Testament. For example, the writer to whom the name Simon Magus is given, is said to have "interpreted in whatever way he wished both the writings of Moses and also those of the (Greek) poets;" and the Ophite writer, Justin, evolves an elaborate cosmogony from a story of Herakles narrated Herodotus, combined with the story of the garden of Eden. But the main application was to the Old Testament exclusively. The reasons given for believing that the Old Testament has an allegorical meaning were precisely analogous to those which had been given in respect to Homer.[24]

One of the theological difficulties modern scholarship faces is the integration that our New Testament corpus employs from various sources being written and compiled from a Judaic religious system, which was overrun by a Roman civil government and operated in an international Greek environment. As this writer pointed out earlier, even the Septuagint had an Egyptian recension, and concepts from the Egyptian Book of the Dead were cited in preaching the early Christian gospel at Ephesus, employing such concepts as a slaughtered lamb, a final judgment hall verdict, anointing the sick, and the doctrines of resurrection, ascension, coronation, and incarnation. This writer believes there was a stronger Egyptian influence by way of the Coptic Christian Church than has been previously recognized. It has long been established, by the internal evidence, that Mark's gospel was written to congregations in lands outside of Judea, including Egypt, but until the pseudepigraphyl writings were discovered, we had little knowledge of Egyptian influence upon the rest of the early Hebrew Christian Church.

> Profound, too, was the myth of Isis, the Great Mother. . . . The Egyptians worshipped her with special fondness and piety, and raised up jeweled images to her as the Mother of God, her

tonsured priests praised her in sonorous matins and vespers; and in midwinter of each year, coincident with the annual rebirth of the sun towards the end of our December, the temples of her divine child, Horus (god of the sun), showed her, in holy effigy, nursing in a stable the babe that she had miraculously conceived. These Poetic-philosophic legends and symbols profoundly affected Christian ritual and theology. Early Christians sometimes worshipped before the statues of Isis suckling the infant Horus, seeing in them another form of the ancient and noble myth by which woman (i.e., the female principle), creating all things, becomes at last the Mother of God. These—Ra (or, as he was called in the South, Amon), Osiris, Isis and Horus—were the greater gods of Egypt. In later days, Ra, Amon and another god, Ptah, were combined as three embodiments or aspects of supreme and triune deity. . . . Even Pharaoh was a god, always the son of Amon-Ra, ruling not merely by divine right but by divine birth, as a deity transiently tolerating the earth as his home.[25]

Once again, Professor Will Durant has presented some evidence for our case. As stated earlier, literary borrowing was done all over the Mediterranean. Even the Egyptian followed the Hebraic practice of allowing only the priests to utter the divine names of deities in the Holy of Holies. The Egyptian deities also had feast days dedicated to their roles of divine activity. One variation the Greeks had from the Egyptian doctrine of the deification of man was that the gods became men, the doctrine of the *kenosis*.[26] This kenotic form expressed a reversal of the Egyptian belief of the deification of man and held that the gods could become men with all of the passions and eros or erotic love and possess all the emotions that the nature of mankind has inherited. Thus kenotic expressions have found their way into New Testament literature without the passions of the Greek gods and are attributed to the divine *Logos*.

He is then redefined as a Hebraic Messianic figure who tabernacled among men. " 'Savior' and 'manifest' (God) became titles of Hellenistic kings. Seleucus himself after death was honoured as 'God the Conquerer' (*Zues Nikator*) and his own son as 'Antiochus-Apollo the Savior' "[27] The Savior God concept was reinterpreted for a Gentile audience in early Christianity. Early Judaism did debate the concept regarding whether or not the Messiah would be God Himself or a Divine Man who would supernaturally perform miracles to establish His right to rule and execute judgment.[28] Some rabbis would answer in the affirmative based on the Greek version of Esther's Prayer chapter 15:2 (*The New Oxford Annotated Bible with Apocrypha*); this verse does show the influence of the Savior God concept due to the fact the All-Seeing is referred to as Savior. Therefore, Will Durant is quite correct regarding early Christianity's use of Mithraism and influences from the Egyptian cults of Isis and Horas. This was retold in new birth imagery to portray the story of the divinity of the Christian Messiah in early church liturgy. Even the school of Zoroastrian thought from Persian had its influence upon early Christianity. They acquired its documentation from the Greeks, who borrowed some of theirs from the Egyptians. Durant continues:

> As this system of belief came from Zarathustra, it bordered upon monotheism. Even with the intrusions of Ahriman and the evil spirits, it remained as monotheistic as Christianity was to be with its Satan, its devils and its angels; indeed, one hears, in early Christian theology, as many echoes of Persian dualism as to Hebrew Puritanism or Greek philosophy.[29]

Even the *Logos* doctrine was entitled the "Good Mind," which was to inspire the wise men or the *Maji*, who were to give inspired scholarly and wise counsel to the divine king. These particular traditions were predominantly powerful in Babylon where the tradition of the *Maji* merged with Hebraic tradition as the Hebrew sages redefined their Jewish wisdom in Babylon.

As Dr. Shea points out, this tradition was carried into the New Testament as the wise men were filled with inspiration and wisdom.

> *Evidence from the Revelation of John.* The clearest case for early Christian equivalents to Daniel's *maskilim* in the New Testament has been made by Gregory Beale, who argues that although the Greek equivalent of *maskilim* is not used in the Revelation, the combination of *nous* (vuc, "mind," "understanding") with *sophia* (ooOia "wisdom") in Rev. 13:18 and 17:9 reflect the same meaning as the combination of the verbs *sakal* "understand, have insight" and *byn* ("understand, gain insights"). . . . "In Dan. 9:22, 23; 11:33; and 12; 10 the combined verbs have the same meaning as in Revelation 13:18 and 17:9.[30]

Dr. Beale also expresses the position that the Greek text of the Apocalypse states in the letter to the seven churches that all those in the Body of Christ who possess the divine wisdom and truth are the *maskilim* of the New Testament.

The Maji and Divine Wisdom

The *maskilim*, often called *Maji*, also counseled the King of Persia in the king's court. Over two million lines have been preserved from Greek sources about Zoroaster. Much debate has ensued regarding the credibility and authenticity of these writings, but nevertheless their influence upon the Greek/Judaism and later, Christianity, was profound, and each of these nations employed *Maji* in the king's court or temple, especially in Babylon.

> Hermippus was a write whose attitude towards history was somewhat credulous, but it may well be that the statement about his setting forth of two million lines of Zoroaster indicated the

existence of these writings in Greek by his time: the number may well be either a scribal error or an exaggeration. As for the idea of genuine translation, it is not likely. Apart from the Septuagint there is very little genuine translation into Greek, only adaptation. The tefnut story is translated freely, the 'Potter's Oracle' may be a translation as it claims to be, and I would remark that Ecphantus *ap.* Prophyry, *De Abstinentia* iv. 10, gives us an adaptation of the Egyptian negative confession of the dead man; what was then meant by adaptation is illustrated by P Oxy 1381, 174f., *a propos* of a work on early Egyptian history. Such a claim could be utterly false, as we see from *Corp. Herm.* xvi., which pretends to be Egyptian but is Greek commonplace, or from Philo of Byblos; and it will be remembered that Plotinus himself detected a late fabrication under the name of Zoroaster. There was popular demand for such literature, and in the third century B.C. the temptation to invent unknown works from the past was intensified by the existence of the Alexandrian Library and its desire for completeness.[31]

This same phenomenon existed in the early Christian Church, with letters from Paul as well as writings from Egypt that allegedly came from patriarchal figures. This places the literary critics and biblical scholars at a disadvantage due to the fact that we can neither confirm or deny the authenticity or the forgery of many of these documents because they come from antiquity and are not always what they report to be. Conversely, some of the internal information may be from a very old transmission line or tradition that may be authentic in and of itself. Therefore, Scripture scholars and theologians do look for consistent main themes to appear out of ancient literature to aid us in our understanding of these ancient witnesses. Such a transmission line exists in tracing the origin of Satan, as Lauran Paine comments:

The diversity of Satan was vague in I Samuel, xvi 14, and the "lying spirit" of I Kings, xxii, 22 was an impersonal metaphor.

In the post-exilic notations, as in Job, Satan assumed a recognizable form and while he was an adversary and antagonist, different in principle from Jehovah, yet he appeared among the sons of God (Job. ii, 1).

His duty was to tempt men, and in the guise he could be said to have been a personification of literal and unequivocal justice—he would not be bribed or diverted, only qualified good was acceptable to him.

In this form he was acceptable to the latter-day monotheism of the Hebrews, but the ultimate nation of Satan as God's rival found in the Apocrypha, and assumed in the New Testament, was undoubtedly a result of influential Persian theological thought on the Hebrews. The Asmodeus of Obit, iii, is an equivalent to Satan, an evil entity, while in Wisdom, ii, 24, he equaled with the serpent of Genesis, iii. In Baruch serpent gods are termed demons, and finally, in the Secrets of Enoch, Satanail is expelled from Heaven.

The Book of Enoch offered an incomplete hierarchy of Hell, from Satan as king through the demons who were fallen angels, the latter, not originally of evil nature, sharing this distinction with Satan before this fall.

From this genesis, then, evolved the source of a personal devil who both tempted and punished those who succumbed to evil, in the Talmudic and Christian theologies. He was an amalgam of pagan myth and latter-day concept, formed to fit, not necessarily new, but certainly altered, cosmogonies.[32]

It is clear that passages such as Ezekiel 28 are a diatribe comparing Lucifer's fall with the King of Tyre's destruction. These diatribes have a broader context than a simile of speech because they are comparing similar literary structures and story lines, but with two opposite figures playing, leading with a common moral or ending. The King of Tyre becomes an adversary to the nations and will be destroyed, *abad,* and decomissioned, as Lucifer will at the consummation of this age. (Ezek. 28:16–19) The "adversary" is the larger character in whom the fall of the King of Tyre is modeled. Thus, the casting out of Satan and the destruction of his deceptive influence over this planet shall indeed be brought to fruition (Rev. 12:9).[33] It is unfortunate that Christianity adopted so much of Zoroastrian thought into her theology, believing in two equal and opposite deities that struggle in combat for the souls of mankind, when the ancient sages along with the biblical text teach that Satan's destructive influences would be dismantled at the intervention of Yahweh's Messiahship and by the filling of His wisdom throughout the earth.

Many humanistic theologians have tried to advance the notion that Christianity was nothing more than an amalgamation of Jewish, Greek, and mystery religions of paganistic thought. However, it can be argued that Christianity simply used the ancient myths and literary forms to advance in a universal *Kerygma* (oral gospel), its own fulfillment of the events looked for by the ancient sages and stoics alike. Therefore it should not be surprising to find our New Testament corpus of literature contains cultural elements and literary forms, which were borrowed from the entire Mediterranean region. This method of literary borrowing techniques were used by the great teachers, not only for the spreading of the gospel, but also to borrow concepts that could be expressed more fully by using the particular literary form that illustrated the theological concept. For example, the Greek language with use of *Omi* is much more able to convey the omniscience of God as opposed to the Hebraic concept of God being *other.*

It was a concept that Jesus borrowed from Qumran when he stated, "I desire love, not sacrifice . . ." which was a reaction in Qumran to the oblations being committed in the temple at Jerusalem. Therefore, Jesus and the Qumran community were in complete agreement on this theological issue. The Wisdom Traditions may have had a small part in the development of the New Testament concept of *logos,* which was a long-held Stoic

Greek doctrine, which was reinterpreted and applied to *"the word made flesh"* against a Hebraism in which God was made flesh and *tabernacled* with us. Therefore it becomes increasingly difficult for the modern scholar to differentiate the multicultural use of ancient literary forms from their original sources, due to the fact they were reinterpreted through such methodologies as the *pesher* (plural—*pesharim,* meaning interpreter of dreams) and *Midrash* techniques in order to be made suitable for the listening and understanding of the students of the rabbi. Dr. Barbara Thiering explains:

> The system works like this. The scroll writer takes an Old Testament Book, such as the minor prophet Habakkuk, which deals with events in 600 B.C., when the armies of the Babylonians were marching toward Judea, inspiring fear and terror. He goes through it verse by verse and after quoting each passage adds "Its pesher is . . .", then explains that it is really about events in his own time. The Babylonians stand for the "Kittim," by which he means the Romans. Some Romans were currently marching across the land, inspiring fear and terror. . . .[34]

These techniques were at their zenith in the first century A.D.; thus, they transcend both testaments. Modern scholars are now beginning to see the *maskilim* or the "Wise Ones" existing in both testaments. Therefore it is not surprising to see this technique being employed by New Testament writers, such as Jesus and Paul, through the entire synoptic tradition, reinterpreted major sections of Old Testament Scripture, such as the cryptic writings of Isaiah and the apocalyptic genre of Daniel 9 through 12, which were retold to a new audience with a different escatalogical application. Again, Dr. Barbara Thiering:

> In simpler terms, the pesher is like a solution to a puzzle. A rough analogy might be the solution to a cryptic crossword. The clues do not look as if they make sense, but anyone who knows

the technique and has the necessary knowledge can solve the puzzle.[35]

This puzzle was understood by the *Majilmaskilim,* who studied the pesher techniques in Scripture and therefore discovered the sacred knowledge of the time of the anointed one's arrival was at hand. This inspired knowledge was also passed on to Jesus' disciples and later, to the church at large, beginning at the day of Pentecost, thereby anointing all believers as the New Testament *maskilim.* Therefore, in the Spirit of the New Age, the church was energized with apostolic mandate to reinterpret the dreams and cryptic writings in the Old Testament, with prophetic utterances, and to provide God's wisdom for the believing community.

The Hellenistic Matrix and Its Influence on the Palestinian Triennial Reading Cycle

Scholarship no longer supposes that any language is pure in origin, for even the Hebrew language contains cognates of earlier Semitic languages, such as Sumarian, Ugarit, Akkadian, Chaldean, and other ancient languages in the Semitic linguistic family, which may have originated from the great Semitic mother tongue. So by the time our Hebrew and Greek canons were in final form of the redaction process, the matrix of intercultural expressions had become so deeply interwoven into the fabric of the text that they became indistinguishable in the culture that grew out of these original patterns. Therefore the knowledge of the transition between the Jewish canon and the Greek canon is crucial to our understanding. During this time of theological and philosophical transformation of thought, such knowledge will aid us well in understanding the struggle of the patristic witnesses as they labored to establish these concepts and early church theology.

Prof. Julia Neuberger writes from the standpoint of Jerusalem and its transition to Islam, to Jewish and Christian eschatology, the prophecy of Christ's return, and its implications for the Jewish people and the Christian Church.

> Jerusalem is central to Jewish thinking and prayer. From its centrality, both Christianity and Islam have derived a Jerusalem theology and made it central to their things. The difference is that for Jews, most of the time, in most places, it has been a physical and geographical reality, however distant it seemed. It encompassed other ideas, other values, and a universalistic message, but in fact it was the real city that was longed for—'Next year in (the real) Jerusalem', a cry which has its roots in the exodus story, and in the prophetic promises of return.[36]

It is to this paradigm that we now give our attention, to the early church and synagogue and its use of the Torah. Another point often overlooked in the Jewish/Christian controversy regarding the application of the Old and New Covenants is in the Old Convenant, the Exodus, and the Passover were seen as the greatest event in Jewish history and, prophetically, a new exodus spoken of by Isaiah the prophet was to happen in the regathering of Israel. Whereas the New Convenant expressly deals with Christ being the center of salvation history and therefore changes the focal point by fulfilling the Old Testament Passover in His ministry and by being the Passover sacrifice for all those who believe. The emphasis is shifted from what God had already done in the deliverance of the Jews to what Christ is working out here below in creating an unleavened people. So our great exodus is out of sin and into the newness of life while Old Testament Israel is waiting for the new exodus and for the Messiah to complete his work in her prophetically whereby both witnesses of god's people will ultimately be saved in the New Convenant. Knowing that all Israel and that God has not cast away his people, Pauline philosophy was for New Testament Christians never to stumble over Old Testament regulations that would keep them from finding their Messiah.

But Paul never states that Jewish practices do not have meaning, as the Law was supposed to serve as the schoolmaster to lead us to Christ, and for ancient Israel, it was a teacher. Western Christianity has erred on the side of anti-nomianism, with its emphasis on Paul being anti-law. Statements, "For the law is just, holy and good," as well as others such as 'by faith we are establishing the Law,' show us that Paul was neither antinomian nor legalistic in his approach to biblical ethics and the spiritual application of God's commandments. As far as Jerusalem is concerned, Julia Neuberger is quite correct in stating that Jerusalem was central to the Old Convenant. As far as our New Convenant is concerned, it is the Jerusalem above which is the mother of us all. Prophetically, we are in route to this city by the leading of the Kings of Kings.

It was the Apostle John who used the commandments to balance the other side of this paradigm of law/gospel to an antinomian people, while the Apostle Paul's message of grace was for legalistic congregations.

The early New Testament church grew out of a matrix of Hellenistic and Hebrew thought and beside gnostism, which had been growing inside Judaism since c. 721 B.C. Against this backdrop, scholars have long debated on how much of our New Testament is Hebraic and how much of New Testament theology extend into the Greek form of universal thought.[37] Dr. Angus offers the following observation:

> Christianity inherited the lofty ethical ideals of Judaism. The Apostle of the Gentiles found it easier to win converts to the new Christian society than to improve their morals. It was the

> Jewish system of ethics intermingled with stoic principles and suffused with the new enthusiasm of Christian love which Paul sought to impose upon the Gentiles. The poorer Jewish-Christian Churches more than repaid the Gentile-Christian contributions in money by the wealth of their ethical heritage. The former were agitated by questions of legalism, while the latter were endeavouring to restrain libertinism by the adoption of the ethical code of Judaism and Christianity.[38]

Modern New Testament scholarship is studying extensively the early church in its relationship to Judaism. It is certainly without question that Judaism is Christianity's mother religion and certainly for the first decade of her existence the church, called the "New Eve," existed within the matrix of the Judean temple cult.

> But it was from the Synagogue that the Christian communities took over the tradition of reciting, chanting, and singing, as more fitting for their simple service than the elaborate rite of the Temple, with its great choirs and instrumental music.
>
> For training Christian congregations in singing, converted readers (αωαψωωοραι) and procentors from the synagogues were chosen. The *schola cantorum* sang from the Psalter, which Esdras is said to have compiled for the Levites. The people answered with response taken from a collection of short verses and liturgical formulae made for the use of the Jewish congregation. The acceptance of the Jewish institution of readers and presenters specially tainted for their office, made it possible to introduce into Christian worship antiphonal singing (as described in Exod. xv, 1 and 21 and Judges v. 1–31), and psalms sung by a soloist with responses from the congregation (as described in the second book of the Apostolic Constitutions: 'after the reading of the two lections someone else must chant the hymns of David and the people must answer with the responses').[39]

The Book of Psalms, as the temple hymnbook, continued to be used in Jewish congregations as well as Christian congregations. The New Testament reading cycle beginning with the Torah, then to the Prophets, and through the Writings continued in the New Testament Church. This liturgical reading cycle would have included within its readings and musical liturgies portions of Psalms containing the enthronement ceremony.

Jewish feast days and their Messianic fulfillment would have enjoyed a special treatment on these high holy days, with the Book of Ruth being read on Pentecost to show the great Christian gleanings that were to take place in the great harvest from the preaching of the Gospel. During the transition period, the New Testament's fulfillment and reinterpretation of Old Testament passages would have resulted in much liturgical celebration. Instead of just a Torah story of God's intervention through the call of Abraham and the deliverance of his people in Egypt, the church celebrated the call of Christ to his church to come out of her bondage and join the exodus to the New Jerusalem. The retelling of these Old Testament events in a new convenant setting resulted in Torah/Christ story being what scholars call today, a summary of salvation history.

Furthermore, Judaism had also undergone a radical transformation in the preceding centuries. She had moved from a Torah-based religion to a Talmudic-based religion, placing her at odds with Jesus over some points of doctrine. However, this also resulted in the Jewish oral traditions, the Mishnah, serving as the oral commentary for the written law while the Talmudic writings from Babylon and Jerusalem, would serve as the hedge in protecting the 613 commandments as well as the Torah, so that Israel would never again be led into captivity by any Gentile oppressor. These early reformers in Judaism were indeed reacting to what they feared as God's judgment had been enacted upon their forefathers because of their refusal to bring justice to the poor, the orphans and the downtrodden.

Such a mandate is also given in our New Testament body of literature in the gospel of Luke 4:16–22. When Jesus stood up to read the Scriptures, it was time for the reading of Isaiah 61 in the synagogue liturgical reading cycle where "acceptable Day of the Lord" was read and the freeing of the captives was proclaimed by this Scripture being "fulfilled in your ears." In that context, the people of God are obligated to obey the Scriptures as they were read in the reading cycle that was established by the Levites in their 120 courses of priestly training for so many generations. What had once developed from the Levites had evolved into a "Palestinian Triennial Cycle" of Torah reading, which was divided into 154 sections. On Sabbaths, during the synagogue service, several members of the congregation, at least seven, were summoned by the ruler of the synagogue to take part in the reading.[40]

> It should be noted that the term "Triennial Cycle" misrepresents the Palestinian Sabbatical readings of Scripture. As has been pointed out above, seven men were called up for the readings and each of them read a minimum of three verses, making a total of at least twenty-one verses for each Sabbath service. Had this computation been followed, it would have taken some five and a half years to complete the Pentateuch, but according to Ta'anit IV, 3 cited above, the section of Genesis recited during the first Sabbath of the Palestinian cycle, consisted of 34 verses (Gen. 1:1–2:3), exceeding the minimum by thirteen lines; and if we take 34 verses as the average weekly reading, it would have taken almost 172 Sabbaths, more than three and a half years, to complete the cycle.[41]

In a similar fashion, the liturgical practices of the Christian church have attempted to develop and maintain an oral tradition alongside the Biblical text, both of them having equal authority. This process is a historical one from which the Creeds and the great church councils have maintained what they believe to be an Apostolic tradition, derived from the apostolic liturgies and constitutions and still having authority for all Christians to this day. This was the process of the liturgical church maintaining its traditions within a historical context that establishes a precedent for the interpretation of Scripture, comprising both oral and written traditions. Therefore, the biblical canon, especially in the New Testament corpus, is in reality the church's book, just as the Torah was the central pivot point around which the structure of Judaism was created.

Then, later, as the widening of the term, *Torah*, was applied to the *Haf-Torah* portions of the Old Testament and then to the entire Old Testament canon, rabbinic schools were formed, with each rabbi being encouraged to develop his own commentaries on the canon. So the methodology in the two systems of theology is quite different because the sacramental approach by the church sees the emblems in themselves as holy, which are expressed through Christian liturgy and systematic theology, while the rabbinic system teaches that as the rabbis are led by the Holy Spirit to interpret Torah with commentary and ethics is the basis of Jewish theology. Due to this paradox, Christians and Jews struggle to understand one another's starting point in this deepening dialogue.

> The New Covenant is a deepening internalizing of the Old. Jesus also understood it this way: "Do not suppose that I have come to abolish the Law and the prophets; I did not come to abolish [*katalusai*], but to complete [*plerosai*]. I tell you this: so long as heaven and earth endure, not a letter, not a stroke, will disappear from the Law until all that must happen has happened. If any therefore sets aside even the least of the Law's demands, and teaches others to do the same, he will have the lowest place in the kingdom of Heaven, whereas anyone who keeps the Law and teaches others so will stand high in the kingdom of Heaven. I tell you, unless you show yourselves far better men than the

> Pharisees and the doctors of the law, you can never enter the kingdom of Heaven." Matthew 5:17–20 N.E.B.[42]

Jesus and His ethical demands, which originated from deep within the original intent of the Torah, was to take his followers to a new level of righteousness due to the fact that He was embodied Torah. With this equation of Torah/revelation embodied by Christ/righteousness, the believer is expected to rise to completeness in Christ's righteousness and was to encourage others in the faith to hold to the same righteousness standard. In traditional circles, these verses have often been overlooked due to our inability, by our own efforts, to uphold this standard. So traditional interpretators have assumed the term *plerosai* denotes a setting aside of the Torah due to Christ's fulfillment, but the original language often includes the meaning "to act out" or, in the believer's case, it is "to be Christlike"; we therefore establish the law through faith.

> The form in Matthew is not, of course, the same as that of the supposed rabbinic debate, and this is due to its "setting in life." The setting in life of the rabbinic form is scholarly exegesis, that of Matthew is Jesus as supreme authority laying down a standard of the proper demand as against those who take the words of the scriptural percept literally as a standard of conduct.
>
> These verses in Matthew are to explain or support Jesus' claim that he has come not to abolish the law but to complete: "For truly I say to you that until heaven and earth pass away, by no means will one iota or one point of the law pass away, until all things come to pass" (Matthew 5.18). Here he is no revolutionary, in no sense from verse 21 onward is he taking anything from the law. He is not destroying the law but upholding it, adding a higher standard.[43]

The disciple of Christ is held more to a moral application or intent of his/her ethical behavior whereas the rabbinic arguments of Jesus' day were oftentimes based on a legal codification of rabbinic exegesis, creating a hedge around the law and thus creating a false standard of righteousness. (v. 17—Μη νομιοηρε οτι ηλθον καταλυσαι τον νομον, & c.)

> In verse 18, the word used is *genetai,* from ginomai, to become, to come to pass, happen. The law thus shall become the reality of the world's life to the end of the world. This gives a very different perspective on the meaning of "fulfil" than those interpretations which see its meaning as ended, ie., the fulfillment of the law as the end of the law. There is no hint of such a meaning in the text.[44a]

According to Philo, the term would be better rendered "until the end of the world."[44b] It is also believed by the rabbis that the Messiah shall reestablish the only true interpretation to Torah[44c] during His Messianic reign and that His followers in this age uphold His standard of righteousness by not teaching others to diminish from this standard in any way. If any teacher shall diminish the role of Torah, his role also will be minimized or least in the world to come.

In the ancient Near East, the royal law word was given as an aspect of kingship and the king's law and edicts could not be rescinded (such as the Persian edicts).

> Thus, the whole of the New Testament speaks as a unity with that law given in the Old Testament. . . . The ancient power of the king, however, was inseparable from his law-making power. His word was literally law. For Jesus to claim to be Messiah-King over all the world meant that He Himself regarded His own every word as inescapable law. For converts in the world of antiquity, Christ's word was law, and to despise the law of a king was a serious offense. Even the thief on the cross had confidence in the law-word of that King (Luke 23:39–43)[45]

For the Jew, the central point is the great Exodus out of Egypt and a greater Exodus yet to come with the rebirth of the New Covenant (Jer. 31:31) and, for the Christian, it is the centrality of the Cross due to the fact the mighty acts of God have already brought our forefathers out of Egypt. Within the Christian dispensation, it has often been assumed that Gentile Christianity has taught a completely separate gospel from that which pertained to Israel. At this date, many New Testament scholars are now questioning this, due to the fact that Christianity, as Dr. Eisenfelt points out, was the largest sect within Judaism in the first decade of its existence. So critics are asking the following questions: Do the two basic covenants represent two approaches to the same deity, and did the church evolve out of the synagogue as a separate institution never to be united with its mother religion? Dr. Baker advances this theological observation:

> a. The relationship between Israel and the Church is a particularly pressing matter for those who advocate the priority of the Old Testament over the New Testament. . . . Van Ruler views the Church as a spiritual repetition of Israel, but does not solve the problem of the relationship of the present-day nation of Israel to that spiritual "Israel". Miskotte . . . on the other hand, affirms that in the Church Gentiles are grafted into the ancient tree of the Covenant people (Rom. 11:12–18) and that it is Israel's election which is the root of salvation of Christendom. Neither Jews nor Christians alone are Israel but rather the church and synagogue together from one congregation of God. The present breach is therefore not to be removed by missions to Jews but by a call to brothers to realise their unity with each other . . .[46]

Modern scholarly investigation does reveal that Pauline theology talks about the "new man," comprised of both Jew and Gentile united together, exemplified by the veil that was rent in two, tearing down the wall of distinction (Eph. 2:15) and formed this new entity, the church.

The "Q" Document and the Gospel of Thomas

For decades scholars have tried to revisit the gospels with a factual emphasis to find the historical Jesus. Dr. Albert Schweitzer, later revised by Robinson, set the path for this modern quest. This gave a real challenge to the traditional historical approach to the gospels and to Christian orthodoxy that emerged from the church creeds and councils. The theological waters had already been muddied by debates over the alleged "Q" document (*Quelle* "source") from the German theological schools, claiming the gospel of Mark should be first in chronological order and this "common source" was fed by the writer of Mark's gospel to inspire the *syn* (synoptic) tradition.[47] Dale Allison Jr. and Vernon K. Robbins offer a three-stage development of the Q ending, with Luke and Matthew, as late as the 90s of the first common century. The three stages are, first, oral traditions; second, the *Kerigma* (A.D. 30–50) or gospel announcement, and third, the gospel in written textual form (A.D. 80–90).[48]

In recent decades, scholars have debated whether or not the historical time lines would have been long enough during the period of the *Kerigma* (A.D. 30–50) to generate an oral gospel tradition by the time the written records would have been firmly established and circulated among the early church canonical lists. This is why the higher critical schools of the documentary hypothesis as well as the *Quelle* theory in the synoptic traditions must maintain a later dating system for the composition and editing of biblical canonization. This also provides a longer time from Jesus' original sayings to the actual composition of the gospels, allowing for greater corruption to take place prior to canonization. These considerations led to the formulation of the first three rules of evidence:

> The oral memory best retains sayings and anecdotes that are short, provocative, memorable—and oft-repeated.

The most frequently recorded words of Jesus in the surviving Gospels take the form of aphorisms and parables.

The earliest layer of the gospel tradition is made up of single aphorisms and parables that circulated by word of mouth prior to the written gospels.[49]

And to add more fuel to the fire, the Jesus Seminar advances the position that the Egyptian Book of Thomas should actually be the lense through which the other gospels are interpreted.

However this may be, an excellent case can be made for the position that the Gospel of Thomas is not fundamentally dependent upon the New Testament gospels, but that it preserves sayings that at times appear to be more original than the New Testament parallels.[50]

Considered to be the *Magnus Opum*, Robert W. Funk and Roy W. Hoover, set out to disprove the validity of the synoptic tradition.[51] Thankfully, the Gospel of Thomas theory has not gained much scholarly support outside of the Jesus Seminar, due to its late documentary composition, and an accurate transmission line back to the words of Jesus has not been firmly established. It is poor scholarly hermeneutical practice to lay an independent document over the top of another independent tradition and use it in the final court of arbitration in advancing the hermeneutic of the passage in question rather than allowing each biblical writer to provide us with their own textual witness.

Scholarly acceptance of the "Q" "*quelle*" hypothesis has been steadily gaining credibility. While it is true that scholars in general are still in search of the source of the early gospel traditions, these traditions draw heavily on reinterpretations of Old Testament passages. A more universal application is used in the final interpretation. Only in a minority of such cases were pagan sources cited directly from stoic hymns, Plato, and other pagan myths and given a gospel reinterpretation.

> A very conservative count lists 295 separate quotations: 224 direct citations prefixed by an introductory formula; 7 additional cases where "and" connects a second quotation to the one previously identified as such; 19 passages where a paraphrase or summary rather than a definite citation follows an introductory formula (e.g., Matt. 2:23); and 45 quotations where the length (e.g., 1 Peter 3:10–12) or the specificity (e.g., Matt. 27:46) makes it entirely clear that a reference to the QT is intended. Since many quotations are fairly extended, these 295 actually occupy some 352 verses of the NT. Two hundred and seventy-eight different verses of the OT are cited (some of them several times): 94 from the Law, 99 from the Prophets, and 85 from the Writings.
>
> As soon as allusions as well as direct quotations are included, the count rises sharply. Toy lists 613 instances; Shires, 1,604; Dittmar, 1,640, and Heuhn yields a count of 4,105.[52]

The Old Testament quotations in New Testament Scripture cannot be overemphasized. Therefore, it is important not to introduce foreign material into the interpretation of the text unless strong literary borrowing and structure is evident and we allow for each writer to act as his own witness to the events described in synoptic tradition.[53] However, this does not exclude the importance in clarifying and enlarging our perspectives in our quest for the Jesus tradition. It is not proper make a correlation between the "Q" document and the Gospel of Thomas.

> Rejecting the customary comparison of the *Gospel of Thomas* with the Q document, Boudewijn Dehandschutter points out that the gospel attributes to Jesus sayings that earlier in the Christian tradition represents a relatively late, rather early, stage in the tradition of Jesus' words.[54]

The Egyptian sources, such as the Gospel of Thomas and the Gospel of Philip and other apocraphyl and pseudepigraphal documents, should be viewed as separate traditions.

At this date, there is increasing emphasis being given to the variant readings of our Eastern and Western recensions of the biblical text. Even the great Egyptian Uncials are now being compared to the value of the Byzantine text.[55] It is now realized by an increasing number of scholars that Western Augustinian Christian thought attempts to view early Christian theology through the lens of a Gentile-based Pauline interpretation, while the Eastern Christian theologians use the Johnine corpus as a lens through which to view the early gospels.

> Concern for unity among the churches was undoubtedly a major factor accounting for collecting the four Gospels into one literary tradition. . . . Initially, there seems to have been considerable resistance in the West to the Fourth Gospel, in part because it was fundamentally different in character from the synoptic Gospels and from the oral tradition concerning Jesus, which the churches in the West had inherited. The inclusion of John's Gospel in the collection of four probably gained for it a wider circulation and eventually a general acceptance beyond the Eastern churches. M. Werner, in his work on the development of Christian dogma, holds that it was the peculiar theological character of John's Gospel—its gnostic-like interpretation of Paul's thought—which many early Christians found objectionable. But it was the affinity of John's spiritual-sacramental doctrine of salvation to the Logos-Christology, which ultimately led to the popularity of John and to its high place in the canon.[56]

One fact worth considering is that Christianity's Eastern counterpart experienced less corruption from the time of the early church until the completion of the New Testament canon. Therefore, Eastern church theology in general followed the early church's traditions more accurately and continued a theology closer to the Jewish frame in the areas of the liturgical practice of ring-circle dancing[57a,b] a holistic view of monotheism in its expression of trinitarianism, and its repudiation of the doctrine of original sin, which gained acceptance in the West due to a misunderstanding and an overdependency upon the Pauline corpus in providing a theological construct, which has been inappropriately applied to the New Testament corpus of literature.

Thus, John, the non-synoptic author, provides us a lens from the synoptics to James, who was the bridge to the Pauline witness. And with this lens, we see a Jewish liturgical cycle that was employed by early Christianity in its Messianic reinterpretations of biblical events.

> 8. The Jewish background. A Contribution to Johannine studies has been made by Aileen Guilding in her research into the influence of the triennial lectionary of the Palestinian synagogues upon the structure and terminology of the Fourth Gospel, built as it is so largely around the Jewish feasts.[58]

Dr. Harrison correctly observes that not all the Jewish feast days are mentioned in John's discourse due to the fact that Pentecost is lacking. However, he fails to advance the concept that the corpus of John is dealing with Jesus' own Messianic identity and Pentecost was the giving of Law, which was reinterpreted with the giving of the Spirit at the birth day of the New Testament Church. Just for the fact Tabernacle imagery with a Messianic fulfillment was employed is enough to tell any scholar which portion of the liturgical year and lectionary readings were referred to in the yearly reading cycle. Therefore we cannot omit any major literary transitions between Jesus and Paul or we fail to reconstruct New Testament theology appropriately.

This is another reason why many textual critics prefer the group of New Testament texts that have arisen from the Eastern portion of the Roman Empire, i.e., the Byzantine group of texts.

Conversely, the Western group of texts had many Latinisms, which found their way back into our later Greek manuscripts. This is not to mention the problem between the Eastern and Western church councils in their respective interpretations of the divine substance of Christ as well as the *philioquae.* For many centuries the Nestorian Church has tried to maintain the Tatian Diatessaron in its Western form of Aramaic, which was originally composed in that language. However, modern textual studies have concluded the Diatessaron was from a Greek recension as well.

It is a little known fact that the Church of the East during the days of Timothy of Baghdad had an educational system that was very advanced. Their curriculum included Greek, Syrian, and Egyptian languages.[59] Other witnesses in the Eastern tradition of Taitan are as follows: the Acts of the Persian martyrs, the Old Armenian and the Old Georgian versions, a number of Arabic manuscripts of the gospels with the liturgical text in karshunic, citations in the Manichaean text, the Jacobite marriage ritual preserved in the Old Osmanic language and a fragment of a lectionary in Sogidian.[60] Furthermore, studies in the Coptic recensions and later Syriac versions are adding a Middle Eastern flavor from earlier Greek recensions to show a more complete reconstruction of our New Testament beginnings. Finally, while the Dead Sea Scrolls contain no direct mention of Jesus and the Apostles, it is plain to see many New Testament parallels were borrowed from Qumran.[61]

6 The Egyptian Recension and Its Influence on the Biblical Text

From the days of the murder of Gedeliah during Jeremiah's ministry, massive trade routes with Egypt continued to be used for Jewish trade and migration. Coptic Christianity would flourish from this when the gospel spread from Jerusalem to Alexandria during the first century and a quarter of the people of Egypt were Christian by ca. 325 and a half by 400.[1] Most scholars believe the Greek text called Alexandrinas, *Alexandrian papyri* (chronologically between Vatacanus and P75) [2a,b] probably began the textual tradition of the Coptic Church in Egypt.

> Among Christian documents which during the second century either originated in Egypt or circulated there among both the orthodox and the Gnostics are numerous apocryphal gospels, acts, epistles and apocalypses. Some of the more noteworthy are the Gospel according to the Egyptians, the Gospel of Truth, the Gospel of Thomas, the Gospel of Philip, the Kerygma of Peter, the Acts of John, the Epistle of Barnabas, the Epistle of the Apostles and the Apocalypse of Peter. There are also fragments of exegetical and dogmatic works composed by Alexandrian Christians, chiefly Gnostics, during the second century. We know, for example, of such teachers as Basilides and his son Isidore, and of Valentius, Ptolemaeus, Heracleon and Pantaenus. All but the last-mentioned were unorthodox in one respect or another. In fact, to judge by the comments made by Clement of Alexandria, almost every deviant Christian sect was represented in Egypt during the second century; Clement mentions

the Valentinians, the Basilidians, the Marcionites, the Peratae, the Ophites, the Simonians, and the Eutychites. What proportion of Christians in Egypt during the second century were orthodox is not known.[3]

Rev. Carlo Martini has stated, "But we should remember that the only MSS surviving from the first centuries are in fact all Egyptian."[4]

Much debate currently rages in regards as to how many of the themes from the mystery cults were borrowed and reinterpreted for liturgical use in church worship as well as for the spreading of the gospel during the period of the Kerygma from circa A.D. 30 to A.D. 50.

During this period, a minority of scholars suggests that the apostle Paul was trained in the mystery schools during the time he reports of his training that he received from the Lord personally in Arabia. Some of their argument comes from Paul's use of the word *mystera* to the Ephesian elders. However, he never mentions the virgin birth, which was very popular in the mystery schools. It was not the gospel teachings that gave Paul his authority, but rather it was his encounter with Our Lord on the road to Damascus. Some scholars feel that Paul didn't know Jesus personally, but Paul refutes this as the basis of his apostleship. Thus, the focal point of the Pauline corpus is the resurrection of the Messiah as our Captain, who will lead us through our death, burial, and resurrection just as the ancient Egyptian schools waited for in the Isis cult.

This cultured, educated Jew, who did not know Jesus personally, identified Jesus as a savior figure of the Hellenistic type, a dying/rising god, such as Osiris in the Isis cult, popular in Egypt.[5]

The popular notion that the writers of the New Testament corpus of literature did nothing but revise the Messianic legacy of Our Lord, as well as reinvent the paganistic notion of the dying/rising god and incorporate it into the resurrection narratives to pull the world's greatest hoax upon the unbelieving world, is a fallacy of concept. Literary techniques used by any Near Eastern writer allows them to quote widely and freely in their use of literary and historical data. It was their literary practice to include contemporary and historical events in the narrative, so the new revelation would have a familiar order while bringing to light new theological truths.

Gentile Christianity through the auspices of the former Hellenistic and Greco thought forms helped phase out almost every remaining strain of Hebrew thought and practice within the first century A.D. due to the fact so many Gentile churches were raised, and the sophisticated schools of Neoplatonic Philosophy would govern the debates over theological concepts in the first four centuries of the common era. Different churches in various geographical areas would make these theological shifts from Hebraic thought forms to the Neoplantonic schools at different times and over different theogical issues. By the fifth century, different churches in Rome and Alexandria shared in different mystery traditions. Socrates Scholasticus (c. 440) reports:

> Although almost all churches throughout the world celebrate the sacred mysteries on the sabbath of every week, yet the Christians of Alexandria and at Rome, on account of some ancient tradition, have ceased to do this. The Egyptians in the neighborhood of Alexandria, and the inhabitants of Thebais, hold their religious assemblies on the sabbath, but do not participate of the mysteries in the manner usual among Christians, in general; for after having eaten and satisfied themselves with food of all kinds, in the evening making their offerings they partake of the mysteries.[6]

The Egyptian church did not follow the Roman tradition of making the Jewish sabbath a fast day, but rather made it a day of feasting on Sabbath and Sunday. This fact alone shows that early Christianity was not in complete conformity in regards to fasting or related sabbath issues. Furthermore, the facts also indicate that Egyptian monasticism would later influence some of the Roman churchmen by the fourth century A.D.

> The revived respect for the Sabbath is clear in *The Lausiac History,* written by Palladius after he traveled from Palestine in 388 and spent 12 years living among the monks in Egypt. He found monks observing both Sabbath and Sunday. Some celebrated communion on Sabbaths and Sundays. Some monks spent the five days alone, congregating for worship only on Sabbaths and Sunday. And two monks in different places fasted five days a week, enjoying food only on Sabbaths and Sundays. (Augustine said in 396 that many monks in monasteries ate only on Sabbaths and Sundays.) Palladius's observations are important, for the revival of interest in the Sabbath that begins around the middle of the fourth century coincides with the spread of monasticism out of Egypt about that same time.[7]

Among the School of the Poor in Jerusalem were those who stayed with the Jewish practice of a twenty-four hour sabbath rest, while the church at Rome reduced the sabbath rest to a fast day by the fourth century A.D.

> That the early Christians adopted this Jewish custom is implied, for instance by Augustine's rhetorical remark, when referring to the Sabbath, he says: "Did not the tradition of the elders prohibit fasting on one hand, and command rest on the other?" Further support can be seen in the opposite to the Sabbath fast by Christians in the East and in some important Western areas, such as in Milan at the time of Ambrose (d. A.D. 397), and in certain churches and regions of North Africa. The transformation of the Sabbath from a day of feasting and joy to a day of fasting and mourning, as we shall see, represents a measure taken by the Church of Rome. . . .[8]

The Ebionites

Some scholars, such as J. L. Teicher of Cambridge, have advanced the notion that the Essenes of Qumran became the Ebionites. They also attempt to link the Ebionites to Torah observance, Judaistic teachings, and the message of the prophets with their ascetical rules of communal life, practices of baptism, and other washings and converted to Christianity. According to Joseph A. Fitzmyer, "we have no evidence for this."[9] The reason for this confusion regarding the Ebionite identity is due to the fact both had some sort of communal meal; bread and wine were used at Qumran while the Ebionites used bread, salt, and water, celebrated the Christian Eucharist and, as Epiphasius tells us, practiced poverty.[10]

Another false assumption is that the Ebionites represent or at least can be related to primitive Jewish-Christians;

> It is true that both stressed the importance of the observance of the law, but they differed radically from each other on their view of the nature of Christ. The Ebionites' Christology was in fact like that of the Gnostics, regarding Christ as a plain and common man "who was the fruit of the intercourse of a man with Mary." Such a Christological error can hardly be attributed to the Primitative Jewish-Christians. Therefore, on account of such a fundamental doctrinal difference, the Ebionites, as well noted by J. Danielou, "should not be confused purely and simply with the heirs of the first, Aramaic-speaking, Christians who fled to Tranjordan after the fall of Jerusalem in A.D. 70." Marcel Simon, in fact, argues on the basis of information provided by Epiphanius that "the sect of the Ebionites appears to be a result of a confluence between original Jewish-Christian and a pre-Christian Jewish sect."[11]

Modern scholarship has discovered some documentation regarding the Ebionite movement called the Gospel of the Ebionites. Epiphanius quotes their gospel in *Against Heresies,*

XXX.16:5: "I have come to destroy sacrifices; and if you do not stop making sacrifices, the wrath (of God) will not leave you."[12] This statement seems to be in agreement with Messaniac Judaism as well as the Qumran convenantors, due to the common theme in the Old Testament, "I desire love, not sacrifice." This theme is later developed by Jesus and Paul when Jesus states, the time is coming and now is when they shall not worship in Jerusalem and he is seeking such to worship Him in spirit and in truth (emphasis added), and Paul's letter to the Romans (16:1) takes this theme a bit further by stating that we are to commit our bodies as a "living sacrifice," as he is attempting to reconcile these theological misunderstandings.

> These Ebionites rejected the writings of Moses, especially the requirement of sacrifice and the use of flesh. They acknowledged only the Gospel of Matthew (which they called the Gospel of the Hebrews), and they rejected Paul as a deceiver. Baptism was part of their practice, and they took the Sacrament of the Lord's Supper annually, using unleavened bread and water. They also observed the Jewish Sabbath and required circumcision. In other practices, they followed the Essene Ebionites.[13]

Further evidence exists in the New Testament text in Paul's writing to Timothy, which speaks directly against the aesthetic practice of forbidding to marry as well the practice of using only water in religious rites and ceremonies whereas he prescribes wine in the use of the Lord's supper as well as for medicinal purposes. Many Jewish and aesthetic groups rejected the Pauline corpus because they felt Paul was giving the things of God to "dogs" or Gentiles. This same argument against Pauline canonization is even used by the Muslims, by whom he is considered to be a traitor. Evidently after Paul's conversion, he faced great opposition, both personally and theologically.

The Nazarenes

One sect that did continue in Jewish practices under a Messianic heading in the first centuries were the Nazarenes. Their biblical history is found in Acts 24:5–26:32, in which Paul was accused of being a ringleader by Tertullus, as Paul was brought before Felix, Festus, and Agrippa to stand trial where he declares, "Neither against the law of the Jews, neither against the temple, not yet against Caesar, have I offended any thing at all" (see Acts 25:8). Epiphanius testifies of them:

> The Nazarenes do not differ in any essential thing from them [i.e., the Jews], since they practice the custom and doctrines prescribed by the Jewish law, except that they believe in Christ. They believe in the resurrection of the dead and that the universe was created by God. They preach that God is one and that Jesus Christ is his Son. They are very learned in the Hebrew language. They read the law. . . . Therefore they differ both from the Jews and from the Christians; from the former, because they believe in Christ, from the true Christians because they fulfill till now Jewish rites as the circumcision, the Sabbath and others.[14]

It's obvious that the early Messianic believers had great difficulty in grasping the transition between Old and New Convenants that was unfolding before their very eyes. The writer of Hebrews states: "The Old Covenant is waxing away" (Heb. 9) with the conversion of some Jewish households into Hebraic Christianity. Ireneus in *Against Heresies* 1:26, states the following in regards to the Nazarenes:

> They practice circumcision, persevere in the observance of those customs which are enjoined by the Law, and are so Judaic in their mode of life that they even adore Jerusalem as if it were the house of God.[15]

Jewish Christianity had many divergent opinions, just as the Gentile church would employ. Many of the Messaniac Jewish groups did not embrace the virgin birth, as we have indicated. They did not wish to be identified with the mystery cults in their day.

The Elkasaites

The Elkasaites claimed they had received revelations by an angel who came in the company of a female of similar dimensions identified as the Holy Spirit (the word for "spirit" in Hebrew, *ruah*, is feminine). They also believe that re-baptism and a confession in this new revelation could remit even the grossest of sins. They observed circumcision, the Law of Moses, and were involved in magic and astrology. They denied the virgin birth, as well as many other Jewish groups. They rejected the major and minor prophets and denied the Pauline corpus altogether.

> They believe that Christ had been born in the ordinary way, but that he had been incarnate before and would be incarnate again on future worlds. (This was a Pythagorean doctrine called *metempsychosis*).[16]

An interesting historical observation is that the Syrian church at Odessa would continue to worship the Holy Spirit as a feminine entity from the document entitled *The Odes of Solomon,* which would influence the Eastern Church for centuries to come.[16a]

The Manichaeans

Beyond Syria, in the land of Persia at the center of philosophical and religious supremacy was Persian Christianity. On one side was Manichaeanism, which may have contained concepts of Egyptian theology and on the other side was Zoroastrianism. These would have a religious clash and begin a great period of religious persecution of the churches of the that region, which was recorded in the Syriac Act of the Matyrs and called this the first persecution of Christians in Persia. This was due to the influence of a great teacher named Mani, who claimed to be an apostle of the Lord, Jesus Christ.

Debates over Modalism grew out the teachings of Mani and would affect the verdict of subsequent church councils. Many of his teachings sounded Christian because of their terminology, but they employed a mixture of heathanism with Christianity[17a-c] which may have led to the first great persecution. These persecutions would continue until the Edict of Milan in A.D. 313. During the period of A.D. 276–293, the Manichaean heretics were attacked for a second time by Kartir and Mobeds. The time of this persecution was during the reign of Mani's successor, Sisin.

The Nestorians

A further fracturing of Eastern and Western churches would occur through the council of Ephesus in A.D. when the Church of the East was declared anathema and the gulf would continue to widen over the expulsion of Nestorious, whom the Persians considered to be a hero and a martyr as well as through the Council at Chalcedon in A.D. 451. The Church of East never accepted the verdict of the Ephesean Council, and they may have been right because, according to some historians, the council's legality is questionable. Other modern Church of the East historians claim Nestorious was not a monophasite theologian, but his followers later attributed those teachings to him.[18] This matter continues to be a topic of much debate between Eastern and Western churches to this very day.[19]

One Christological point is clear: Nestorious truly believed in the deity of Our Lord Jesus Christ through the doctrine of "deity by *kenosis*," God "emptying" himself and being born in the likeness of men (Phil. 2:7). Then the "exaltation" of man is accomplished. This theological view is as old as Origen and Athanasius and was begun by Monotanus (circa A.D. 155), who claimed to be the paraclete. His proclamations began the controversy over the John 14 recording of the high priestly prayer and the giving of the paraclete to the church.[20] However, there may be a problem with the Nestorian theology as concluded by A. Grillmeier. . . .

> was neither a theology of a two-headed Christ, nor of a Jesus who earned his way into Godhead, but rather a failure to take the church's ancient tradition of the *communicatio idiomatum* seriously enough.[21]

The Western church would maintain that the descent of the Holy Spirit would be from the Father and the Son in a unified purpose. The monophasite and Nestorian churches of the East would hold to the descent of the Holy Spirit from the Father through the Son to the congregations. It is this historical controversy that led to universal theological schisms between East and West over the issues of the substance of the Holy Spirit and the functions of the Godhead. Modern theologians, such as Karl Barth, believe that God is an ontological trinity who is free to appear to us in an economic form of being.[22]

Meanwhile, the monophasite churches of the East, which originally held the belief in conditional immortality,[23] had been growing at a steady rate, with as many as 120 ships yearly sailing for India. Moffett cites Strabo as follows:

> Strabo did not exaggerate when he reports that on a visit to Egypt about the time of Christ he found as many as 120 ships

a year sailing for India from the Egyptian head of the Red Sea. Among the surviving documents of the first century, in fact, is a mariners' manual, *The Periplus of the Erythraian Sea,* written by an Egyptian Greek about A.D. 60, which corresponds closely to the traditional date for Thomas's mission (between 50 and 72). With the precision of one who had made the voyage himself, the author of the *Periplus* describes the route in detail, with a wealth of helpful hints on wind and tides, harbors and flourishing markets, and local tribes and rulers.[24]

Notice the trade routes that existed between Egypt via the Red Sea to the nations of India. Could trade routes such as these have helped to establish the Egyptian theological schools for the training of Indian priests in Egyptian traditions, as discussed by B. J. Wilkenson?

In spite of the diversity of the Eastern churches, whether Orthodox or Nestorian, a Hebrew church flavor still continues to thrive in their history, liturgy that is their legacy from which the Western Church has much to learn.

The wide application of Hebraic traditions is evident in the early church, which extended from Britain to the Far East before the domination of the Roman Empire would take place. These Hebraic literary traditions were much more widespread than traditional scholars have believed.[25]

According to a tradition cited by Bishop Papias in the mid-second century C.E.., the Jew Levi, who later became the apostle Matthew, compiled the "Logia" or sayings of Jesus and edited them "in the Hebrew language." Eusebius also cites the church father Irenacus as saying: "Matthew published a gospel for the Hebrews in their own language." And also Jerome, when studying in Antioch about 380, compared the Greek and Latin versions of the Gospels with the Hebrew text, which he had found among the Ebionites of Aleppo.

Epiphanius writes that the "Nazoraioi," the second Jewish-Christian sect, "carefully cherished the Hebrew language" in which they read both the Old Testament and the Gospel of Matthew. Eusebius relates that Pantaenus found the Hebrew Matthew in use among the people of India . . .[26]

Debates in modern scholarship range from a Hebrew origin of the Gospel of Matthew due to its Jewish emphasis and content, but the majority of scholars feel that Aramaic was the original language due to its sociological use in Judian society while first-century Hebrew was mainly spoken in the Hebrew Synagogues during liturgical worship.[27]

There is great unity of spirit between Egyptian and Syriac Christianity. The Syrian churches rejoice in the fact that their language is the closest to the Aramaic spoken by Jesus.[28]

The original language that underlies the Greek recension of Matthew is no doubt Semitic, and the Hebraic thought forms would have still been transmitted to Greek the receiver language, through the auspices of the Aramaic tongue.[29]

Coptic Greek, which originated in Egypt, was commonly used in the early Coptic Church where they employed a *Logia* tradition of the "Sayings of Jesus," 114 of which are recorded in the Gospel of Thomas. In this tradition, there was also a Greek/Coptic edition of Matthew's Gospel, which dated from the first and second century A.D., and it should be noted that when Origen lived in Egypt, he drew up a compilation of the Old Testament Canon consisting of twenty-two books.[30] Both Hebrew and Egyptian *Logia* were believed to be from oral traditions. The Egyptian traditions are held by many scholars to be older than many Western textual traditions.[31]

Seven Christian copies of Old Testament texts have been attributed to the second century, and four copies of the New Testament texts. Depending as they do upon paleographic comparison with other papyri, the datings must remain vague.

But given that a half-dozen other biblical texts are assigned to the second or third century, and dozens more to the third, the general conclusion is clear. The presence of an active Christian community in Egypt is well established by a strong wave of biblical fragments that precede the emergence of early Christianity in the mid to late third century.[32]

However, some Messianic Jewish sects did believe the report of Matthew's gospel that they felt was ostensibly Jewish, and therefore, they accepted the virgin birth of the Jewish Messiah.

In their description of the sects they considered Judaizing, the church fathers reported that they did not believe in the virgin birth of Jesus, but they thought he was a human being like other men. They kept the law just as other Jews did, to the extent of observing Jewish days and keeping the Sabbath, even if they also observed the Lord's Day as well. They circumcised their males, practiced ritualistic abulations, and believed that the Kingdom of God or Christ would take place here on earth, centered around Jerusalem. Some of them believed Jesus had not yet been raised from the dead, and many accepted only the Gospel of Matthew as authoritative. Some believed in angels, and some worshipped facing Jerusalem (see also note p. 19–2).[33]

It appears the Nazarenes continued in their attempts to place Christ as the Son of God under Jewish monotheism. No exact Christological formula has been found in early Jewish Christianity, but from the preceding quote, we do see every attempt by the School of the Poor at Jerusalem to retain aspects of Jewish monotheism. However, Bible scholars should not assume there existed a Jewish purism, but rather a syncretism from the blending and reinterpretation of old pagan rites, which were interwoven within the matrix of Judaism from which Christianity borrowed.

> If the old rites were softened into sacraments for the mystical, the hope was till that something would really be effected by them: the devotee would be changed into a Bacchus, a divine being. He would be raised from spiritual death, like the seeds, and—for there is good reason to assume that the hope included this also—would be born again as a result of fertilization by the divine fluid which had been earlier represented by the leather phallus of the primitive rites, or in the orgiastic drinking of wine. The new conception did not entirely replaced the old. The old survived, and still survives in rural fertility festivals in certain localities. But intelligent men were seeing deeper possibilities—men of sufficient breadth of view to see the values in the religious ideas of other peoples, and so to be inclined to syncretism.[34]

These new interpretations from the old myths were to bring to new reality elements of truth that the old myths didn't contain. So for Jesus to be seen as a fulfillment of Bacchus was to be the firstborn of many brethren (Rom. 8:29), who would also pronounce judgment upon this "evil and adulterous generation" (Matt. 12:39–41), which is a type beginning with the New Year's judgment, beginning with the blast of the shofar, bringing in the Sabbath rest with the final enthronement of Yahweh.[35] Both the Early Church and Judaism had differing schools of thought regarding the question of whether the Messiah would be God's agent in the world to come or Yahweh Himself mainfesting Himself as Savior. Some scholars have stated the Savior-God concept was only in Greek tradition and not a Hebriac concept. However, in the Deuterocanonical traditions of Esther's prayer (Esther 15:3, Greek Version, NRSV, Oxford Annotated), the concept is present. But the earliest Jewish formula of monotheism that emerges in history is the great Jewish Monad. The nature of the great Jewish Monad came to be viewed with a triadic nature.[36]

Yet later on, especially in the century of the trinitarian councils, the lack of a trinitarian creedal formula in the NT was felt to be a serious impediment. An attempt to remove this impediment is the so-called '*Comma Johanneun*'—an addition to the I John 5:7f, which originated in Spain in the fourth century. The original text of I John 5:7f dealt with the unanimity of the witness of the Spirit, the water and the blood (ch 64). This original form of the text is to be found in the Egyptian and Syrian manuscripts, in the earliest Fathers and the whole of the East.[37]

The Church in Odessa worshiped the Great Triad with a feminine spirit while the Gospel of the Egyptians declared from Alexandria by Clement, "I have come to destroy the works of the female," which was a commentary of Matthew 19:12. (*Miscellanies* III.9:63).[38] Historians are increasingly aware of the diversity that existed in early Christianity throughout the Middle East. This is not to mention the differing canonical lists that were used in the formation of each community's canon, which was standardized by that local church community. While the School of the Poor in Jerusalem did not accept the deuterocanonical Jewish writings as the Jews in the diaspora did, the same canonical problems were inherited by the early church from Judaism. The subject of contention that has always confronted the people of God throughout the centuries is how to determine the point of corruption in the canonical process.

The Jewish sects, like the Sadducees, would hold the point of corruption at anything beyond the Torah and would therefore reject the writings of the major prophets as well the sacred writings, whereas the Pharisees would accept all of these documents as being authoritative and would hold the point of corruption at the beginning of the Mesianic Jewish church's canon, which Christians called the Greek Bible or the New Testament. And as we have seen, some Jewish groups would only accept the Gospel of Matthew and would see the Pauline corpus as at the point of canonical corruption. Then, in later centuries, when the Arabic world be under the conquest of the Muslims, there a different point of corruption would be established under the auspices of Muhammad.

Many Western Christian historians have generally accepted the view that Jewish Christianity was "gentilized" into a Western tradition very early on in the Christian tradition. But new textual and historical information now reveal the Hebrew Church of the East as well as the North African traditions in Ethiopia and the Coptic Egyptian churches did not just fade away and cease to exist as Western Christian traditions would grow to preeminence.

> The world of the Hebrew Bible clearly has much in common with African cultures, in the importance placed on dreams and visions, and the felt need to establish boundaries with ritual prohibitions. Many modern African prophetic churches keep the sabbath holy, and adopt dietary and other prohibitions similar to those laid down in Leviticus, as the Ethiopians do.[39]

And the Sabbath-Sunday controversey would not materialize in Africa until the followers of Teka Haymanot, based on Shoa, and those of Ewostatewos, based in Tigre, whereas in the West, the Sabbath-Sunday controversey would have occurred much earlier during the reign of Hadrian, with the final expulsion of the Jews from Jerusalem.

The Africans also maintained a strong tradition of eliminating the deification of pagan deites while maintaining their social framework, given from former world religions that would provide them with that voice from within, which would lead them into the fullness of truth contained within the life, death, burial, and resurrection narrative.

> Sykes, in a thoughtful reflection on these issues, writes, 'the contestants are held together by the conviction that the contest

has a single origin in a single albeit internally complex performance . . . the life, death and resurrection of Jesus Christ.'[40]

Contrary to current practices, the Eastern church traditions developed and maintained a strong emphasis on Hebraic worship styles, which continued to be practiced and were re-established at the Council of Laodicea in A.D. 365.

Italy and the East. 'It was the practice generally of the Eastern churches; and some churches of the West . . For in the Church of Milan; . . . it seems that Saturday was held in far esteem . . . Not that the Eastern churches, or any of the reset which observed that day, were inclined to Judaism; but they came together on the Sabbath day, to worship Jesus Christ the Lord of the Sabbath.' *History of the Sabbath,* part 2, pages 73, 74 paragraph 5. Dr. Heylyn, London: 1636.

Council of Laodicea. A.D. 'Canon 16–On Saturday, the Gospels and other portions of the Scripture shall be read aloud.' 'Canon 29—Christians shall not Judaize and be idle on Saturday, but shall work on that day; but the Lord's day they shall especially honour, and, as being Christians, shall, if possible, do no work on that day.' *Hefele's Councils,* volume 2, page 6.

The Council of Laodicea was an Eastern gathering which represented Greek Orthodox attitude. An Eastern Church was revising the celebration of the Lord's Supper on the Sabbath at the about the time this council was held. The Council of Laodicea attests to the reestablishment of Sabbath observance in the East. This was one factor which led to the split in Eastern and Western branches of Christianity.[41]

Throughout church history, anti-Semitic pressure has driven the Gentile church to separate itself from its Hebrew roots in many theological areas. We have overlooked the original size and influence of the original Hebraic church, which reached from India and China in the East, across North Africa to Egypt where Sabbath celebrations continued along with Sunday observance until A.D. 300.[42]

A Gnostic influence was felt from Egypt according to a treatise called "On Style," ascribed to Demetrius Phalereus, who suggests the Egyptian magic ritual was adopted by the Gnostics from the liturgy that the Egyptian priests celebrated to the gods.[43] There is very little doubt that the Gnostics had a great deal of influence over Judaism and the early Christian church. Professor Bultmann observes that a former cultic legal tradition was supplanted by an historical tradition[44], which began with the Osiris Myth and was absorbed by the Gnostics. This resulted in liturgical chanting "show downs" between the School of the Poor and the Gnostics priests. This practice is reminiscent of competing choirs, which were extent in temple hymnity from the Psalter and other temple cults. This liturgical practice had a long transmission into Early Church liturgy due to the fact that the Early Church was part of the Hebrew temple cult.[45]

> In pagan religions transmission is confined primarily to cultic acts and the liturgical formulas which accompany them; there may in addition be an etiological myth, which tells of the origin of the cult. In a more developed stage, cosmogonic myth may also enter in to replace the old formulas, as in the religion of Egypt or in so-called Orphism or in Gnosticism. Then one may properly speak of doctrine and theology, and these, too, may be transmitted as tradition. However, they are subject to great variability, as is indicated, for instance, in the manifold allegorizations of old myths in the Gnostic systems or in those of the Osiris myth (Plutarch; *de Iside et Osiride).*[46]

They were the first heretical group to whom the apostle Paul targeted his ptomelic arguments in his letter to the Colossians. And new evidence seems to suggest the Jerusalem church as well as the Churches of the East continued in many of the chants and hymns from the Book of Psalms. It should be noted that in Zoroastrian rituals from Persia, it was believed that chanting from a written document gave magical powers while the Egyptian priests believed according to the cosmological doctrine of

> . . . Anaximander adopted and elaborated by Phythagoras and a later generation of his followers, the spheres carry the heavenly bodies in their revolutions around the earth. The vowels therefore are also symbols of the planets. Thus there are following correspondences between planets and tones that have been established by the Gnostic writers.[47]

At this juncture, it should be kept in mind that liturgical planetary worship was part of the battle that Paul confronted in dealing with the Gnostics within the first-century Christian church. The theme of Colossians takes the object of worship away from planetary powers and places it in the supremacy of the Son of Man who in Egyptian traditions they call Son of the King.

Egyptian apocryphal traditions were very popular within the Coptic Church. Among the most widely used was the Apocalypse of Peter. This document mentions breast milk becoming sacred substance and the symbolic baptism and hell. Another major document that influenced the theology of Egyptian Christianity was the Apocalypse of Elijah, which contains internal evidence from a curious legend of a transmission line of Arabic history of Alexandrian patriarchs.

> It is this horror that presumably led to the invention and transmission of a curious legend in the Arabic *History of Alexandrian Patriarchs,* in which a woman baptizes her children by cutting her breast and anointing them with drops of her blood. As in the *Apocalypse of Peter,* which describes as sour the milk produced by woman in hell whose breasts are tortured by animals,

the positive maternal symbolism of breast milk is negated in this martyrdom legend: it is blood that becomes the sacred substance. In these two contexts—symbolic baptism and hell—blood or sour milk from breasts is appropriate. In contrast, $D.d of ApocEl 2 attributes an entirely negative significance to the drawing of blood from breasts. The power of this image in ApocEl 2 and its evocation of the *Chaosbeschreibung* tradition arises precisely because under the "demon-faced" king's reign, blood would replace breast milk—because such an inversion as is acknowledged in the stories of the baptizing mother and the hell of the *Apocalypse of Peter* might actually happen in Egypt under a cruel king.

The use of *Chaosbeschreibung* in ApocEl 2 is therefore both explicit and implicit. That these terrors stem directly for vicissitudes in the kingship implies a continuity of Egyptian kingship ideology into the description of woes in the Apocalypse of Elijah. The details of the fate of women and maternity in these times also recall a basic motif of social chaos in *Chaosbeschreibung*; although it must be acknowledged that $D.f bears a form-critical resemblance to some contemporaneous Jewish literature concerning the eschaton.[48]

Even the words in the Apocalypse of John have a eschatological liturgy that matches Egyptian literature regarding the order of the seals as well as Elijah's Apocalyptic writings that feature a "man of sin" as an "antichrist" figure.[49] Another literary connection in the genre of apocalyptic writings is the term "woes," referring to a latter-day alignment of kings. And a "King of Peace" who arises into the West and "who runs over the sea like a lion" and who is a successor to four Asian empires. Then, finally, Alexander is a "Savior King."[50]

One could certainly surmise that localized eschatology, pioneered by C. H. Dodd in 1935, does have relevance here. The legends begin with a local fulfillment; then change the actors and players while retaining the motif structure as they take on and embody a worldwide fulfillment. This is exactly how the Savior uses the Daniel prophecies in Matthew 24 regarding the "Abomination of Desolation," which took place on Keslev 25, and begins with Jerusalem, then extends to all of the known world. However, certain errors did infiltrate Egyptian Christian thought. The gospel of Mark was written to correct those theological errors upon which Peter expounded in his public addresses, which Mark recorded using Greek shorthand to be read by an Egyptian audience and audiences other than Judeans.[51] Great attention in this gospel is given to the teacher/disciple cycle, which follows the plot of a Platonic rhetorical play. This is the role where Mark leads the student or the reader into the drama based on his oral enactment where he is asking them to take part in the oral drama.[52]

Even as late as the fifth century, in Lister and Iona near the Irish Seas as well as in the British Isles under direction of Patrick and Columba, Christian groups continued most of the Jewish church practices. This is attested to in part in the document *Liber ex Lege Moisi,* Ms CCCC 279 (part of the *Canones Hibernenses* in the Corpus Christi College Ms. 279) where a partial commentary regarding the Ten Commandments is listed. This manuscript contains the first three commandments and part of the fourth. These commentaries contained a Book of the Law and the Book of the Gospel. One of the most respected scholars in the field of Celtic students is Dr. Leslie Hardinge. In his Ph.D. dissertation for King's College in Britain, he asserts the following:

> Not only were Patrick and the framers of the *Senchus Mor* interested in the Decalogue, Brigit was also a "keeper of God's commandments," and Columba was likewise credited with teaching "the books of the Law completely," for "Christ's law they used to chant, with mysteries they used to search it out, with their host no heedlessness was found." As Fournier long

ago pointed out, this little book apparently played an important part in the framing of the laws of Ina and hence of those of Alfred the Great and later legislators.

> The significance of the *Liber ex Lege Moisi* has been overlooked in studies of Celtic beliefs and practices. Not only were laws modified by it, but also theological concepts and many practis show direct dependence upon its regulations.[53]

It was not until the conquest by Roman Catholicism that the Celtic churches' original Jewish position would be virtually eliminated and Patrick would be honored as a saint under their banner.

Therefore it is simply undeniable that the traditions of primitive Christianity were not simply abandoned immediately within the early church, for as Dr. Maxwell points out, many of the Jewish practices in some form continued in Eastern Christianity until the eleventh century A.D. and were part of split of the Eastern and Western Church. Strains of Jewish thinking and Sabbath observance continued in Constantinople. It is in this period when the first use of the term *Christianorum Sabbatum* occurs, used by Petrus Alfonsus, which shows that these debates over Jewish/Christian thought still continued and did not die out with the early church councils. It is also true that during the church councils, many Old Testament concepts were debated by the church fathers in regards to their application within the New Covenant.[54]

> They observed the Sabbath and also the Lord's Day. They celebrated Passover on the fourteenth of Nisan, but they may also have celebrated the resurrection at Easter. They may or may not have observed the Jewish Feast of Weeks instead of, or in addition to, Pentecost. It is uncertain whether they observed New Year's Day, the Day of Atonement, and the Feast of Tabernacles with popular Judaism in the fall. The number of feasts celebrated may have varied from church to church. At any rate,

> Jewish-Christians were closer to popular Judaism in their observance than Gentile-Christians were, but Gentle-Christians were just as traditionally Jewish in their calendrical observances as were either Jews or Jewish-Christians.[55]

It is doubtful that unless the early church, if it had not fulfilled the prophecies of the Old Testament in Ruth, Isaiah, and Deuteronomy and grafted in Gentile believers, that it would have grown beyond the borders of Jerusalem and Pela.

7 The Witness of the Early Church Fathers and the Exegesis of First Peter

Greek philosophical thought had unindated the Western church during this period far more severely than it had take a foothold in the Eastern church. The Eastern churches would come under Greco-philosophical thought later. One of the theological doctrines that underwent much scrutiny and debate was the doctrine of origins of life. Origen had stated the *logos* became man so man could become god, while Justin argued that the process of begettal began the origin of life and all truth came to the church via the prophets rather than from Greek philosophical doctrine.

> Now the soul partakes of life, since God wills it to live. Thus, then it will not even partake [of life] when God does not will it to live. For to live is not its attribute, as it is God's' but as a man does not live always, and the soul is not for ever conjoined with the body, since, whenever this harmony must be broken up, the soul must cease to exist, the spirit of life is removed from it, and there is no more soul, but it goes back to the place from whence it was taken.[1]

Many traditional exegites of the church fathers have stated erroneously that all of the patristic fathers held to the Greek philosophical model of death being a separation of soul and body. Until Athenagorus changed his view from his earlier *Plea, mortality of the soul* (c. A.D. 177) to his later *Plea, innate-immortality of the soul* (c. A.D. 187), no major ecclesiastical or historical writer/theologian of the Ante-Nicene fathers advocated this position.[2] In Justin's exception of this oversight along with the witness of Tatian, ". . . and through death existing no longer . . ."[3], Theophilus, "For God will raise thy flesh immortal with thy soul . . . "[4] and Melito, Arnobius of Africa (A.D. 297–310), the last spokesman for conditional immortality, ". . . that that, on the contrary, cannot be immortal which does suffer pain . . .",[5] Tertulian, ". . . truth compels us—that truth which God reveals, but the crowd derides, which supposes that nothing will survive after death.";[6] In Irenaeus of Gaul,[7] Novatian of Rome,[8] and Clement[9] we see the patristric fathers held opposing views regarding the origin of life and the nature of Christian thought in dealing with its completion of Greek dualistic thought or its separation form these philosophical constructs, with pleas to abandon the aestic dualistic model and to return to a biblical view.[10a-i]

The doctrine of Plato, which was rejected, was the concept of the reincarnation of the soul, but his idea of the immortality of the soul was historically maintained. During the infancy of Egyptian, Arabian, and Greek theological development, the "sleep of the dead" was a very common belief, as we have seen in the Book of the Dead, The Coffin Text, and the historical references by Eusebius, the Father of Church History, who held the immortal soul postion as did Origen, whom he quoted regarding Arabian Christians who held "false opinions" regarding conditional immortality.[11]

By the time of Muhammad, the Arab communities would adapt the Platonic doctrine of the separation of the soul from the body, but maintain a limited duration, *abqab* (meaning years or long years), for the punishment in Hell (Surah 4:169, 33:65, 70:23, 78:23).[12] There remain echoes of the sleep of the dead prevalent in the writings of the Quran in which the body is seen

(Surah 39:20) as having a new starting point in the resurrection, which corresponds to Hebraic thought regarding the body, soul, and spirit comprising a unity and the destructive hell fire being of limited duration, *olam*. The same is true in other Semitic traditions as well. In terms such as *pi* and *hi* meaning "to destroy" and the QRT text (Ugarit), *smd*. These terms show that Yahweh is the direct agent of destruction, *baddon* "destruction or ruin." Also, conditional curse threats from the blessing/curse formula found in Leviticus 26:38 and Deuteronomy 28:20, sermons Deuteronomy 4:26, 8:19, 20:11–17, Joshua 23:13 and also 1Q22:1–10 are remarkably similar to the Near Eastern texts. They also bear some resemblance to the curse formulas and descriptions applying to man's destruction (*wy'bd yi*), which have been found in a Phoenician burial inscription from Cyprus. These Semitic burial inscriptions from Nerab near Aleppo, says "and may his posterity perish" (*t'bd pe*). This is an Akkadian curse formula. Prophetic threats are also found in such Old Testament passages as Isaiah 29:14; Amos 1:8; 3:15; Isaiah 26:14, Jeremiah 12:17;

> . . . *'bd* and *'baddon* are not yet used in the OT (or in the available texts from Qumran) for an otherworldly, eternal destruction, even when accompanied by expressions for "eternal" (*Ianesah* Job 4:20; 20:7; cf also the Mesha inscription *wysr'l 'bd 'bd 'im* "while Israel hath perished for ever." ANET 320b: KAI No. 181.7).[13]

The church's historical theological views did not always return to the prophets as the final court of arbitration due to the influence of the Neoplatonists. However, one Semitic doctrine through Greek philosophical thought was maintained, namely, the doctrine of the Heavenly Council or the "lessor gods" being under the direction and authority of *Theos*.[14] "The true God, then is, 'The God' and those who are formed after Him are gods, [Δογοι] images, as it were of Him the prototype . . . but admitting other beings besides the one true God, who have become gods by having a share of God."[15] Origen has often been misunderstood in his explanation of the *Logos* doctrine.[16] It is apparent he believed in lessor gods of The Mighty Council, but he also maintained the fact just as the *logos* was in God, the Father's image and essence, that we were divine beings by having a share in God's divine image, *icon.* Is it possible that Origen helped to reestablish the Orthodox doctrine of deification from man's sharing God's essence in a state of glory?

At first the doctrine of death may not seem to have much theological importance in regards to which view the ecclesiastical church or individual theologians may take as long as the resurrection of the dead is maintained, but consider the facts of these paradigm shifts that have resulted in blocking the original intent of early theological and patristic writers and historians in each of these cultures. Thus, as Christian theologians, we are often at a disadvantage working from an isolated perspective, not seeing the historical development and trying to judge these matters by data having only been transmitted to us in recent times, having been filtered through the eyes of Western culture as well as ecclesiastical theology.

Another fact often overlooked by proponents on each side of this debate is that there was no uniform position that the church as a whole adopted on this theological issue and there was little agreement among church theologians until the Middle Ages. During this period of time, debates still continued regarding the question of the soul existing in contrast to the body, but the Greco-Roman philosophy held a stronghold upon Christian theologians as they attempted rapproachment with Greek philosophy, especially Platonism. Thomas Aquinas (c. A.D. 1225–74) rejected Platonism in favor of a synthesis of Greek and Hebraic notions based on his reliance on Aristotle. But the church in general would follow a Neo-Platonic line of theological development.

After the Protestant Reformation in the Neoreform Movement, there would once again be a challenge to the Neo-Platonic theological leanings of the ecclesiastical church. This challenge was generally over the concept of the immortality of the soul due to the fact it was considered unbiblical and led to a depreciation of the body and our physical existence.[17] It would not be until A.D. 1522 that Martin Luther would revive the doctrine of the mortal soul after the Fifth Lateran Council of A.D. 1512–1517 had rejected this position in favor of the immortality of the soul.[18]

Today, various attempts are being made to revive the doctrine of the holistic view of resurrection and the doctrine of man[19] that is even affecting our holistic view of diety and man's relationship to Him. These new approaches to biblical studies are resulting in a holistic reading of the text. Hopefully, the journey of historians, theologians, and scholars will be to find relative material regarding the origins of our suppositions resulting in a new quest for biblical truth.

The Alexandrian schools in the time of Philo may have acted as the capstone that championed a redefinition of Platonic doctrine, which found its way into Judaic, Christian, and Islamic thought. It is a tenable assumption to make, that much of the life, death, burial, and resurrection material has been lost, and only by exploring new possible paradigms based on new documentation can we even begin to understand these ancient theological shifts from culture to culture. Therefore, it is not a fallacy of concept to advance the notion that original Egyptian and ancient Semitic documentation needs to be revisited through the auspices of the biblical writers who knew of these traditions rather than viewing these ancient doctrines through the eyes of the Platonic/Alexandrian lense that we have inherited.

One thing we may conclude is that the biblical writers employed a much wider use of multi-cultural theological beliefs than scholars have previously supposed, and in this milieu, we are only beginning to uncover the literary traditions from which they borrowed so extensively to apply to their own interpretation. Therefore the world that shaped our New Testament theology was on a much broader scale than any one of the theological biases that we have inherited contain. Even when great scholars examine these questions, they interpret the data to fit the matrix that they believe existed in the sociological makeup of the society in which Jesus lived. As Xavier Leon-Dafaur correctly observes, they often overlook the fact that Jesus and the Apostles challenged many of the theological norms of their day. Thus, the sociological norms are often seen by scholars to be in harmony with the biblical text even though there may be appropriate tension between the two.

> These rituals, as elsewhere in the East, went to excess, and the Old Testament already struggled against their deviations, perhaps because Yahwist faith and worship was opposed to any worship of the dead. It is a fact that the gospel stories reported the turmoil that went on around the deceased. Jesus, for his part, manifested great calm and tried to make the tumult stop:
>
> He saw a tumult and people weeping and wailing loudly. And when he entered, he said to them, "Why do you make a tumult and weep? The child is not dead, but sleeping." And they laughed at him. But he put them all outside. (Mark 5:38–40)[20]

It is the opinion of this commentator that when Jesus, through the auspices of New Testament writers, speaks about passing from death unto life, two possibilities exist. Number one, it was a promise to that generation as the preterist claim or; two, the writers may be expressing the belief that all who die in the faith possess eternal life as a promise (Heb. 11:32). And we also need to remember these eternal concepts deal in a terminology of the eternal with time due to the fact that, as expressed in rabbinic tradition, we have this world (*ha olam hazeh*) and the world to come (*ha olam habba*). Therefore, the community of believers exists truly in this world and attempts to live in the spirit of the age to come.[21]

Just as the fullness of a revelation is revealed from a former social framework derived from a common origin shows us some of the amalgamation of former beliefs into the new body of truth to express its value, when we add foreign material from outside this paradigm, which the Western church has done to the life, death, burial, and resurrection motifs, thus we weaken the very doctrine that the progressive revelation is supposed to provide. By denying the sleep of the dead between the intermediate state of death and resurrection, we have opened the ecclesiastical church to the former pagan practices of and the belief of communication with the dead, leading to many of the modern occult revivals in our day. While it is certainly true the Christian church rejects divination as a practice due to the Deuteronomy 18 mandate, and has correctly rejected Plato's doctrine of reincarnation, with this compromise and departure from Hebraic Christianity, we have confused the real essence surrounding the Christ event and His victory over death.

> Salmond points that Paul, who gives more 'of a seeming psychology' than any other New Testament writer, 'never contemplates a simple immortality of soul: he never argues for man's survival merely on the ground that there is a mind or spirit in him. He proceeds upon the Old Testament view of man,' that view, Salmond continues, 'is essentially different from the Hellenic idea, which ruled the scholastic theory, and has exercised a deep and unfortunate influence on modern systems of doctrine.'[22]

M. J. Harris agrees with the emninent scholar Dr. Fudge in stating that the New Testament speaks of the immortal, but this concept clearly does not mean endless personal survival through the avoidance of physical death. Rather it involves the participation in the eternal life and therefore immunity from eternal death. This is suggested by the etymology *athanasia* (1 Cor. 15:53f; 1 Tim. 6:16).

> The Gk. pagan of the 1st cent. would probably have understood *he anastasis ton nekron* as "the standing up of corpses" (Acts 17:32a), whereas others in the tradition of Judaism may have had some idea of the new body as a permanent home of the soul which had been preserved intact in the heavenly treasuries since the time of death (cf. P. Volz, *die eschatolgie der judischen Gemeinde,* 1934, 117–21, 249–55).[23]

Ascension and Descension Themes in the Theology of Peter

It was a common practice for the New Testament writers to apply universal themes as a fulfillment of Old Testament expectations in apocalyptic literature. The same holds true for the doctrine of resurrection in which it is not just the "standing up of corpses," but this event will include the transformation of the entire person as we are conformed into the image of Christ by the power of the Holy Spirit that saves us from the intervention of death. It is this body that is fashioned without hands that is being currently reserved for us in heaven with our reward (2 Cor. 3:18; 1 Cor. 15:50).

It was in this model that Jesus passed through His life, death, burial, and resurrection, for indeed He was in the heart of the earth just as we are in the intermediate state between this present life awaiting our resurrection (Matt. 12:39–40). But the early church fathers advanced a different commentary regarding this event. They used 1 Peter 3:19–21, 4:6, 3:10 in conjunction with the resurrection narratives to show that during this intermediate state Christ preached to spirits who were in prison. Dalton states the word "proclamation" can mean question, however, there is no example anywhere in Greek where it means request.[24]

If this alternative meaning is plausible, then the traditional interpretation may be questionable. Thus it would be plausible for the pre-existent Christ to have examined the condition of the spiritual personages as opposed to preaching to them in His intermediate state. The only statement of time in First Peter was that these spirits were unruly during the days of Noah. No internal evidence suggests that Peter is linking this preaching event during the days of Noah with the resurrection motifs contained in the gospels, but rather, he is stating that the eight souls saved by water and the angelic host both received their witness from God during the days of Noah.

However, the descent clause has long been neglected in the Western creeds. Rufinus records in c. 404 that the Aquilleian Creed contained the descent clause, which he connected with First Peter 3:19 in his attempts to explain what Christ had accomplished for spirits in prison. It is interesting to note that First Peter 3:19 is missing in the oldest Christian manuscripts and no writer before Hippolytus (c. 200) and Clement of Alexandria (A.D. 150–215) and Origen ever makes an allusion to the descent passages in First Peter.

According to Kathleen Thomas, this descent narrative may have been transmitted from an ancient Syrian rite that was linked with the rite of baptism, which does fit the previously stated material regarding the rite of baptism as representing the saving power by which Christ is now seated at the right hand of the Father; v. 21 contains elements of ascension, exaltation, and subjugation.[25a,b] Could these descent passages have been a textual interpolation that found its way into Christian tradition which are not included in the Apostle's Creed in the

Forma Recepta, which we call the received form, neither are they included in the Old Roman and African forms?

However, it does appear in the Apostle's Creed according to Rufinus and Fortunatus A.D. 390–570, *descendit in inferna* (Ecclesia Aquileiensis circ. A.D. 390), *descendit as infernum* (Venantius Fortunatus cir. A.D. 570).[26] Perhaps a solution can be found in the heavy use that Peter employs of the prophet Isaiah (Isa. 40:6–8 in 1 Peter 1:24–25, then again in Isa., 28:16) which is mentioned twice in First Peter 2:6–8. Then the puritia of Christ and the atonement is borrowed from Isaiah 53 and is in First Peter 2:22–34.

Peter's dependency on the enthronement/servant song of Isaiah 53 is most striking. Other passages that employ enthronement terminology are as follows: death, resurrection, exaltation: Romans 8:35, Acts 5:31; resurrection, exaltation, subjugation, Ephesians 1:20–21; resurrection, exaltation, Acts 2:32–33; death, exaltation, Hebrews 1:3b; 10:12; 12:2; exaltation, parousia, Mark 14:62, Colossians 3:14 (cf. Heb. 9:28); exaltation alone, Acts 7:55, Hebrews 8:1 (cf. Rev. 12:5b).

The evidence from the passages just cited is clear that the New Testaments writers were familiar with the enthronement that they attributed to the ascension of Christ to His Father to receive His glorification. In like manner (Acts 1:7–8), He shall descend to meet His elect and share with them His glorification. It is this faith in the parousia that compels Peter to exhort the believers in First Peter 3:14–15, not to be afraid but to sanctify the Lord in their hearts. This may be a loose paraphrase from Isaiah 8:12 and 13, in which Judah was commanded to be brave and sanctify the Lord. Perhaps this Isaiah material, which surrounds the passages in questions, will provide a better hermeneutic for future New Testament expositors.

8 Between Jesus and Paul: That Scripture Might be Fulfilled

The order of events in the trial, the mocking and scourging, the crucifixion followed by the resurrection of Our Lord was by no means accidental, especially when we consider, as shown earlier, the cultic legal traditions from the Egyptian temple liturgies being followed by Isaiah in his servant songs (Dr. Ludlow). Thus contained in the statement that "Scripture might be fulfilled" may take on a much broader shade of meaning than has been previously realized by traditional exegites. Therefore, understanding Isaiah's use of the "Opening of the Mouth" rite (Dr. Gileadi) becomes central to our comprehension regarding how Christ fulfilled the events foretold in the Old Testament and how He announced His kingdom rulership in the New Testament. It is not by accident that the Egyptian background to Matthew's Gospel has become increasingly investigated by scholars such as Burton H. Throckmorton, Jr. It cannot be overemphasized that the effect of the Hebrew culture was greatly felt within Egypt's literary traditions as well.

The Prominent Literary Influence of Isaiah and the Psalter in the New Testament Church

It is interesting to note that the two most quoted books in the New Testament from the Hebrew Scriptures are Isaiah and Psalms. It is even more compelling when we consider that these two books contain direct references to the Egyptian enthronement ritual patterns specifically in the Servant Songs of Isaiah and the Enthronement Psalms. Scholars such as Thomas M. Finn in studying early Christianity and ritual combat affirm the fact that early church congregations chanted a combat ritual within an interpretative psalm. In this ritual the exorcist assaults the devil and seeks to drive him out in the name of Christ, the Redeemer.[1]

The New Fulfillment of the Torah

As we have previously established, the meaning "to fulfill" is not to destroy or to dismiss, but to bring to pass or to act out in a present fulfillment or with an eschatological completion yet to come. Thus, the salvational acts of God in fulfilling Torah are past, present, and future. Take, for example, Jesus's statement in Luke 24:44–48.

> Then he said to them, "These are my words which I spoke to you, while I was still with you, that everything written about me in the law of Moses and the prophets and the psalms must be fulfilled." Then he opened their minds to understand the scriptures, and said to them, "Thus it is written, that the Christ should suffer and on the third day rise from the dead, and that repentance and forgiveness of sins should be preached in his name to all nations, beginning from Jerusalem. You are my witnesses of these things."[2]

Terms such as "it is written" and "that Scripture might be fulfilled" shows us the role Jesus played as the Messiah fulfilled very ancient prophecies as well as the words he was speaking to his disciples just prior to his death, burial, and resurrection. At this juncture let us turn our attention briefly to the biblical data regarding the meaning of Christ's death due to the fact that a differentiation of meaning is applied to the death, burial, and resurrections motifs between the pagan world view and the biblical text regardless of the fact that many popular writers are trying to combine the two world views from a single source. First, our sins are laid on Christ as opposed to the death, burial, and resurrection being a method of righteousness through the ritual. Because Christ is already perfect, He leads us from condemnation to His righteousness (2 Cor. 5:21, Heb. 9:28, 1 Pet. 2:24) via a substitutionary death for our sins or "ransom," "redemption," *apolutrosen* (Eph. 1:7, Gal. 3:13, John 11:50, Mark 10:45, Heb. 4:15), which was the price paid for the satisfaction of divine justice or "expiation." *hilasmos* (Rom. 3:25, p. 451; 1 John 2:2, p. 705; 1 John 4:10,)[3] (Heb. 2:17, Rom. 3:25, 1 John 2:2; 4:10).[4]

> In Mark 10:45 a clear connection is made between the theme of *diakonein ro* service on Jesus' part and that of an expiatory death; "For the son of man also came not to be served but to serve, and to give his life as a ransom for many."[5]

The central point of this passage is that Jesus fulfilled the entire body of the law and the prophets/servant songs and the writings, which make up our corpus of Old Testament literature. Therefore, this includes the enthronement literary genre contained in the Psalms, but it is not necessarily limited to them.

> *hoti on sum humin 'viz.* that must be fulfilled', summarizing what Jesus had told the disciples during his lifetime. for *dei* cp. on 9:22; for *plerou* cp. on 1; 20
>
> *panta to gegrammena . . . peri emou* 'all that has been written . . . about me.'
>
> *en to nomo Mouseos* 'in the law of Moses', i.e., the Pentateuch.

tois phophetais kai psalmois '(in) the (books of the) prophets and the (book of) psalms."[6]

Have we as Christian exegetes failed to notice the literary correlation in this passage, Luke 24:44–48, and the fulfillment of the genre of enthronement Psalms as well as the servant songs of Isaiah? Both of these texts have literary links with the enthronement rituals dedicated to Yahweh as well as the servant songs that were reinterpreted to show our Messiah would open not his mouth. These were identifying signs of his Messiahship, in addition to the prophetic message regarding the events that he would suffer as our servant as well as the life, death, burial, and resurrections motifs, which show him as King of Kings and Lord of Lords, the only Messiah figure who has the right to rule and fulfill Scripture.

Another example of the reinterpretation of the Psalter found in New Testament literature is contained in Paul's Ephesians letter, chapter 1, verses 22a, 22b, and 23.

> 1:22–23, vs. 22a is quoted with only slight variations from Ps. 8:6 LXX, but vss. 22b–23 move far beyond the psalmist's perspective and set forth the overall theme of Eph.; God has enthroned Christ as the **head over all things for the church, which is his body, the fulness of him who fills all in all.** This particular statement about Christ's relationship to the church has been framed in a way which leads to profound results for an understanding of the nature of the church.[7]

This is a clear indication that Paul of Tarsus possessed the understanding of enthronement theology contained in the Book of Psalms. Psalm 8 is not an enthronement psalm per se, but the concept is certainly enthronement theology.

Was Paul a Jewish or a Gentile Theologian?

The greatest contribution to Gentile Christianity would have been from a Jew of Tarsus of the tribe of Benjamin named of Saul, who would claim to receive an Apostleship from Jesus Christ directly while in the Arabian desert. But not everyone would be totally convinced of the apostle's claim. Some would say that he borrowed his theology from the mystery cults during this period, then added his version of a death/burial/resurrection motif, and fused it with Hellenistic Judaism to establish his own apostolic authority and develop Gentile Christianity.

> According to H. Seyrig, the images on the coins with the alleged pyre which were thought to show that he was a dying and rising vegetation god indicate an architectural structure widespread in this area. Far less was Heracles Sandon a 'mystery god.' Bohlig makes the quite misleading suggestion with 'with this Sandon-Heracles of Tarsus we have in the Augustinian era the same deity who otherwise is designated Adonis in Syria, claiming that the celebration of the burning of his effigy and his ensuing resurrection in Tarsus, is, like that of Adonis in Heirapoilis, 'a preliminary stage to a mystery religion.' Such conjectures remain a sheer unprovable construction, typical of the speculations of the history-of-religions school. There were no Heracles mysteries in antiquity, and it is still questionable whether oriental gods already has any kind of 'mystery' character in the first half of the first century.[8]

The Apostle Paul was obviously familiar with Jewish and Gentile theology and philosophy. This is why he felt so free in re-establishing the historical validity of Christ's resurrection while simultaneously employing Greek thought forms and resurrection motifs from the Hellenistic world that he was attempting to evangelize.

For decades scholars have vacillated on the extent of the emphasis of Pauline theology. Some have suggested that Paul's theology as "a Hebrew of the Hebrews and a Pharisee from the tribe of Benjamin," would reflect a foundation of Jewish with a transcendent universal Gentile approach at the apex. But one thing is abundantly clear: the writings from this Apostle as well as the historical accounts compiled by Luke the historian in the Book of Acts, do reflect Paul of Tarsus as honoring Jewish times and seasons. In the last chapter, we noted in the conclusion the early church continued in their liturgical use of Jewish festivals and Torah readings. Since 1940, scholars have been studying the Palestinian Triennial reading cycle in which there is a strong parallel between Our Lord's visit to the synagogue in Nazareth, recorded in Luke 4:16–19 where he reinterprets Isaiah 61 and applies it to his own mission. In a similar liturgical manner, Paul of Tarsus in the synagogue at Antioch, upon the conclusion of the reading of the Law and the Prophets, delivers a homily with many allusions to Scripture.[9]

> First he quotes verses directly from the Book of Psalms, intermingled with a citation from Isaiah (Acts 13:33–35, quoting Ps. 2:7, Isa. 55:3; Ps. 66:10), and he concludes the sermon with a discussion of Hab 1:5. It is an intriguing question of whether Paul's sermon is an example of a formula of citing various parts of Scripture, attested in the later midrashic and liturgical texts. Essentially, however, Paul's speech appears to be a Jewish version of the Hellenistic homily rather than a type of homily found in the Qumran or midrashic texts.[10]

In recent decades, scholars have found that other worship traditions existed in New Testament Christianity alongside the formal synagogue service. In the household codes traditions, when the early church met in private assemblies, it is quite plausible that, in these local traditions, a synagogue type of liturgy was employed. Bernadette Brooten explains,

> There is a general tendency among scholars to assume that it is not an actual synagogue service which is meant, but rather some sort of outdoor prayer meeting. The reasons for the hesitancy to translate *proseuche* as "synagogue" are: 1) the "we supposed" (*hou enomizomen*) of v. 13; 2) the use of *proseuche* instead of *synagoge*, which is the usual term in Acts (Acts 6:9; 98:2; etc.); and 3) the fact that the congregants are women. As to the first reason, it does not seem unusual that the missionaries would not know the site of the synagogue in a strange town. Secondly, the term *proseuche* perhaps goes back to the sources of the author of Acts (the same term occurs immediately following in 16:16) or is perhaps a simple variant in the author's usage. It is in any case well-attested as meaning "synagogue."[11]

This broadening of our application of the synagogue order of services being employed in public synagogues as well as previously believed private assemblies, which have been shown to be actual synagogue services, gives us more evidence to believe that synagogue services grew into a much wider variation of liturgical styles according to cultural, geographical, and religious application.

Paul's Liturgical and Holy Day Cycle

In this transitional period, the early church still continued in telling the stories of the great exodus with a possible reinterpretation of Christ being their captain to lead them out of the spiritual bondage as well as to lead them out of Roman captivity into the Kingdom Age. Christ would have been looked upon as their Passover (I Cor. 5:7–8).[12] Traditions within Holy Day observances would have continued to be emphasized along the lines of Christian development as with the day of unleavened bread when the symbol would have been reinterpreted to be the unleavened man with a new nature and a new citizenship and clothed with the new righteousness. Western evangelicals have de-emphasized Paul's use of the Greek word ηεροταε, to keep a feast, and ηερατιζζο, the keeping of a festival. While evangelical theologians emphasize the spiritual significance of what the festivals days pointed to in shadows and typology, Paul uses the reality of Christ to deepen their original application for the church age, exemplified by his use of the *present active subjunctive volitive*[13] in I Corinthians 5:7–8, with the statement, "Let us continue in the keeping of the festival, not with the leaven of malice and wickedness, but with the unleavened bread of sincerity and truth"—*"hoste heortazomen en zumei kakias kai ponerias en azumois eilikrinias kai aletheias."*[14]

Exegetes have held different opinions regarding the linear action of Paul's thinking when he uses the phrase, "let us celebrate the festival." Even in the Old and Later Latin translations, the Latin counterparts to the Greek convey essentially the same lexical definitions, "**festiuitas,** (= πανηγυριζ) (*among the Christians or Jews*) feast, sacred day . . . **festiuo,** (*intr.*) keep a feast."[15] "**festino** (adv.)"[16] Traditional commentators have interpreted this statement to imply that one keeps a festive attitude all year long as one becomes a new lump in Christ. This interpretation has some merit regarding the activity that one pursues in a Christian walk, but the term "keeping of a festival" does employ a delineation of time (7 εκκαθαρατε aor. imp. act. εκκαθαιρω (#1705) to clean out, to purge thoroughly). For the Jewish regulation regarding the removal of all leaven from the house before celebrating the Passover s. SB, 3:359–60, the prep. in compound is perfective (MH, 309f). Aor. Imp. calls for a specific act with a note of urgency (RWP). παλαιοζ (# 4094) old; that is, the leaven used in the period before Passover (Barrett). μτε pres. subj. act. ειμτ (#1639) to be. αζυμοζ (#109) unleavened. The purpose is that they might be a people with the leaven of such sin in their midst (Fee; Barrett)[17], as well as liturgical celebration.

Classical exegetes Conybeare and Howson deal with this controversy in their footnote of 1 Corinthian 5:7–8 regarding the time of writing of Paul's epistle to the Corinthians because some objections have been advanced regarding the fact Paul must have used the term *paschal lamb* and *feast* metaphorically. This school of thought feels the latter would not have been read at the time of the Passover season.

> In spite of the opinion of some eminent modern commentators, which is countenanced by Chrysostom, we must adhere to the interpretation which considers these words as written at the Paschal season, and suggested by it. The words *leaven, lump, Paschal Lamb,* and *feast* all agree and most naturally with this view. It has been objected, that St. Paul would not address the Corinthians as engaged in a feast which he, at Ephesus, was celebrating; because it would be over before his letter could reach them. Anyone who has ever written a birthday letter to a friend in India will see the weakness of this objection. It has also been urged that he would not address a mixed church of Jews and gentiles as engaged in the celebration of a Jewish feast. Those who urge this objection must have forgotten that St. Paul address the Galatians, (undoubtedly a mixed church) as if they had all been formerly idolators (Gal. iv, 8); and addresses the Romans, sometimes as if they were all Jews (Rom vii. 1), sometimes as if they were Gentiles (Rom xi. 18).
>
> If we take "as ye are unleavened" in a metaphorical sense, it is scarcely consistent with the previous 'cast out the old leaven;' for the passage would then amount to saying, 'Be free from leaven (metaphorically) as you are free from leaven (metaphorically);' whereas on the other view, St. Paul says, 'Be free from leaven (metaphorically) as you are free from leaven (literally)'. There seems no difficulty in supposing that Gentile Christians joined with the Jewish Christians in celebrating the Paschal feast after the Jewish manner, at least to the extent of abstaining from leaven in the love-feast. And we see that St. Paul still observed the 'days of unleavened bread' at this period of his

> life, from Acts xx.6. Also, from what follows, we perceive how naturally this greatest of Jewish feasts changed into the greatest of Christian festivals.[18]

Most commentators in the Orthodox community correctly observe that the term for bread in Christian worship should be leavened because of the new lump that is the result of the leavening process, which begins with unleavened bread. So what we have is a paradigm shift between the Messianic church and Gentile Christianity.

> An alternative way of reconstructing 5.8 is "When we celebrate our Passover, let us not do it with malice and evil, which are like bread make with yeast, but rather use sincerity and truthfulness, which are like unleavened bread."[19]

At other times, the Apostle Paul simply uses the Jewish holy days as a liturgical calendar and time reference point as in Acts: "We waited to set sail until after the Days of Unleavened Bread," in his journeys to Jerusalem. Then, at another time in the Book of Acts, the voice of Paul through the pen of Luke, the historian, uses the term *herotae* when he states, "I must by all means, observe this feast," although he does not specifically tell us why he must observe this festival. Dr. Bacchiocci, in his Ph.D. dissertation, also agrees with the fact of Dr. Luke's respect for Jewish time reckoning in the Book of Acts. In regards to Jewish as well as Gentile Christians, they were observing times and seasons under the Jewish reckoning and not exclusively under the Roman calendar as has been previously supposed.

> In Acts also he repeatedly shows his respect for the Jewish calendar and religious customs. He mentions for instance that Herod arrested Peter "during the days of Unleavened Bread" and that he intended "after the Passover to bring him out to the people"

(12:3, 4). He reports that he himself left Philippi with Paul on the morrow of the complete rest which marked the last day of the Unleavened Bread (20:6; cf. Luke 22:1,7). He doesn't hesitate on repeated occasions to show how Paul respected Jewish customs (Acts 16:1–3; 18:18; 20:16; 21:24). He says, for instance, that Paul was "hastening to be at Jerusalem, if possible, on the day of Pentecost." (20:16). Later he reports how in that city, the apostle under pressure purified himself, and "went into the temple to give notice when the days of purification would be fulfilled:" (21:26). To these could be added Luke's frequent references to the Sabbath meetings which Paul attended with both "Jews and Greeks" (Acts 18:4; cf. 17:2; 16:13; 15:21; 13:14, 42, 44). In the light of these indications, it would appear that Luke respected the Jewish liturgical calendar and used it quite consistently when reckoning time.[20]

It is also abundantly clear that Dr. Luke as well as Mark and other writers of the New Testament all shared in the use of Jewish theology, literature, and religious practice as the roots of the Christian theology. It later centuries, a growing separation between East and West, Jew and Gentile, would even make this theological bridge much more difficult to maintain. The Apostolic writers never succeeded in closing the Jewish/Gentile gap. Therefore, only since the time of Davies have Western commentators sought to give the Apostle Paul his Jewishness at the root of his philosophy, which extended into Hellenistic sophistication with his use of transcendent vocabulary and a reinterpretation of Hebrew metaphors.

And then after his day, when his letters came to be read by Gentiles who little understood Judaism, the misinterpretation of Paul became almost inevitable. These Gentiles often approached the epistles as outsiders incapable of appreciating their setting within what we may call a family dispute, which could explain both their extreme bitterness and, at times, their fine sensibilities. The disputes over the true interpretation of their common

Jewish tradition between Paul and his kinsmen, both those who accepted and those who rejected the new faith, were expressed with intensity, not to say ferocity. As long as they were seen as being *intro muros,* they remained endurable. But once removed from this setting they took on a radically negative character. They no longer appeared as attempts at the reinterpretation of a shared tradition but as forages in hostility. In time, though the process was not rapid, what was a disruption among Jews came to be spelled out at the denigration and rejection of Judaism and of the people of Israel as a whole. Paul's criticisms of the Law were intrinsically difficult to understand and, when wrenched from their familial context as read by Gentiles largely untouched by Judaism, were ascribed a rigid coldness and a clinical, a surgical, and a unified antithetical purpose.[21]

With the Torah being disconnected from its original Hebraic culture, the Gentile Christians viewed Christ as the completion of the Torah (τελσζ γαζ νσμσυ) Romans 10:4.[22a-c], but with the marriage of Judaism and the Hellenistic world, which had created a religious of syncretism and had mysteriously adopted Jewish elements. This would cause a new stream of syncretism, which would overlay the Torah with a Hellenistic philosophy.

Modern critics now feel the Greek term νσμσζ is a direct equivalent of the Hebrew term for law the Jews call Torah that in later Judaism would refer to God's entire revelation in the entire Hebrew Scriptures. The Pauline use of the term would imply general instructions as well as being summarized with the designation, "the Law of Christ." And with this new interpretation, of the term νσμσζ would have a different application to Gentile Christians. What was once a required national day of rest, such as annual festivals and Shabbat, became a part of the early church's liturgical and eschatological patterns for instructions.

In addition to 1 Corinthians, the portrait of Paul and Christian communities in the Book of Acts demonstrates that Christians adhered to the Jewish calendar. Paul enters the synagogue at Antioch of Pisidiea on several Sabbaths and proclaims the Gospel (Acts 13. 14, 44). According to Acts, it was Paul's custom to enter the synagogue on the Sabbath, and in Thessalonica, he reasoned for three Sabbaths from the Scriptures (Acts 17.2). Paul addresses the community at Troas on the first day from Sabbath (Acts 20.7). Concerning feasts, Paul sets sail from Philippi after the days of unleavened bread (Acts 20.6) and intends to arrive in Jerusalem by the feast of Pentecost (Acts 20.16). The portrayal of Paul in Acts supplies clear evidence that Christians mark time by the segments of festivals and Sabbaths.[23]

A similar problem exists in Christianity's traditional interpretations of passages such as Romans 14:1, Colossians 2:16–17, Galatians 4:6.

Some scholars regard the Colossians false teachings as an offshoot of the teaching of the Qumran community. They point out that the emphasis on dietary rules, festal calendar, and the veneration of the angels, tallies completely with the practices of the Qumran community. The term 'law' (γνομεο) is absent anyway from the controversy in which Colossians is engaged. The most plausible conclusion held by most scholars is that the false teachings and practices at Colossi were of a syncretistic nature, containing both pagan and Jewish elements. The Old Testament was apparently invoked to provide a justification for their sincerity beliefs and practices.[24]

The Colossian Heresy and Galatian Bondage

Traditional Christian exegesis has long since held that the shadows referred to verse 16 were always viewed to be in the past referring to the Mosaic law and to the sacrificial system employed by ancient Israel. While there is very little doubt that these two divisions of biblical law do overlap in their applications as shadows of the Messiah and His kingdom, Troy Martin points out that there is a present reality to this existing shadow that has fulfillment in the age to come. Therefore, the Church represents the eschatological age to come within this present age that we now occupy. So the church is a type of the Kingdom of God whose fulfillment will be consummated at the second coming of Christ when the ultimate reality will fulfill the shadows and types in its totality.

> Furthermore, some commentators subtly shift the tense of εατιν in the relative pronoun clause at the beginning of v. 17. The tense is present and affirms that these things are now shadows. These commentators translate that past tense and conclude that these stipulations have ended now that the true substance has arrived since they were only shadows. This shift of tense is evident when Lohse states, "The regulations are merely shadows of things to come. . . . Since reality is with Christ alone, the shadowy appearances have lost all right to exist. . . . The reality that exists solely with Christ is shared only by those who, as members of the body of Christ, adhere to the head (2:19). Therefore, for them the shadows have become completely meaningless, and the 'regulations' to which the arrogant exponents of the 'philosophy' refer, *have lost* all binding force (Colossians, 117). In spite of this exegesis, the test affirms a present, albeit temporary, validity to the shadow. H. A. W. Meyer correctly argues, "The μελλονια have not been manifested at all, and belong altogether the αιον μελλον, which will begin with the coming again of Christ to set up His kingdom. . . ."[25]

This traditional error has resulted in Christian commentators making the wrong assumptions by presuming that any Old Testament or Jewish practice is the shadow in a past tense and no longer holds any relevance to the Christian experience or to our eschatological hope to come.[26a,b] They have oftentimes missed the paganization of times, days, seasons, and years that has resulted in a breaking of the biblical canon rather than building the New Testament on its proper foundation of the Old Testament. Therefore it is crucial that we understand why Paul uses neutral verbs that pertain to a participation in a feast or a new moon or a Sabbath. These things are a shadow of future realities. Dr. Bacchiocchi explains,

> The verb is neutral and it does not mean "to condemn" but "to judge" whether approvingly or disapprovingly. Paul uses the same verb repeatedly in Romans when dealing with a similar problem; "let him who abstains pass judgment (μη κρινετω) on him who eats" (14:3). "One man esteems (χρινει) one day as better than another, while another man esteems (χρινει) all days alike" (14:5). The meaning of the verb "χρινει" according to its common usage is not "to condemn," but rather to express an opinion, to resolve, to pass judgment." Note then that the verb used indicates that Paul is considerably tolerant on this question.[27]

It appears that traditional commentators may have missed the real focal point of Colossians 2:16–17. The issues that Paul raises in these passages are the proper motivation for acts of worship and Christian conduct as well as a non-judgmental attitude regarding the conviction of others, in addition to dealing with the emphasis on the former shadows becoming the latter realities.

> . . . As reason for the warning, it is adduced that all the rules and regulations cited in 2:16 are but a shadow of what is to come. That which is to come (ταμελλουτα) is the designation for the future age, for the eschatological completion of salvation (in the framework of the same picture, Heb. 10:1; in apocalyptic

e.g., 2 Bar. 4). Both the writer and the opponents were concerned with this reality. Thus the first part of the sentence contains no criticism yet. The opponents, too, viewed their regulations as a shadow of the redemptive reality. In metaphorical language, "shadow" indeed was no derogatory designation. The important issue is to what the shadow points. Shadow and reality are two poles of a semantic axis influenced in antiquity by Platoism and described as σκια and εικφυ (shadow and archetype) but sometimes also as shadow and body. The contemporary reader has to remember that the reference is to an image and that the shadow has an objective and concrete form, while the archetype, as the true reality was the idea. In the Hellenistic environment Jewish conceptions were also interpreted in this manner (cf. Philo, Conf. Ling. 190; Heb. 8:5), and the false teachers evidently also viewed their religion as a way into the spiritual world.[28]

Paul seems to be using an eschatological type and shadow approach as did the Old Testament writers employing a Jewish literary technique while using Greek vocabulary in dealing with Judaizers.

The verb is neutral: "Judge with approval or with disapproval"; to say that only condemning is intended here is not tenable. The Colossians are not only to avoid what such a judge forbids, they are also not to do what such a judge approves. The latter would be as serious a mistake as the former. The reasons for which such a judge approves a thing are just as wrong as the reasons for which he forbids it. For he is not prompted by the gospel nor by Christ's words but by his vapid philosophy and empty deceit (v. 8) and would make booty of us either way. The main concern is always, not *what* we do or avoid, but the *inner reason* for our conduct.[29]

Dr. Troy Martin provides us with a possible resolution,

The resolution of the grammatical and syntactical problems of the clause to δε σφμα του χριστσν, supports the following translation of Col. 2:16–17: "Therefore do not let anyone critique you by [*your or her/his*?] eating and drinking or by [*your or her/his*?] participation in a feast, a new common, or sabbaths, which things are a shadow of future realities, but *let everyone discern* the Body of Christ by [*your or her/his*?] *eating and drinking or by* [*your or her/his*?] *participation in a feast, new moon, or sabbaths, which things are a shadow of future realities.*"[30]

Further investigation regarding the exegesis of this parallelism in the final reality is needed. Martin and Bacchiocchi definitely have provided us with strong evidence that our traditional renderings under close scrutiny do not stand due to the tension that this places in Paul's subject matter as well as the tension it places within the biblical canon. Furthermore the possibility exists that the Colossian heresy may have borrowed some secret instructions regarding the Torah, which were hidden from the rest of Israel.

The Qumran texts also contain evidence of secret instructions concerning holy sabbath and festivals which remain hidden to the rest of Israel. (cd 3:14; 1 Qs 9-26-10.8).[31]

Again, Troy Martin concludes the following,

In future studies, exegetes should seriously consider the possibility that Christian practices, and not those of the opponents, are criticized in Col. 2:16, 15. The exegetical tradition's failure to adequately consider the grammar and syntax of το δε σωμα του χριστου in Col. 2:17 results in a misunderstanding of this clause along with the whole of Colossians.[32]

George Eldon Ladd submits that Galatians is a reinterpretation of biblical law recodified and interpreted for a Gentile audience with a Jewish factions, but Paul is also striving to protect the biblical from corruption of human traditions (Col. 2:8)[33] The beggarly elements referred to in Galatians 4:9 is well demonstrated by Orthodox scholar, Paul Nadim Tarazi, over the issue of slavery and the Galatian church's poor decision to return to that yoke.

> The "again" evokes the thought that if the Galatians do make the wrong decision they will in effect be returning to their previous condition of slavery. The warning in 4:9 against returning to serve the "weak and base elements" expressed the same thought. In both cases the "wrong decision" Paul has in mind is to endorse the Law as obligatory for Christians. Not only do the following verses provide direct evidence of this but also v. 1 itself provides indirect evidence in the expression "a yoke of slavery." In Paul's day, Jews commonly use the work "yoke" to refer to one's duty to fulfill the Law's requirements, and this explains why he added it to "slavery" which would otherwise have sufficed by itself.[34]

Paul uses the expression "to know" γιγνοστω, (in Hebrew, *yadah, to be known of God*) a stronger term than the Hebrew, *hikkir,* meaning *to acknowledge,* used in Old Testament literature, *of one who recognizes a relative and redeems him from a strange master.* In context, Paul is simply asking the question to the Galatian church as to why, after having *known,* not merely to acknowledge God's existence, but to be known of God by the election of one's calling, would they return to slavery once again?[35]

Paul's frequent use of the Midrash in the Book of Galatians is an indication of his desire to see the Galatian church freed from the bondage of slavery and to be transformed into slaves of righteousness as free men. David Daube adds that, "If Paul is familiar with this or a similar Midrash, his choice of argument in Galatians becomes even more understandable,"[36] due to the fact the Galatian church was to be freed from bondage under the Law so they could be free among men while they are slaves to God. We cannot arrive at this theological balance unless we are familiar with the Jewish Tractrates and other sources that Paul makes reference to in the construction of his epistles.

In summary, both the Colossians and Galatians letters may have been influenced by a document out of the famous philosophy of Pythagoras. Swiss scholar E. Schweizer states this text was written a century before Paul in the 500's B.C. This recently seen document goes beyond the geometry into the worlds of spirits and souls. Schweizer endeavors to show us that erroneous worship must be mainly Hellenistic. Another common theme in both letters is the term "elements," *stoicheia,* found in Colossians 2:8, 20. This term may be understood in two ways, which basic components may refer to an elementary or juvenile doctrine taught either by Jewish or Pagan ritualists. The second competent may employ concepts of a *pernicious* and false philosophy employing "elemental spirits of the universe" (agreeing with the RSV) *stoicheia tou kosmou.* Therefore these letters are not simply an expression of aesetic dualism as traditional commentators suggest, but confront with an extreme dramatic opposition of this age ruled by spirit forces versus Christ himself.[37]

Paul's Battle with Flesh and Spirit and the Desire to Depart

But in a larger context, Christianity has been influenced by aesetic dualism. Being caught in this dilemma of body and spirit, the Apostle Paul would have rather departed and be with Christ because he longed for His presence during Paul's life's troubles (Phil. 1:21–24). Even though Paul knew the righteous dead all died having not received the promises (Heb. 11:13) and both the righteous and unrighteous have the same sleep [*rephiam*] (Dan 12:2) and know not anything (Ps. 136:3), Paul looked forward to the reward that God, who only has immortality (1 Tim. 6:14–16) would grant him at His coming (2 Tim. 4:8) when he would be resuscitated [*neshamah*] (Job 33:4).[38] This anointed God gives life to all of His creatures (Eccles. 9:5); . . . "who gives breath [*neshamah*] to the people upon it, and spirit [*ruach*] to those who walk in it" (Isa. 42:5).

Modern scholars, such as Clark Pinnock, Dale Bruener, John Stott, L. E. Froom, Hans Kung, and Ellis echo some of Dr. Bacchiocchi's conclusions regarding the conditional view of immortality and hell, and the New Testament corpus of literature speaks primarily of our relational position in Christ after death rather than an anthropological one. This growing body of scholarly evidence is bringing New Testament exegesis far closer to the Semitic model of eternal destruction discussed earlier in the covenental curse concept.[39a-c] As Alan E. Bernstein has stated, the excluded die, are destroyed or annihilated.[40] Scholars such as Murray J. Harris maintain the historical position against the growing tide of non-traditional interpretators in dealing with the duration and the nature of eternal punishment.[41]

Along with these changing eschatalogical trends, our understanding of the Kingdom of Heaven is also under scrutiny by such scholars as R. G. Beasley-Murray, John Bright, and Herman Ridderbos. Theologians such as those mentioned previously maintain an eschatalogical perspective of the Kingdom of God, descending from heaven and bringing all nations into the Kingdom of God. (Rev. 21:1–2). Rather than the redeemed ascending upward into His presence, He will make His home and tabernacle with the redeemed. Dr. Dale Breuner explains:

> We moderns, "schooled in Greece," tend to see in God's "I am" a present-tense *spiritual* presence of Abraham with God, which

need not be disputed since there is in the New Testament a connection of some kind between the faithful dead and the Lord (cf. Luke 23:43; 2 Cor. 5:8, Phil. 1:21–23). But even the Humanist-trained sixteenth-century Calvin was sufficiently at home in Hebraic thought to see Jesus's resurrection is eschatology here: "God does *not* promise souls the survival of death, glory complete and *immediate,* and [full] enjoyment of blessedness, but delays the fulfillment of their hope *to the last day* [at the general resurrection.]"[42]

This modern view by Breuner is a compromise between the pansoulist position, which maintains soul sleep during the intermediate state of death and resurrection. Bruener's compromise deals with the connection of this intermediate state during this journey in which the Pauline corpus uses figurative language, such as a ship departing from a port journeying to a far country. The soul sleep position maintains the travel of the spirit back to God as an act of preservation of the departed one rather than the spirit separate functional entity, which is separate from the body. In the final eschaton, heaven will not represent a place to which we ascend, but the presence of God will bring the heavenly dimension to His people as the waters of healing heal the nations. Again, Dr. Bruener explains,

> Jesus, then does *not* say the faithful will be *in heaven* like angels; he says that they will be "*like* angels," that is, the faithful will become very different from what they now are; they will be wonderfully transformed human beings. (Since Sadducees did not believe in angels at all, Acts 23:8, Jesus' analogy of angels is provocative. Cf. Sand, 444.) The goal of the work of God is not angels or heaven but humanity on earth (schl., *der,* 653).[43]

Our Western theological views of the Kingdom of God have garnered a great deal of mystical concepts that have been brought into the Western churches' theological frame. When one examines the *Tibetan Book of the Dead* in regards to the judgment scenes that began at the moment our pre-existent soul was assigned a definite body, this theological construct is echoed when a particular appeal is made at the Egyptian ritual to the god Khnemu, the creator of bodies, who is fashioning man upon the potter's wheel. And on this wheel, we have the four circles of heaven, purgatory, earth, and hell. As this cycle of rebirth by ascent into the heaven world and by descent in the hell world, this timeline is circular.[44] Whereas the Hebraic model is linear, with a created beginning, ascent to the apex and descent into the final eschatological outcome of all things.

> In the second phase, after the general resurrection of the dead, the Last Judgment will ensure that anybody whose name cannot be found written in the Book of Life will be thrown in the burning lake. The others will be granted eternal life on a renewed earth. The center of this world will be the new and eternal Jerusalem which the visionary sees descend from heaven and situate itself on earth.[45]

Notice once again the common imagery, the biblical writers using eschatological language borrow from pagan literary traditions of ancient Egypt and redefine them to fit within the parameters of salvation history. While they reveal a similar literary order, the events are applied to a biblical revelatory timeline that will be completely fulfilled with a recreated heaven and earth.

The Theology of Romans 14: Fasting Before the Gods or Esteeming All Days Alike

Modern studies in Romans 14:1 to indicate that some early Christian congregations were indeed influenced by Hellenistic fast days due to the fact that the original Jewish congregation founded by Priscilla and Aquilla had long since apostatized and by the time of the authorship of Romans 14 A.D. 56 or 57, all vestages of this Jewish faction were gone, leaving only the vegetarians and the planetary worshipers of the Saturnalia. Paul's general counsel to the Roman, Colossian, and the Galatian churches was not to fall back into the beggarly elements/pagan lists found in Galatians 4:10: "the years are then grouped into Olympiads of four years or eras of varying lengths."

When Paul refers to days, months, seasons, and years in Galatians 4:10, he lists categories most characteristic of a pagan time-keeping system.[46] Neither did he wish to see the corrupt Hellenistic forces within the remaining synagogue congregations seize control and place a yoke of bondage upon the Galatian church once again. No wonder Paul asks the question, "Oh, foolish Galatians, who bewitched you?" (Gal. 3:1) This is a hint of the occult forces that he felt lay behind the scenes of planetary worship. So Paul's counsel continues by saying for the sake of unity in these dividing congregations, let every man fast or esteem one day above another and another man esteem all days alike. Paul's attitude is similar in dealing with the Colossians when he exhorts them to let no man or teacher judge them in regards to their religious practices. One consideration worthy of contemplation is that the early church would have been attempting to continue in the time-keeping practices by marking festival seasons with Jewish holy days for the following reasons:

1. A New Year's Day to begin the new life cycle for the community for the purity of their religious life and rituals.
2. All major cultures in the surrounding nations did continue in their appointed times and seasons that were dedicated to their deities.

3. Attempts to prevent further syncretism and integration with pagan cults.
4. The festival days would play a key role in understanding Christianity's biblical identity and destiny as well as preparing the early church in its evangelism to the Jewish people.

Consequently, a reinterpretation of the fulfillment of these Jewish festival days was in the making due to the fact that the Christ event had already happened for the early church and Christ was seen as our Passover who would draw all men to himself, thus symbolizing the water-drawing rite, which was performed in the middle of the Feast of Tabernacles. This symbolic act would correspond with Jesus beginning his public call for all men who are thirsty to come unto him and drink.

> 4. That the Solemn Worship in the Solemn Assemblies Weekly to be carry'd on after Christ had fulfilled his Week of Tabernacling in the flesh should be on the eighth day of the Week. & for this end we many. Consider, that on this eighth day of this Feast the last & great day of the Feast, Christ to draw all to himselfe, & to attend his Gospel Worship on it, John 7:37. stood and cryed, saying, If any man thirst, let him come unto mee, & drink. v 38. for he that believeth on mee, as the Scripture, saith, out his belly shall flow rivers of living Waters. They had a Custom on this day to fetch much Water out of the River Shilo, a type of Christ, & the Priests poured it on the Altar, & they then Sung Isa. 12:3: With joy shall ye draw water out of the Wells of Salvation. It is though, that Christ in respect unto that Custom presents himselfe to them now on this day, as being the Day, that Christ, upon his Tabernacling in the Flesh Should have Evangelicall assemblies of his people weekly Constituted to carry on Divine Worship upon. Hence this day was to be kept holy to God & a Solemn assembly was now to be held. & with respect thereunto is that Ezek. 43:27. & upon the eighth day, &

so forward, the Priests shall make your Burnt Offerings upon the Altar & your Peace Offering.[47]

This festival was held annually from the 15th to the 21st of Tishri and was celebrated for seven days, which ended in a solemn assembly with a peace offering on the last great day. The eighth day, as the Last Great Day, pictured the eschatological hopes of Israel as the cisterns from which they drew water would go forth, heal the nations, and never run dry. However, by the birth of the Earth Church, Israel's cisterns had indeed run dry. Therefore Israel's eschatological hopes would hang in the balance and have to be fulfilled in a victorious Messiah who had previously fulfilled the meaning of the Feast of Tabernacles though the development of his church and would later, during the Days of Awe, come to rescue Israel from her tribulation.

"According to Rabbi bar-Kahana (c. A.D. 130) the feast [of Tabernacles] holds within itself the promise of the Messiah. . . . Again, the tractate on this feast in Jerusalem Talmud explains the name of the [water] ceremony by referring to the Isaian te[x]t . . . explaining the name 'Place of Drawing' from the fact that it was "from there that they drew the Holy Spirit." Most Jews, however, rejected the message of Jesus to "draw water of the wells of salvation" (Isaiah 12:3). Instead they forsook "the fountain of living waters, and hewed them out cisterns, broken cisterns, that [could] hold no water" (Jeremiah 2:13).[48]

It should be noted that John the Revelator mentions the waters that flow from the rivers of life to heal the nations metaphorically, showing these cisterns were replenished through the Messiah.

This, as will be seen is relevant to our interpretation of the 'last day of the feast, the great day' (7:37). The leafy huts were seen as an image of eschatological salvation, cf. Pesiqta 187b: 'If any one filfils the commandment of the feast of Tabernacles in this world, God will in the time to come give him a share in *sukkoth* in the territory of Sodom, which God will divide among the tribes of the just. . . . (Ps. 60:8) 'I will exult', and when I exult, when his kingdom shines forth in the world, then I will divide Sichem, I will divide it among the tribes of my children' (Billerbeck II, 779). But we must not try to accommodate too wide a range of ideas in this third great pilgrimage feast, celebrated with such jubilation; as far as John was concerned, it was the outpouring of water and the use of festal lights which provided symbolic links with the self-revelation of Jesus cf. the commentary on 7:37–39 and 8:12.[49]

In New Testament literature, again and again we see repeating echoes of salvation history themes, which are reinterpreted and given new definition as they placed in their locations in salvation history. These themes include the Tree of Life, recurring themes of light, the symbolic purification of water, the new Eden, the new Exodus, as well as the unleavening process.

Then, as the community grows and becomes unleavened with sin and leavened by the Holy Spirit, we become a new man with a new nature. Pentecost would be seen as the beginning of the liturgical year when the Spirit would fall upon the believers who gathered to hear Peter preach. This would correspond to the giving of the Law at Sinai, but fulfilling this prophetically by a grafting in of Gentiles and by writing the laws not on tables of stone, but on men's hearts. The sounding of the *shofar* would not only represent a call to battle as in Ezekiel 33 with the work of the watchmen, but the trumpet would represent the sounding of gospel and a call for every man to repent (Acts. 17). Christ's atonement would fulfillment *Yom Kippur* by providing a perpetual atonement for all those who believe. Historically, God's people were led as a nation as God tabernacled with them. Today we don't build booths in the wilderness due to the fact that our body is the tabernacle of God. This has been the case since the *logos* became man and tented with us that someday we would also tabernacle with God when He returns to dwell with men in the Last Great Day that fulfills the Holy Day cycle of the New Year.

> The references to time in Paul's First Epistle to the Corinthians exclusively reflect the adoption of a Jewish Calendar. Even in a place like Corinth, Paul speaks of the first day for Sabbath (Κατε μαιν οαββστον; 1 Cor. 16:2), not the day of sun. He builds an elaborate argument based upon the festivals of Passover and unleavened bread (1 Cor. 5.6–8) in order to exhort the Corinthians, 'Let us keep the festival' (1 Cor. 5.8). Although the emporal references in Paul's letters are sparse, 1 Corinthians provides strong evidence for the Pauline adoption of the Jewish practice that marked time by Festivals and Sabbaths.[50]

It should be clearly indicated that the New Covenant deals with the Jewish festival days as symbols of the present and future realities that will take place at the final wedding feast, which is memoralized by the Lord's Supper. The Jewish festival days are a wonderful illustration of God's redemptive plan of salvation, but they are not included in the New Covenant contract between the Lord and His church. This is why the Pauline corpus of literature appears at first glance to be neutral regarding Jewish festival days and other Mosaic practices; but he, himself uses them as illustrations and as time-keeping schemes as well as eschatological fulfillment for the church and Israel. For even the rabbis have said that one can add to the revelation of Torah with liturgical practices, but one cannot go contrary to it, so using this paradigm, the New Covenant is built upon the foundation and the passing of the old. The New Covenant shall someday encompass all Israel.

Notice, Paul does not condemn any Jewish Holy Day practices, but he simply shows we are not compelled to observe them, and therefore, he adds we are not to sit in judgment upon those who may possess a different conviction. In spite of this tolerance, Paul does see that the Old Testament does have a message for Christians. Again, Dr. Bacchiocchi observes,

> In this perspective Paul sees that not only the observance of holy days, but that even dietary scruples can serve as a shadow, preparing Christians for the realities of the world to come. Old Testament festivals have a message for Christians. The Passover (which today we call Easter) commemorates Christ's atoning sacrifice and proclaims His coming (Mark 14:25; I Cor. 11:26); the Unleavened Bread typifies "sincerity and truth" (I Cor. 5:8); Pentecost, the outpouring of the Holy Spirit (Acts 2:4); the Sabbath, as we have seen, the blessings of salvation, which are a foretaste of the eternal rest of God's people.[51]

In referencing Conybeare and Howson and the Jewish New Testament by Dr. Stern with contributors such as Roy Blizzard and Dr. David Biven, both Hebrew and Semitic scholars, this writer is advancing the following observation: when the terms ηεροταε (Acts) and ηερταζζο (1 Cor. 5:7–8) are employed in the New Testament, this denotes a quality of linear action of the party who is being addressed; and in a Middle Eastern frame of reference, they would always associate a feast with a literal meal and a liturgical observance with priestly songs, celebrated at an appointed time;

> Among the feasts already mentioned the 'origies of Maioumas' seem to have occupied a prominent place at Antioch. They were ordered by Commodus in the same edict by which he had instituted the Olympic games. The Orgies of Maioumas were a nocturnal feast connected with scenic performances in honour of Dionysus and Aphrodite. The feast was celebrated every third year in May. In the reign of Theodosius I, the Great (379–95); it was forbidden on account of its orgiastic character, but reinstituted by his son and successor Arcadius in A.D. 396. It spread

> over all the provinces of the Empire and left many traces in several feasts, which were celebrated throughout the whole period of the Byzantine Empire. According to V. Cottas, the ιαλανικοω ιπποδρομι, the 'Hippodrome of Vegetables,' described in "Constantine Porphyrogennetus, *De Ceremoniis,* had absorbed some of the features characteristic of the Mauoumas, and of the 'Feast of the Roses'—called *tns hastrns*—a variant of the Moioumas. On the day of the 'Hippodrome of Vegetables,' the races were followed by performances by the mimes (οι του λογιου). The Hippodrome was adorned for the occasion with a cross of roses, and vegetables and sweets were distributed among the crowd.[52]

Just as the Feast of Celebrations occurred on the first of March in Rome to begin the new year, the sacred new year would also begin with feasting to the purification and renewal of the emperor worshiped in the imperial cult. This patternism was borrowed from the Greeks, when at the beginning of the sacred new year, Dionysus would be reborn in the wine through symbolic ritual to newness of life.

The preceding examples of Greek and Roman festivals show conclusively that a full liturgical celebration was practiced by followers of the cults in an active ritual. This weakens the position advanced by most evangelical theologians who often suggest that the feast days referred to by Paul have just a marking in time with no permanent theological importance for the early church. If this indeed were the case, then the Apostle John, in the Book of the Apocalypse, would have never used eschatological symbols such as woes, seals, and trumpets in his literary structure around such festival days as the Day of Atonement and the Feast of Trumpets.

9 Our Pilgrimage from Egypt to the New Jerusalem

Part of our theological problem has been that not until the 1960s, with the work of scholars such as D. T. Niles, were the Jewish patternisms contained in the Book of Revelation known to the average scholar. Debates still rage regarding whether the text in its present form contains the correct order of Trumpets, Woes, Heavenly Visions and Signs, and Courtroom Scenes. Scholars have surmised that some of the Greek syntax is suspended in the middle of some of the sentence structure, showing them we do not have a complete diagram of the book's structure. Both Daniel and Revelation were compilations of letters, so therefore it would not be absurd to think some of the chronological order may indeed be misplaced. There is enough of the structures intact to give us the essential information regarding the Jewish apocalyptic message that lay behind many of John's concepts and ideas, which are enlarged in this document and even pagan Canaanite sources were consulted and added to the cosmic drama.

Annual Feasts in Revelation. Equally striking is the evidence that the Book of Revelation appears to be patterned also after the annual feasts of the Jewish year.

Passover. The letters to the seven churches are reminiscent of the Passover, the primary feast of the spring season. For example, nowhere else in Revelation are there such strong concentrations of references to Christ's death and resurrection (cf. Rev. 1:5, 71–18). Christ's intense scrutiny of the churches reminds us of each Jewish household's search for leaven to remove it just before Passover (Exod. 12:19; 13:7). Since Passover is the only festival fulfilled by the earthly Christ (1 Cor. 5:7), it is fitting that it would be associated with that portion of the book where He is portrayed in His ministry to the churches on earth.

Pentecost. As the inauguration of the heavenly sanctuary, the throne-scene of Revelation 4:5 is fittingly associated with Pentecost, the first Pentecost took place during the time when the law was given to Moses on Mount Sinai (Exod. 19–20). As the new Moses, Christ receives, as it were, the new Torah from God (Rev. 5). Exodus 19 also involved the inauguration of Israel as the people of God (Exod. 19:5–6, cf Rev. 5:9–10). The Jewish liturgy for the feast of Pentecost included the reading of not only Exodus 19 but also of Ezekiel 1, a major literary background to Revelation 4–5.

Feast of Trumpets, Day of Atonement. The blowing of seven trumpets—near the center of the book (Rev. 8-9, 11)—reminds the reader of the seven monthly new moon feasts that climaxed in the Feast of Trumpets, marking the transition between the spring and fall feasts. The Feast of Trumpets itself, falling on the first day of the seventh month (corresponding to the seventh trumpet) ushered in the time of judgment that led up to the Day of Atonement (cf. 11:18–19). There is an increasing focus on the concept of judgment from that point in the book.

Feast of Tabernacles. The last of the five basic feasts of the Levitical system (cf. Lev. 23) was the Feast of Tabernacles that followed the Day of Atonement. Harvest was over (cf. Rev. 14–20). God was not "tabernacling" with His people (Rev. 21:3). The end-time celebrations of Revelation are filled with images of feasting, palm branches, music, and rejoicing before the Lord. The primary images of the Feast—water and light—find their ultimate fulfillment in Revelation 22:1,5.[1]

At the end of the preceding liturgical Holy Day cycle, a newborn king ushers in a new righteousness and a renewed creation. At this juncture, the redeemed will experience the completion of their new birth, which will bring about the consummation of their righteousness. During this event we shall see our Divine Warrior, the first born of many brethren (Rom. 8:29) face to face, and we shall be like Him. We follow Him to the marriage supper where the tabernacle of God is with men, and we shall be His people and He shall be our God. We shall be like Him.

> For the aorist indicative with *oupa* with a future outlook, Brooke notes Mark 11:12; 1 Cor. 8:2; Heb. 12:4; Rev. 17:10, 12. *What we shall be* (*ti esometha*). Not *tines* (who), but *ti* (what) neuter singular predicate nominative, "This *what* suggests something unspeakable, contained in the likeness of God" (Bengel). *If he shall be manifested (ean phanerothei*). As in 2:28, which see. The subject may be Christ as in verse 9, or the future manifestation just mentioned. Either makes sense, probably, "it" here better than "he." *Like him (homoioi autoi). Autoi* is the associative instrumental case after *homoioi.* This is our destiny and glory (Rom. 8:29), to be like Jesus who is like God (II Cor. 4:6). *We shall see him even as he is* (*opsimetha auton kathos esitin*). Future middle indicative of *horao.* The transforming power of this vision of Christ (I Cor. 13:12) is the consummation of the glorious process begun at the new birth (II Cor. 3:18).[2]

Both Egypt and Israel employed apocalyptic prophecies that surrounded each nation's liturgical new year. The temple and the altar symbolize in Egyptian theology royal purification rites while the temple in the Book of Revelation associates the activities of a high priest performing a daily *tamed* (Seville), which typifies the intercessory activities of Christ's ministry as High Priest. These images of the temple are associated with the Day of Atonement.

> It is interesting, therefore, to find in chapter 11 that the book moves to the explicit language of the yearly services of the Day

> of Atonement. Kenneth Stand has pointed out that Revelation 11:1–2 contains a strong allusion to the Day of Atonement, which comes immediately after a reference to the completion of the time prophecies of Daniel (Rev. 10:5,6). In Leviticus 16—the major Day of Atonement chapter—atonement is made for the high priest, the sanctuary, the altar, and the people.[3]

In biblical theology, Egypt was seen as a type of sin or leaven that God's people are now symbolically required to come out of in our lifestyle and religious practices. Egypt, like Sodom and Gomorrah, is seen as the land of corruption that has experienced God's judgments. This symbology falls between the Days of Unleavened, which illustrate coming out of sin to be a holy people, and Yom Kippur, a time of covering and atonement for the people of God and judgment upon God's enemies. Egypt is referred to in Revelation 11:8.

Notice the phrase "where our Lord was crucified." This is a metaphorical allusion applied to Sodom and Gomorrah and to a type of Egypt's condemnation and is being compared to the place of Our Lord's crucifixion at Golgotha. Also, in old covenant theology, rain and blessings are withheld from Egypt and God's judgment is provoked if she will not share with Israel in celebrating the Feast of Tabernacles (see Zech., 14:4–8). Egypt had only a ritualistic formula for installing a righteous king as perfected by ceremony. They had never experienced the sacral kingship, which would bring in complete justice and righteous to herself and other nations, as the prophetic work of the Messiah that would bring righteousness to all nations in the Kingdom Age (Dan. 2:44).

> Another interpretation was proposed by S. Mowinckel in a series of *Psalmenstudien* in the 1920s. . . . He saw them as reflecting the heart of traditional festal celebration, actualization of the primeval victory over chaos. . . . All was again made new, and the cry sent up 'Yahweh has become king!' Mowinckel filled out

his account of this celebration of God's kingship from other appropriate texts, such as those depicting God's festal procession (24; 68; 132).[4]

As far as Egyptian theology is concerned, they did believe in an all-knowing creator god, whom Isis and Thoth and Ra and other deities actually represented. Feast days were also dedicated to these Egyptian gods. It is also true that the ritual taken up in Egyptian temples was not that of Osiris; he would appear at the end of time when all wisdom would be declared from the tree of life. It is also worthy to note that judgment hall speeches, hymns, and a crowing of the cock initiated by a temple priest were given as a part of Egyptian ceremonial rites.

It has been shown already that Thoth (honoured in Egypt as the Founder of ritual) played a great part in Egyptian court-ceremonial. The fixing of the royal names, the determining of the years of reign, the foretelling of royal feasts and victories—all these are functions assigned to Thoth in the coronation-ceremonies. They are fully illustrated on the monuments. In the actual coronation-ceremonies, the priest, of course, took the part of Thoth. Even in the joyful liturgy of coronation, there are echoes of the funerary, or Osiran, ritual.[5]

These elements were applied universally at New Year's celebrations when the names of the deities were changed to represent the local deities of tyrannical gods. In the religious spectrum, Thoth was seen as the creator of divine liturgy, and whatever liturgy the Egyptian priests developed would have been enacted by the priests and congregations in acting out their divine roles in celebration of the divine acts to come. The divine right of kings in Babylon and Egypt were extensions of the divine order in the cosmos.

In Egypt, enthronement and its renewals were enacted in the ceremonies for the beginning of winter and there linked to the renewal of cosmic order[6] or as one has stated, "The king is removed . . . the King is established."[7] And by divine decree the Book of Revelation declares, "The kingdoms of this world shall become the kingdoms of our God" (Rev. 11).

Meanwhile in Christianity, the church would debate the role of Jewish liturgy and its place in the corpus of New Testament doctrine and worship. Just as in the third century A.D., the Alexandrian scholars translated the Hebrew Old Testament into Greek, the international language, a similar situation transpired for the literature of Egypt as the Alexandrian scholars were attempting to establish a Greek translation of all the world's known literature. Therefore, understanding these Greek recensions is crucial to the reexamination of the textual data and its theological influence upon the early patristic writers of the New Testament. Is it then possible that the New Testament writers were actually attempting to combine together these elements of thought? A growing number of scholars agree with this premise as they read Ephesians 2:15 in regards to the reference to the Jew and the Gentile forming the new man. Incidentally, Ephesians 2:20 is referencing the Tractate Shebiith 1:6, as well as most other books in the New Testament also referenced this tractate hundreds of times. Ephesians 2:25 corresponds to Sotah 3:4; the Tractate Sukah 3:2 with Ephesians 4:28, Sukah 3:3 with Ephesians 4:28, Sukah 3:5 with Ephesians 4:28, Sabbath 23:2 with Ephesians 4:14.[8] This is just a small example of the Hebraic foundations behind the structure and ideology of our Greek New Testament.

Among the scholars on the cutting edge of the Jewish background to the New Testament and the Dead Sea Scrolls integration is R. P. R. Murray;

> Christians of the first three centuries have left us no continuous commentary on any biblical book to compare with the examples of interpretation, which, especially by being found at Qumran,

are proved to have existed already in the Jewish world, such as in the Targum of Job or the sectarian *pesharim* on prophets and psalms. NT writers consistently claim to know and give the 'true meaning' of a scriptural text or figure, in ways like that practiced at Qumran, and they similarly weave unconnected texts into chains of *testimonia*; but until Origen, Christian writers, Jewish or Gentile, rather *exploit* the Bible for their own purposes that attempt continuous exposition. Nor do we find Christian 're-writing' of biblical narratives as in the 'genesis Apocryphon,' or claims to produce a new edition of Mosaic revelation as in Jubilees or the 'Temple Scroll.' Christians, of course, claimed new revelation, mediated both by Jesus and by others through a renewed gift of prophecy, expressed in new messages and also in re-interpretation of biblical texts with reference to Christ and the life of the church; but the focus is on the new context.[9]

Early Christian theologians interpreted the biblical text with a new application that was relevant to the new Christian community. The new interpretations were viewed as a re-telling of God's mighty acts towards this community. The Holy Spirit was seen as the power of the coming age, and the structure of this community would extend into that eon. In this pilgrimage to the New Jerusalem, new prophetic enemies of this community must be identified and the conflict of who is to be worshiped must be identified in the final conquest before the consummation of this present age.

No small part of the difficulty of interpreting apocalypses such as Revelation has to do with the way in which they make use of mythological symbolism. The apocalyptic authors used the ancient Near Eastern combat myth, which saw the formation of the world as the result of the victory of the divine warrior over the monsters of the watery chaos, to give meaning to present and future events.[10]

This is typified by Deborah's song of victory that is restated in the Apocalypse.

The Apocalypse of John contains enthronement material from the liturgical cycle of Spring and Fall Feast Days. The enthronement of Christ's redemptive ministry would begin in the Spring Feast of the Passover redemptive cycle and the Judgment/Harvest cycle would be fulfilled in the typology of the blowing of the shofar during the Fall Feast of Trumpets.

> The crowning of Christ's Paschal sacrifice occurred at Pentecost when he was officially enthroned at the right hand of God (Acts 2:32; Rev. 5:9–12) and began His intercessory ministry in the heavenly sanctuary on behalf of believers on earth. . . .[11]

Revelation 11:17 is the theme that is a celebration of God's enthronement.

> The first theme is the celebration of God's enthronement: "We give thanks to thee, Lord God Almighty, who are and wast, that thou hast taken thy great power and began to reign" (Rev. 11:17). This reminds us of the blowing of the shofar on *Rosh Hashanah* which was seen as we noted in chapter 2, as a symbol of God's enthronement. The themes of judgment and kingship are closely related because the king was enthroned to judge over his people.[12]

At the beginning of the Fall cycle, with the announcement of the enthroned deity's arrival at the consummation of this age into the age to come, this event marks God's savings acts by completing the resurrection cycle in the house of His redeemed people. In like manner, we go through our death, burial, and resurrection as Christ, our Captain, passed through His own death, burial, and resurrection as the firstborn of all brethren (Rom. 8:29).

As we mark the beginning of our born again experience and hope for the fulfillment of the eschatalogical promise of rebirth/resurrection to come, so the seventh trump will announce the consummation of the age and the fulfillment of the promise of new life in the new heavens and new earth. At the sounding of the seventh trump, Christ will return as a Mighty Warrior leading His army into victory, restraining the powers of chaos and the beast and bringing the world to judgment.

> A cylinder seal found in Tell Asmar in Mesopotamia shows a seven-headed dragon being subdued by two deities. This is the type of monster which raged against the prevailing gods in Canaanite mythology, the Leviathan to which the Old Testament alludes.
>
> Thus the Old Testament Leviathan exists as part of the widely spread dragon theme. However, the treatment of this mythological monster in the writings of the O. T. and in subsequent Apocraphyl and Rabbinical literature gives a unique place. It is the purpose of this article to show that the Leviathan concept underlies the usage of the Beast in Revelation.[13]

At the pinnacle of his power, the Beast knows he has but a short time before the Conquering King returns in judgment with His vindicated saints, and John reinterprets the beast to be "that old devil who is Satan who deceives the whole world" (Rev. 12:9) when the powers of chaos will be destroyed and the new creation will be ushered in.

The Creation Judgment Motif

Biblical parallelism often works in models of one pair of subjects, which are layered side by side, which affect the level of meaning, which an interpretator extracts from the passage or a given holy day. For example, Yom Kippur called the Feast of Trumpets models creation and, at the seventh trumpet, announces the beginning of judgment followed by a Messaniac reign with a new creation motif. While parallel to this concept is Yom Kippur or the Day of Atonement, which pictures judgment being brought to the earth by the divine warrior and the dragon being slain and destroyed. Such is the case for the creation/judgment model, which parallels darkness to light, night to day, and the individual professes faith in creation while petitioning God's forgiveness in the judgment.

In the wake of the Bible, Jewish tradition has faithfully interpreted the Day of Atonement as a double reference to Creation and Judgment.

There was an evening, there was a morning, unique day, this means that the Blessed be He, gave them (to Israel), a unique day which was nothing but the Day of Atonement (*midrash Rabbah,* Gen. IV, 10)

The reference to Gen. 1:5 in connection to the Day of Atonement suggests that actually the birth of Kippur coincides with that of the universe. Creation and Day of Atonement belong to the same world of thought in Jewish tradition. Moreover, the tradition links the Day of Atonement to the Day of Judgment, the moment when God's forgiveness seals the destiny of the repented.

To average people, who are neither perfectly righteous, nor totally wicked, will be granted a delay of 10 days (from the first to the tenth of Tishri); they have then until Kippur to repent, in which case they will live; otherwise death will sanction their bad behavior (T. B., *Roash Hashana* 16b)

Parallel to these traditions, the prayers which are said during the Day of atonement testify, this time on a liturgical level, to this double reference to Creation and Judgment. The first prayers carry the believer into the spirit of the festival, professing faith in Creation and hoping for forgiveness in Judgment.

Blessed be thou, Lord our God, King of the universe, who opens the doors to mercy and gives light to the eyes of those who expect forgiveness from the One who created light and darkness, and creates everything. (Yotser leyom Kippur)

Throughout the liturgy the awarement of the God-Judge who disclosed everything is paired with the truth that He is the Creator;

How could man be just before his Creator, as everything is disclosed to Him? (Mosaph leyom Kippour)[14]

This also parallels with Egyptian prophecies from the King's chamber, as Smyth illustrates. After the reinterpretation of the combat ritual and the descent into the Abyss, the reborn king rises from his grave to embrace the new righteousness, which will bring light over darkness and judgment/repentence over chaos over which our Risen Lord has already claimed the victory. Then, at the seventh trumpet as the judgment period begins. He will lead the nations from darkness to light through His righteousness. Biblical writers do not borrow exclusively from one ritual pattern, but borrow elements from various patternisms and cultural expressions to build the new literary structure that is needed to bring forth their new interpretation as the writers advance the new revelation. Therefore, the combat ritual is used as a model for Christ's ultimate victory over the dragon and the descension narratives are reinterpreted to show us Christ's victory over the grave; and by His righteousness, we will share this same experience at the seventh trumpet. In the same manner as He ascended to His Father, we shall to Him.

But it was not Hebrews alone, descended from those under Moses, who were to be saved by Christ; for besides the special Hebrew passage—another, though far less conspicuous mode of escape from the descent into the bottomless subterranean pit, was also eventually provided, to prevent any immortal soul being necessarily lost. Ford, before reaching the dismal abyss, there is a possible entrance, though it may be by a strait and narrow way, to the one and only gate to salvation through the death of

Christ—viz. the peculiar, deep but dry, well representing His descent into Hades.

This Hades locality is not the bottomless pit of idolaters and the wicked, lying at the lowest point of which the entrance-passage subterraneously descents, but a natural grotto, rather an artificial chamber, in the course of the well's further progress to the other place. It is in fact the Paradise of the dead, which is stated to be within the earth; and where they wait in unconscious condition, either the rapturous awakening to meet their Lord in the air, before His visible return to all men as Millennial King; or, the final trump of the day of Judgment and the great white throne.

Meanwhile here at the Pyramid, the stone which one covered that well's upper mouth is blown outwards into the Grand Gallery with excessive force (and was once so thrown out, and is now annihilated), carrying part of the wall with it, and indicating how totally unable was the grave to hold Him beyond the appointed time.[15]

In the cosmic struggle over kingship, the Sun god of Egypt struggled with the Arabian Moon god for supremacy. As we study the ancient king list of each of these nations, the divine right of kings is appropriated to the progeny or descendants of the purified king. This cosmic struggle continued with the rise of Egyptian Christianity over the deities of pagan nations, and even the Christian liturgy was renamed from its originator, Thoth. Following the formula, the victorious god, who was previously the adversary becomes the righteous god, and his enemy, the dethroned deity, descends into Hades to become the Satan.

It is likely that the author intended the obscure image of the son "appear[ing] beneath the sun and the moon" (C.c, 2:27) as an explanation for the son's anti-Christian depredations. Although Schrage interpreted the image as a euphemism for self-exaltation (in the spirit of Isa. 14:13–14 and Dan. 8:10–11), it gains greater contextual meaning when interpreted within Egyptian Christian cultural categories, as allegiance to the sun and the moon as cosmic powers in the Greco-Egyptian sense and therefore as emblems of the son's primary allegiance to a high ritual "paganism"—the antithesis of Christianity in third-century Egypt. "Appearing beneath" in this sense could signify either iconographic representation (e.g., on stelae or amulets) or a public ritual. The use of "sun and moon" as emblems of "high" paganism would therefore belong to the *interpretatio* Graeca of Egyptian religious cosmology: Re and Thoth as successive lords of the sky, whose counterparts in Greco-Egyptian ritual spells received considerable devotion.[16]

Christ's parousia divides the church age from the Messianic age to come when Christ shall put all enemies under His feet, and He will overcome the powers of darkness after the Anti-Christ figure is dethroned and shown to be the Great Adversary. In the Hebrew lunar calendar, this event is pictured as the Feast of Trumpets when Christ will reign over the cosmic powers and will bring all things unto the governance of the Father. This writer has shown how the biblical authors employed various aspects of Canaanite and Egyptian rituals to explain the mighty acts of God in salvation history. Paradoxically, the Coptic Church reverses the literary whereby the biblical narrative is reshaped and reinterpreted to fit the pagan orientation of the church.

The solar association of the king from "the City of the Sun" (G), who functions as penultimate benefactor to the "saints" and their shrines, reflect a syncretism pervading the Apocalypse of Elijah—and not doubt much of early Egyptian Christianity—at the broadest level: that is, the conceptualization of Christ and the eschatological Adversary in terms of classical Egyptian mythology. It has been noted that Christ's parousia follows upon a series of alternating cycles between woe and benefience; this makes Christ the ultimate restorer of the order, fertility, and power that the King from the City of the Sun approximated and the Lawless One subsequently banishes. Christ's function reflects native traditions of a salvific restoration of the cosmos after a period of chaos—traditions that derived from the kingship ideology.[17]

In this present church age, this community of believers goes through its Garden of Gethsemene followed by Christians being brought to trial, persecutions, and final judgment, as this community is being fashioned into the complete image of Christ. The heavenly court has decreed that the curse reversal of God's covenant lawsuit be implemented, which makes provision for repentance and for justice to come to fruition in the new age due to the fact God's enemies, such as false religion, false spirituality, false Christ, and the evil global economy have been identified and overcome by the blood of the Lamb.[18] In this section of Scripture, Old Testament passages are reintroduced into the text, but with a prophetic and cosmic reinterpretation of their original meanings. Babylon would not be the same nation in the literal coronation that historically enslaved Judah, but at this juncture becomes a symbol of captivity for the people of God in a false religious system.

However, John does not bring unmodified a single Old Testament symbol (or even a scriptural reference) into his revelation, whole or complete. Shadows and echoes from the Old Testament abound in over half of the verses in Revelation. Images and figures come particularly from Daniel, Isaiah, Ezekiel, and Zechariah. But in the whole book, there is only one explicit reference to an Old Testament passage. Revelation 15:3, referencing to the song of triumph sung by those who overcame the beast, state that "they sing the son of Moses the servant of God" (KJV), but what follows is neither the song found in Exodus 15 nor that of Deuteronomy 32. Rather, it is an amalgamation of several Old Testament themes. Old Testament symbols are modified, reworked, and shaped to meet the special needs of the vision.[19]

In a similar literary style, John reinterprets the Sabbath Songs in the Hallelujah chorus of the Apocalypse. In 4 Q 403, over eighty small fragments exist from the sixth scroll. Further evidence exists in forty small fragments in the second Scroll titled 4Q 400. Therefore, there is ample evidence to show that John knew of material similar to the Dead Sea Scrolls that he used for his reinterpretation when creation would break forth in praise to its Mighty God.

Therefore, Pilate becomes a type of Anti-Christ who enacts wrath on the people of God who have been led into false worship by counterfeit miracles, and his judgment speech before the crucifixion would be reinterpreted in a new literary form in Revelation 13,[20] with a new song of deliverance[21] climaxing in Revelation 14.[22] Christ was seen as the new Adam, with a new prophetic history, and a new period of Sabbath rest would spring forth into the reign of the Incarnated King. After the hour of his judgment,

"The hour of his judgment" is not *karios* (a fixed time), or *chronos* (time), but *ha hora* (the hour), which is a very important concept in the New Testament. Apart from its general usage it has a specific application to the Day of Atonement, both in its soteriological fulfillment on the Cross, and in its eschatalogical consummation at the close.[23]

Not only Christianity misunderstood the nature of God's judgment by viewing it an axiomatic condemnation whereas God's intervention in human affairs is to correct sinners and to lead them to righteousness whenever possible and to commit wrath upon the rebellious nations for attempting to fight Our

Lord on His return. Desmond Ford quotes E. Bevan on this point,

> Greek philosophy had long ago repudiated emphatically the conception common to primitive and popular Greek religion and to the Old Testament. Anger was a weak and discreditable emotion; it taught, in men, and to attribute such an emotion to a divine being was absurd and blasphemous. Deity, every novice in Greek philosophy knew as an axiom, must be spathes, without disturbing emotions of any kind. The idea of the Divine anger was not something which penetrated into Christianity from its pagan enformonment; it was something which the Church maintained in the face of adverse pagan criticism.[24]

The Jewish imagery reflecting the Day of Atonement in reference to judgment in the Hebrew concept is one of bringing God's righteous judgment and vindication to His people rather than a wholesale condemnation. These prophetic movements in the Book of Revelation depict the mighty acts of God as He unfolds like a scroll the drama of salvation.

To back up this literary structure, we have Dead Sea Scroll fragments, which were decoded in 1959. These fragments also have an allusion to the Day of Atonement, the sanctuary, Sabbath and all holy things,

> Col. II (= Jub 1:7–15) . . . 8[they have forsaken] my laws and [my statutes, the festival]s of my covenant [and my sabbaths and my holy things] 9 which they have dedicated to me in [their] mid[st and my tent and my] sanctuary [which I made holy for myself in the midst of] 10 the earth. . . .[25]

The first fragment dates its Sabbath sacrifice and exhorts seven angels to praise God. William H. Shea states as follows:

> Materials from Qumran, as they are studied and published, continue to widen our understanding of biblical times and teachings.

A doctoral dissertation by Carol Newson (published later as a hardback under the title, *Songs of the Sabbath Sacrifice: A Critical Edition*) analyzes a Qumran author's view of the heavenly sanctuary. The Qumran document is represented by Fragments from six scrolls and is organized around a quarterly cycle of 13 Sabbaths, probably intended to be repeated four times in the sect's liturgical year.

The *Songs of the Sabbath Sacrifice* is most similar to the Book of Revelation. Both have a chiastic literary structure, focus on the heavenly sanctuary, and give a strong emphasis to the number 7. This remarkable document evidences the interest of at least one of Judaism in the heavenly sanctuary, understood largely in terms of OT description of the earthly.[26ab]

At this juncture, we shall explore a broader literary structure which originated from the intricate patternisms that were transferred into this new literary form. The old form was from creation to judgment while the expanded from is from creation to kingdom.

It is also noteworthy that this particular way of introducing and concluding is repeated with the Bible. John probably had this principle in mind when he introduced his gospel with the miracle of Creation (John I) and concluded Revelation with a calling for the coming Kingdom (Rev. 22:17–21). Similarly, the Pentateuch begins with Creation (Gen. 1 and 2) and ends with the hope of resurrection (Deut. 34:6; cf Jude 9) and the prospect of the Promised Land (Deut. 34:1–3). This can also be seen in the Book of Isaiah which starts with a reference to Creation (1:2) and ends with the hope of the Kingdom of God (Isa. 66:22–23).[27]

Many other themes are broadened as well. Armageddon is no longer just the Valley of Megiddo, but is reinterpreted to stand for the cosmic struggle between good and evil. In a similar fashion, Gog and Magog would represent a northern evil power that will be destroyed in the great final conflict during the consummation of this age. Even the Sabbath concept is taken from a Creation model and expanded from a day to a cosmic rest in the new Creation under the righteous reign of God Himself, providing a rest of all creation.

Just as ancient Israel employed liturgical sabbaths throughout the liturgical new year, depicted by the annual festivals, which are revealed in the *Sedur* (their order of worship), these events also take on a prophetic and cosmic application, which transcends national Israel and was reenacted by our Messiah during his ministry and in his trial death, burial and resurrection;

> . . . at the end of the cycle, when the soul attains liberation, and the lower Self and the higher Self become one on the higher mental plane. The "srauta sacrifice" signifies the final abandonment of the lower nature; this is equivalent to the crucifixion and resurrection of Jesus.[28]

where he was humiliated, denied after the third crowing of the cock, stripped of clothing, scourged, spat upon, His beard pulled, the crown of thorns, the royal robe, the walk showing a descent into Sheol, death, resurrection, and followed by coronation and deification, the scared marriage, and the renewal of the covenant.

This imagery shows that with prophetic voice the writers of the both Old and New Testaments used literary devices just as the patriarchs would have borrowed Canaanite literary structures to follow the Lord's inspiration for the building of the temple. The New Testament writers employed a similar literary borrowing technique by taking the cycle of coronation events and applying it to the trial, and the life, death, and resurrection narratives of Our Lord to show his divine kingship as well as a prophetic foreshadowing of what is ahead for the New Testament church as we are fashioned into the image of our Father's dear Son.

> For Christians the resurrection was not merely an object of hope. After the resurrection of Jesus, it was a present reality. In the resurrection it was revealed that the Messianic age, the αιφν μεδδφν, had begun. Believers were now linked with the risen Lord by His Spirit. They had tasted the powers of the αιφν μελλφν (Heb. 6:5). The new birth for which the Jews hoped was for them in some way a present reality.[29]

This is followed by our sacred marriage ceremony and a renewing of all creation. These events will be followed by a sacred marriage of Christ to His church, which corresponds to the final ritual act of the incarnated king when he marries creation, and this is the end of the ritual cycle that corresponds to the end of salvation history when a righteous king rules with God over His entire creation.

The Church and Sacral Kingship

The subject of sacral kingship did not come to completion with the passing of the feudal system in Europe. The Church, through the precedent of canon law, still believes in its divine mandate from God to influence and establish righteousness by divine decree.

> An Anglo-Saxon commenting on the duties of a Christian king projects the same image: "Thou wilt have at God's judgment to produce and lead forth the flock of which thou hast been made the shepherd in this life, and then give account how thou heldest that which Christ afore purchased with his own blood." The

eschatological mission is that of *pastor*, leading his flock to the Divine Shepherd.

In the Christian concept of monarchy, as in its northern heathen background, it must be noted again that kings gain their realms by God's favour and lose them by His disavour. It is 'Jesus Christ, the Savior of the World, . . . through Whom kings rule and divide the kingdoms of the earth.' So, for example. 'He has given and granted to King Edward the fair island of Britain, as he did of yore to his kinsmen.' But it is not only their ancestral realms which God gives to monarchs. He increases the earthly power of his faithful vice-regents.[30]

The structure of hierarchical rights did not cease with a royal mandate as applied to a king over his society, but in the feudal system of church and state, this divine decree extended to subordinates and sub-kings as well in both the church and the sociological structures at large.

In feudal society the customs which developed at the most basic level of lordship were gradually extended upwards until they came to include the supreme overlord, the king. The obligations and legally binding force which existed in the contract between lord and vassal came to be applied gradually also to the relations between a king and even the most powerful of his subjects, men who sometimes had as much resources in land and movable wealth at their disposal as the king himself.[31]

The custom that originated from ancient vassal treaties are still evident here with the concepts of an overlord subjecting a defeated king to vassal kingship. This defeat also resulted in the subjugation of the entire feudal state. In the feudal system, not only did there exist the ancient right of divine warfare from a church-state economy, there was also the right of a king who was the head ruler over the church hierarchy to publish the king's edition of the Holy Scriptures due to the fact the Scripture in liturgical traditions the sacred canon is seen as the church's book. Therefore, the church is the custodian of the truths contained in Scripture.

Summary and Conclusion

In recent decades there has been a revival of interest regarding the Bible's relationship to Egypt and its semitic counterparts, including the origins of the Great Semitic mother tongue in addition to the religious systems that may have given birth to Egypt as well as inspired the Hebrew prophets to express themselves in the literary forms that were common in the ancient Near East. Consequently, this modern research indicates the Middle Eastern literary traditions were by and large one general culture in which all the neighboring nations played an integral part in producing the literary traditions as a whole. But when major powers rose to the forefront, such as Greece and Rome during the latter portion of Axial Period, from which most of our classical literature is derived, and produced a literary smokescreen, it has affected our Western lense in trying to understand these philosophical paradigm shifts to this very day. This smokescreen affected Egyptian and later, Jewish thinking regarding these issues. Western Christianity continued in this vein under the auspices of Neoplatonism.

The ancient common use of myth and ritual took on a local application within each nation as their gods would either be victorious or vanquished into the adversaries of the victorious deities. Common ritual themes were used in the international wisdom schools and apocalyptic traditions and were referred to by the biblical writers as a literary device in telling of the royalty of the Messiah. However, a common patternism emerges more frequently found in the writings of Isaiah, the enthronement Psalms, and the Gospels as well as combat ritual themes, which are also found in the writings of John, the Revelator, in the Apocalypse, which he borrowed from Isaiah, the Prophet. This helps establish the ritual and the liturgical as well as the eschatalogical patternisms that were employed by the Gospel writers to identify the Suffering Servant during Passion week. Common vocabulary also exists throughout the ancient Near East, with terms such as Son of God, or Son of the King, a Lamb led to the slaughter, judgment hall speeches, descension into the grave as well as resurrection motifs, procession and ascension to the royal throne, royal marriage and deification (*theosis*), Holy War, and an eternal kingdom.

> Some observers, beginning with Wilhelm Boussett, see the depiction of Christ going to the underworld as the tailoring of an old myth of a redeemer figure asserting his authority and subduing demons, to fit a story about Jesus. There are similarities between the myth and the ritual dramatizations that were enacted during the new year festivals. The temple and ritual motifs may have seemed similar to myths, yet no doubt to the early Christians, the *descensus* of Christ was the real event and was not perceived merely as the recasting of prevailing lore.[1]

This motif was borrowed from the Near Eastern ritual patternisms and employed by the biblical writers, not only in establishing the divinity of Jesus followed by His descension and ascension to deity and resulting in a deification of saints (Rev. 3:9), but also using a common vocabulary for Near Eastern readers to help them grasp the complexity of salvation history, from the prophetic utterance of the Hidden Messiah who would be revealed in the fullness of time to the nations that have not heard of His fame shall declare His glory (Isa. 66:19–20) and fulfilling quest of the writers of the ancient Vedas who were in search of the perfect man. These universal themes were helpful in the spreading of the church's Kerigma, resulting in massive conversions into the early church. It is essential for future scholars to continue to endeavor to uncover this art of literary borrowing because locked within the structures, there may be windows to ancient witnesses, which will lead us to the literary environment from which the patristic authors wrote these themes in their original autographs. But until that time arises, we are forced to use the methodology of source criticism and reconstructing the universal themes in attempting to determine their origins.

Notes

Introduction

1. Currid, John D., *Ancient Egypt and the Old Testament,* pp. 22–25.
2. Bright, John, *The History of Israel,* p. 120.
3. Perdue, Leo G., et al., *Archaeology and Biblical Interpretation,* p. 88.
4. Bimson, John J., *Redating the Exodus and Conquest,* p. 51.
5. Hester, H. L., *The Heart of Hebrew History, A Study of the Old Testament,* p. 43.
6. Ibid., p. 60.
7. Sayce, A. H., and Peterson, R., *Race in Ancient Egypt and the Old Testament,* p. 68.
8. Maier, John, and Toller, Vincent, Eds., *The Bible in its Literary Milieu,* p. 11.

Chapter 1

1. Edelman, Diana V., *The Triumph of Elohim,* p. 65.
2. Deuel, Leo, *Testaments of Time—The Search for Lost Manuscripts & Records,* p. 210.
3. Budge, E. A. Wallis, *The Book of the Dead—The Hieroglyphic Transcript and Translation Into English of the Ancient Egyptian Papyrus,* pp. 106–107.
4. Ibid, flyleaf.
5. Ibid., pp. 202–203.
6. Ibid.
7. Rollins, Rev. G. S., "*The Principle of Adaptation in Revelation,*" reprint, *The Biblical World—July/December 1990.,* p. 25.
8. Lang, Bernhard, *Monothesism and the Prophetic Minority,* p. 15.
9. McKenzie, John L., *Myths & Realities, Studies in Biblical Theology,* p. 136.
10. Wenham, Gordon, J., *Word Biblical Commentary,* pp. 17–18.

11. Elwolde, John, trans, Saenz-Badillos, *A History of the Hebrew Language,* pp. 32–33.
12. Dakenbring, William F., *The First Genesis,* pp. 183–204.
13. Smith, George, *The Chaldean Account of Genesis,* p. 66.
14a. Rahlfs, Alfred, ed. *Septuginta:* Brenton, Gen. 1:2–3.
14b. Lancelot C. L., *The Septuagint with Apocrypha: Greek and English,* p. 1.
15. Gordis, Robert, *The Book of Job: Commentary, New Translation and Special Studies,* p. 280.
16. Wofters, David, *Deep Things Out of Darkness,* p. 213.
17. Thiele, Edwin and Margaret, *Job and the Devil,* p. 14.
18. Boeeterweck, G., Johannes, and Ringgren, Helmer, eds., Willes, John T., Froniley, Geoffrey Ward and Green, David E., trans., *Theological Dictionary of the Old Testament, Volume III,* p. 229.
19. Thiele, Edwin and Margaret, *Job and the Devil,* p. 15.
20. Mangan, Celine, OP, *The Aramaic Bible—The Targums, Volume 15, The Targum of Job,* pp. 61–63.
21. Deuel, Leo, *Testaments of Time—The Search for Lost Manuscripts & Records,* pp. 249–250.
22. Ibid., pp. 242–243.
23. Saenz-Badillos, Angel; Ewolde, John, trans., *A History of the Hebrew Language,* p. 33.
24. Lange, John Peter; Schaff, Philip, trans, *Lange's Commentary on the Holy Scriptures: Critical, Doctrinal and Homiletical: Job,* p. 9.
25. Ibid., p. 171.
26. Ibid., p. 281.
27. LaRondelle, Hans K., *Deliverance in the Psalms,* p. 37.
28. Kent, Charles Foster, *The Growth and Contents of the Old Testament,* p. 23.
29. Ibid., p. 255.
30. Faulker, R. O., *Ancient Egyptian Pyramid Texts,* p. 93.
31. Ibid., 144.
32. Ibid., p. 169.
33. Ibid., p. 257.
34. Carter, Howard, and Mace, A. C., *The Tomb of Tut-ankh-Amen,* p. 77.
35. Maspero, Gaston, and Sayce, A. H., eds., *The Dawn of Civilization—Egypt & Chaldea,* p. 623.
36. Horne, Charles F., *The Sacred Books & Early Literature of the East,* pp. 158, 270.
37. Rawlingson, George, *The Five Great Monarchies of the Ancient Eastern World,* pp. 43–69.
38. Ibid., p. 51.
39. Ibid., p. 55–56.
40. Nibley, Hugh, *Since Cumorah,* pp. 52–53.

41. Kent, Charles H., *The Growth and Contents of the Old Testament,* pp. 267–268.
42. Deuel, Leo, *Testaments of Time, The Search for Lost Manuscripts & Records,* pp. 209–210.
43. Cathcart, Kevin; Maher, Michael, and McNamara, Martin, eds., *The Aramaic Bible—The Targums, Volume 15—The Targum of Proverbs,* pp. 47–51.
44. Hallo, Wiliam W., Moyer, James, C., and Perdue, Leo G., *Scripture in Context II: More Essays on the Comparative Method,* p. 84.
45. Ibid., pp. 85–86.
46. Skousen, W. Cleon, *The Fourth Thousand Years,* p. 266.
47. Childs, Brevard, *Biblical Theology in Crisis,* pp. 186–188.
48. Ibid., p. 189.
49. Perry, T. A., *Wisdom Literature and the Structure of Proverbs,* p. 23.
50. Gordodn, Cyrus, H., and Rendsburg, Gary A., *The Bible and the Ancient Near East,* p. 63.
51. Pritchard, James B., *The Ancient Near East,* pp. 87–93.
52. Maspero, Gaston, and Sayce, A. H., eds., *The Struggle of the Nations, Egypt, Syria and Assyria,* p. 495.
53. Hengel, Martin, *Judaism and Hellenism,* p. 28.
54. Butler, Alfred J., *The Arab Conquest of Egypt and the Last Thirty Years of the Roman Dominion,* pp. 408–409.
55a. Rahlfs, Alfred, ed, *Septuaginta,* Gen. 1:1–2.
55b. Brenton, Charles Lee, *The Seputuagint Version of the Old Testament and Apocrypha with an English Transition,* p. ii.
56. Lundquist, John M., and Ricks, Stephen, D., eds, *By Study and Also By Faith, Vol. 1,* p. 12.
57. Ibid., p. 15.
58. Whiston, William, *Josephus—Complete Works,* pp. 33–34.
59. Dummelow, Rev. J.R., ed., *The One Volume Bible Commentary,* pp., 19–20.
60. Neusner, Jacob, trans. & ed., *Genesis and Judaism, The Perspective of Genesis Rabah, An Analytical Anthology,* p. 33.
61. Nibley, Hugh, *Abraham in Egypt,* p. 355–360.
62. Charles, R. H., trans, *The Book of Enoch or 1 Enoch,* p. 223.
63. Charlesworth, James H., ed., *The Old Testament Pseudepigrapha, Testament of Abraham,* note "b", p. 887.
64. Froom, L. E., *The Conditionalist Faith of Our Fathers,* p. 685.
65. Ibid., note 22.
66. Nibley, Hugyh, *Enoch, The Prophet,* p. 122.
67. Froom, L. E., *The Conditionalist Faith of Our Fathers,* pp. 688–689.
68. Fudge, William Edward, *The Fire That Consumes,* p. 83.
69a. Elliger, K., and Rudolph W., eds., *Encyclopedia Judaica, volume 15, Sm-Un,* p. 177.

69b. Eiblfedt, O., *Liber Genesis, Biblia Hebraica, Stuttgartensia,* p. 3.
70. Schmithals, Walter, *The Apocalyptic Movement, Introduction and Interpretation,* p. 20.
71. Ferguson, Everett; McHugh, Michael P., and Norris, Frederick W., *The Encyclopedia of Early Christianity,* p. 455.
72. Barthelemy, Dominique, et al, committee members, *Preliminary and Interim report on the Hebrew Old Testament Text Project, Volume 5, Prophetical Books, II,* p. 225.
73. Hanson, Paul D., *The Historical and Sociological Roots of Jewish Apocalypic Eschatology,* p. 9.
74. Charlesworth, James H., ed., *The Old Testament Pseudepigrapha, Testament of Abraham,* 8:5–6, 10, 10:1.
75. Froom, L. E., *The Conditionalist Faith of Our Fathers,* p. 637.
76. Hess, R. S., et al, eds, *He Swore an Oath,* p. 125.
77. Bradford, Charles E., *Sabbath Roots, The African Connection,* p. 89–92.
78. Nibley, Hugh, *Nibley on the Timely and the Timeless,* p. 137.
79. Baker, Margaret, *The Great Angel: A Study of Israel's Second God,* p. 70.
80. Ricks, Stephen D., Parry, Donald W., and Hodges, Andrew H., eds, *The Disciple as Scholar, Essays on Scripture and the Ancient World,* p. 497.
81. Cross, Frank Moore, *Canaanite Myth and Hebrew Epic,* p. 187.
82. Collins, John J., *Hermonia,* p. 199.
83. Dahood, Mitchell, *Psalms II,* 51–100, p. 270.
84. Ricks, Stephen D., et al, eds, *The Disciple as Scholar,* p. 546–547.
85. *The New Jerusalem Bible,* note u, p. 1829, note b, p. 1203.
86. Kimbrough, S. T., Jr., *"Theological Table Talk," Theology Today, Vol. XLVI, No. 2,* July 1989, p. 195.
87. Ibid., pp. 196–197.
88. de Jone, Henk, "Sonship, Wisdom, Infancy, Luke II 41–51a"., *New Testament Studies, An International Journal, Vol. 24, No. 3, April 1978,* p. 351.
89. Vine, W. E., and Bruce, F. F., eds., *Vine's Expository Dictionary of Old and New Testament Words,* p. 193.
90. Burgess, Stanley M., *The Holy Spirit: Eastern Christian Traditions,* p. 228.
91. *New Jerusalem Bible,* note g, p. 2007.
92. Hurtado, Larry W., *One God, One Lord: Early Christian Devotion and Ancient Jewish Monotheism,* p. 61.
93. Ricks, Stephen D., et al, eds, *The Disciple as Scholar,* pp. 487–488.
94. Waddell, L. A., *The Makers of Civilization in Race and History,* p. 149.
95. Harrison, R. K., *Introduction to the Old Testament,* p. 555.
96. Deuel, Leo, *Testaments of Time: The Search for Lost Manuscripts & Records,* pp. 242–247.
97. Alter, Robert, and Kermode, Frank, eds., *The Literary Guide to the Bible,* p. 548.

98. Parry, Donald W., and Ricks, Stephen D., eds., *The Temple in Time and Eternity*, p. 310.
99. Trymer-Kinsky, Tikva, *In the Wake of the Goddesses*, pp. 86–87.
100. Ching, Julia, *Confucianism and Christianity: A Comparative Study*, p. 117.
101. Parey, Donald W., *Temples of the Ancient World*, pp. 119–120.
102. Falkner, R. O., *The Ancient Egyptian Pyramid Texts*, utterance 408, pp. 133–134.
103. Smith, George, *The Chaldean Account of Genesis*, p. 89.
104. Strand, Kenneth, H., ed., *The Sabbath in Scripture and History*, pp., 21–22.
105. Smyth, Piazzi, *The Great Pyramid: Its Secrets and History Revealed*, p. 448.
106. Parry, Donald W., et al, eds., *The Temples of the Ancient World*, p. 119.
107. Lundquist, John M., et al, eds, *By Study and Also By Faith, Vol. 1*, p. 597.
108. *Ibid.*, p. 599.
109. Doukhan, Jacques, *The Literary Construction of Genesis*, p. 207.
110. Deuel, Leo, *Testaments of Time*, p. 247.
111. Cross, Frank Moore, *Canaanite Myth and Hebrew Epic*, footnote 37, p. 123.
112. Bright, John, *A History of Israel*, p. 222.
113. Wallenkampf, Arnold V., et al, eds., *The Sanctuary and the Atonement*, p. 59.
114. Halioni, David Weiss, *Revelation Restored: Divine Writ and Critical Responses*, p. 89.
115. Parry, Donald W., et al., eds, *Temples of the Ancient World*, pp. 260–262.
116. Steinberg, Naomi, *Kinship and Marriage in Genesis: A Household Economics Perspective*, p. 11.
117. Ibid., p. 137.
118. Weiser, Arthur, *The Psalms: A Commentary*, p. 36.

Chapter 2

1. Eichrodt, Walther, *Theology of the Old Testament, Volume 1*, p. 126.
2. Gehman, Henry Snyder, ed, *The New Westminster Dictionary of the Bible*, p. 775.
3. Bultmann, *Theology of the New Testament*, p. 53.
4. Knight, Douglas A., *Rediscovering the Tradition of Israel*, pp. 393–395.
5. Layman, Charles M, ed., *The One Volume Commentary on the Bible*, pp. 254–255.

6. Ibid., p. 255.
7. Ibid.
8. Hengstenberg, E. W., *Christology of the Old Testament,* p. 85.
9. Lundquist, John M., and Ricks, Stephen D. eds, *By Study and Also By Faith, Vol 1,* pp. 209–215.
10. Ibid., pp. 532–533.
11. Padinjarekara, Joseph, *Christ in Ancient Vedas,* p. 130.
12. Laymon, Charles, M, ed., *Interpreter's One-Volume Commentary on the Bible,* p. 132:1–5.
13. Brattier, Robert G., and Rayburn, William D., *A Translator's Handbook on the Book of Psalms,* p. 1088.
14. Leslie, Elmer A., *The Psalms, Translated and Interpreted in the Light of Hebrew Life and Worship,* pp. 103–104.
15. Gerstenberger, Erhard, S., *Psalms, Part I with an Introduction to Cultic Poetry,* p. 197.
16. Riken, Leland; Wilhoit, James C., and Longman, III, Tremper, eds, *Dictionary of Biblical Imagery,* pp. 741–742.
17. Freedman, David Noel, ed, *The Anchor Bible Dictionary, Volume I,* p. 46.
18. Froom, L. E., *The Conditionalist Faith of Our Fathers, Volume I,* pp. 742–743.
19. Martinez, Florentino Garcia, *The Dead Sea Scrolls Translated, The Qumran Texts in English,* pp. 303–316.

Chapter 3

1. Parry, Donald W., ed, *Temples of the Ancient World,* pp. 126–146.
2. Lundquist, John M., and Ricks, Stephen D., eds, *By Study and Also By Faith, Vol. I,* p. 201.
3. Ibid, pp. 431–432.
4. Wallenkampf, Arnold V. et al, eds, *The Sanctuary and the Atonement: Biblical, Historical and Theological Studies,* p. 47.
5. LaRondelle, Hans K, *Deliverance in the Psalms: Message of Hope for Today,* p. 187.
6. Nibley, Hugh, *Temple and Cosmos,* pp. 71–72.
7. Breuggermann, Walter, *The Message of the Psalms,* p. 171.
8. Telushkin, Rabbi Joseph, *Biblical Literacy,* p. 492.
9. Wenham, Gordon, J, *Word Biblical Commentary, Volume I,* p. 9.

Chapter 4

1. Deissman, Adolf, *Light From the Ancient East,* p. 407.
2. Alter, Robert, *The World of Biblical Literature,* p. 71.

3. Smith, George, *The Chaldean Account of Genesis,* p. 49.
4. Ibid.
5. Russsell, D. S., *The Method and Message of Jewish Apocalyptic,* p. 125.
6. Moore, Carey A., *Daniel, Esther and Jeremiah, The Additions,* p. 127.
7. Schmithals, Walter; Steely, John E., trans., *The Apocalyptic Movement: Introduction and Interpretation,* p. 15.
8. Nichol, Francis D., ed, *Seventh-Day Adventist Bible Commentary, Vol. 4, Isaiah to Malachi,* p. 85.
9. Hanson, Paul D., *The Dawn of Apocalyptic,* p. 37–38.
10. Gileadi, Avraham, *The Literary Message of Isaiah,* p. 141.
11. Pritchard, James B., ed., *The Ancient Near East, Vol. II,* p. 52–69.
12. Mendenhall, George E., *The Tenth Generation—The Origins of the Biblical Traditions,* pp. 81–82.
13. Buttrich, George Arthur, et al, *The Interpreter's Bible in Twelve Volumes, Vol. V,* p. 412.
14. Nyman, Monte, S., ed., *Isaiah and the Prophets,* pp. 122–123.
15. Pritchard, James B., ed., *The Ancient Near East,* p. 62.
16. Reumann, John, *Righteousness in the New Testament,* p. 13.
17. Sanders, James A., *Torah and Canon,* p. 75.
18. Ibid., pp. 74–75.
19. Pate, C. Marvin, *Communities of the Last Days: The Dead Sea Scrolls, the New Testament & the Story of Israel,* p. 161.
20. Ibid., pp. 164–165.
21. Ibid., pp. 103–104.
22. Ibid., p. 87.
23. Tvedtnes, John A., Ezekiel's "Missing Prophecy," Wright, Dennis A., et al, *Symposium Committee, Voices of Old Testament Prophets: The 26th Annual Sidney B. Sperry Symposium,* pp. 110–121.
24a. Arndt, W. F.; Gingrich, F. W., trans. & eds., *A Greek-English Lexicon of the New Testament and Other Early Christian Literature,* p. 154.
24b. Zorwick, Max, and Grosvenor, Mary, *A Grammatical Analysis of the Greek New Testament,* unabridged, 5th revised edition, Pontifico, Instituto Biblico, Roma, 1996.
25. Souter, Alexander, compiled by, *A Glossary of Later Latin to 600* A.D., p. 159.
26. Childs, Brevard S., *Introduction to the Old Testament as Scripture,* p. 322.
27. Parry, Donald, *Temples of the Ancient World,* p. 247.
28. Ibid., p. 248.
29. Thiele, Edwin R., *The Mysterious Numbers of the Hebrew Kings,* p. 71.
30. Nyman, Monte, S., *Isaiah and the Prophets,* p. 47.
31. Christensen, Allen, J., "The Waters of Destruction and the Vine of Redemption," Draper, Richard, ed., *A Witness of Jesus Christ, The 1989 Symposium on the Old Testament,* p. 41–42.
32. Nibley, Hugh, *Abraham in Egypt,* p. 626–627.

33. Christenson, Allen J., *The Waters of Destruction and the Vine of Redemption,* p. 45.
34. Frazzer, Sir James G., *Folklore in the Old Testament: Studies in Comparative Relative and Law,* p. 223.
35. Christenson, Allen, J., *The Waters of Destruction and the Vine of Redemption,* p. 48.
36. Gileadi, Avraham, *The Literary Message of Isaiah,* p. 78.
37. Budge, E. A. Wallis, *The Book of the Dead: The Hieroglyphic Transcript and Translation into English of the Ancient Egyptian Papyrus,* p. 250.
38. Gileadi, Avraham, p. 78.
39. Ludlow, Daniel H., *A Companion to Your Study of the New Testament,* p. 99.
40. Malina, Bruce J., *The New Testament World: Insights from Cultural Anthropology,* pp. 62–68.
41. Ludlow, Victor L, *Isaiah—Prophet, Seer, Poet,* p. 31.
42. Ibid., p. 32–37.
43. Froom, L. E., *The Conditionalist Faith of Our Fathers,* p. 638.
44. Waxman, Meyer, *A History of Jewish Literature, Volume I—from the Close of the Canon to the End of the Twelfth Century,* p. 51.
45. Dorothy, Charles V., *"Did Ezra Edit or Author the Law?" The Law of God—Part 4, The Association for Christian Development Newsletter,* pp. 3–6.
46. Friedman, Richard Elliott, *Who Write the Bible?* p. 159.
47. Rahner, Karl, E., *The Encyclopedia of Theology: The Concise Sacramentum Mundi,* p. 1730.

Chapter 5

1. Laetsch, Theodore, *Jeremiah,* p. 316.
2. Ibid., pp. 303–315.
3. Robertson, A. T., *A Grammar of the Greek of the New Testament in Light of Historical Research,* pp. 91–92.
4. Nibley, Hugh, *Since Cumorah, the Collected Works of Hugh Nibley, Vol. 7,* p. 149.
5. Fell, Barry, *America B.C., Ancient Settlers in the New World,* pp. 57–58.
6. Brough, R. Clayton, *The Lost Tribes - History, Doctrine, Prophecies and Theories About Israel's Lost Ten Tribes,* p. 83.
7. Olson, S. Gusten, *The Incredible Nordic Origins,* p. 14.
8. Fell, Barry, *American B.C., Ancient Settlers in the New World,* p. 142.
9. Gordon, Cyrus H., *Before Columbus - Links Between the Old World and Ancient America,* p. 136.

10. Ibid., p. 159.
11. Ibid., p. 166.
12. Cryer, Tom, *Visual Testament and the Israelite Indian,* p. 303.
13. Ibid.
14. Ibid., p. 205.
15. Ibid., p. 360.
16. Gordon, Cyrus, *Before Columbus,* p. 158.
17. Hopkins, Richard R., *How Greek Philosophy Corrupted the Christian Concept of God,* p. 73.
18. Nibley, Hugh, *Since Cumorah - The Collected Works of Hugh Nibley, Vol. 7,* pp. 272–274.
19. Parry, Donald W. and Ricks, Stephen, D., eds., *The Temple in Time and Eternity,* p. 74.
20. Ibid., p. 81.
21. Russell, D. S., *Between the Testaments,* pp. 22–23.
22. Martinez, Florentino Garcia, Tichelaar, Eibert, J. C., *The Dead Sea Scrols, Volume 2 (4Q274-11Q31),* p. 825.
23. Gannie, John G., *Holiness in Israel,* p. 79.
24. Hatch, Edwin, *The Influence of Greek Ideas and Usages Upon the Christian Church,* pp. 69–71.
25. Durant, Will, *The Story of Civilization, Vol. I, Our Oriental Heritage,* pp. 200–201.
26. Mikels, Leroy, *The Kenosis, An Exegetical Analysis,* pp. 60–72.
27. Angus, S., *The Religious Quests of the Graeco-Roman World,* p. 25.
28. Doukan, Jacques, *Daniel: The Vision of the End,* p. 41.
29. Durant, Will, *The Story of Civilization, Vol. I,* p. 368.
30. Merling, David, ed., *To Understand the Scripture - Essays in Honor of William H. Shea,* p. 218.
31. Jackson, F. J. Foakes and Lake, Kirsop, *The Acts of the Apostles, Vol. V,* pp. 179–180.
32. Paine, Lauren, *The Hierachy of Hell,* p. 51.
33. Dankenbring, William F., *Satan's Fate,* pp. 68–74.
34. Thiering, Barbara, *Jesus and the Riddle of the Dead Sea Scrolls,* p. 20.
35. Ibid., p. 21.
36. Neuberger, Julie, Jerusalem, Coggins, R. J. and Houlden, J. L., eds, *Dictionary of Biblical Interpretation,* p. 338.
37. Engberg-Pederson, Troels, *Paul in his Helenistic context,* p. xvii.
38. Angus, S., *The Religious Quests of the Graeco-Roman World,* p. 54–55.
39. Schurer, Emil, *A History of the Jewish People in the Time of Christ, Vol. II,* pp. 80.
40. Welesz, Egon, *A History of Byzantine Music and Hymnography,* pp. 34–35.
41. Mann, Jacob, *The Bible as Read and Preached in the Old Synogogue, volume I, the Palestinian Triennial Cycle: Genesis and Exodus, The Library of Biblical Studies,* ed. Harry M. Orlinsky, p. XXI.

42. Doukan, Jacques, *Drinking at the Sources,* p. 75.
43. Wilson, Alan, *Jesus and the Law,* p. 101.
44a. Ruchdooney, Rousas John, *The Institutes of Biblical Law,* p. 698.
44b. Allen, Willoughby, C., *A Critical and Exegetical Commentary on the Gospel According to S. Matthew.*
44c. Bornkamn, Gunther, Barth, Gerhard and Heinz, Joachim Held, Scott, Perry, trans., *Tradition and Interpretation in Matthew,* p. 157.
45. Rushdooney, Rousas John, *The Institutes of Biblical Law,* p. 796.
46. Baker, L., *Two Testaments, One Bible,* pp. 142–143.
47. Kelber, Werner, H. *The Oral and the Written Gospel,* pp. 44–80.
48a. Allison, Dale C., Jr., *The Jesus Tradition in Q,* pp. 49–54.
48b. Robbins, Vernon, K., *Jesus, the Teacher,* pp. 25–48.
49. Funk, Roert W., Hoover, Roy W. and the Jesus Seminar, *The Five Gospels - What Did Jesus Really Say?* p. 28.
50. Meyer, Marvin, Bloom Harold, inter., *The Gospel of Thomas - The Hidden Saying of Jesus,* p. 13.
51. Funk Robert W., et al, *The Five Gospels - What Did Jesus Really Say?* p. 128.
52. Gaebelein, Frank E., gen. ed., *The Expositor's Bible Commentary,* p. 617.
53. Childs, Brevard, S., *Biblical Theology of the Old and New Testament: Theological Reflection on the Christian Bible,* pp. 86–89.
54. Meier, John P., *A Marginal Jew, Rethinking the Historical Jesus, Volume One: The Roots of the Problem and the Person,* p. 129.
55. Wisse, Frederik, *The Profile Method for Classifying and Evaluating Manuscript Evidence,* p. 5.
56. Tanner, Obert C., et al, eds., *Toward Understanding the New Testament,* p. 407.
57a. Nibley, Hugh, *Old Testament and Related Studies,* p. ix.
57b. Parry, Donald W., and Ricks, Stephen D., eds., *The Temple in Time and Eternity,* p. 79–98.
58. Harrison, Everett F., *Introduction to the New Testament,* p. 231.
59. Wilkinson, B. G., *Truth Triumphant,* p. 287.
60. Metzer, Bruce M., *The Early Version of the New Testament,* pp. 19–20.
61. Fujita, Neil S., *The Crack in the Jar - What Ancient Jewish Documents Tell Us About the New Testament,* pp. 109–155.

Chapter 6

1. Ferguson Everett, McHugh, Michael P. and Norris, Frederick W., eds., *The Encyclopedia of Early Christianity,* p. 687.
2a. Ehrman, Bart E., *The Orthodox Corruptioin of Scripture: The Effect of Early Christological Controversies on the Text of the New Testament,* pp. 225–226.

2b. Metzger, Bruce M., *The Test of the New Testament: Its Transmission, Corruption and Restoration,* pp. 213–219.
3. Metzer, Bruce M., *The Early Version of the New Testament,* p. 101.
4. Martini, Rev. Prof. Carlo M., *Is There a Late Alexandrian Text of the Gospels?, New Testament Studies: An International Journal, Vol. 24, No. 3,* p. 288.
5. Funk, Robert W., *Honest to Jesus,* p. 35.
6. Strand, Kenneth, *The Sabbath in Scripture and History,* p. 171.
7. Holbrook, Frank B., ed., *Symposium of Revelation - Book II,* p. 85.
8. Bacchiocchi, Samuele, *From Sabbath to Sunday,* p. 188.
9. Fitzmyer, Joseph A., *The Semitic Background of the New Testament,* p. 479.
10. Ibid., p. 478.
11. Bacchiocchi, Samuele. *From Sabbath to Sunday,* p. 154.
12. Throckmorton, Burton H., Jr., *Gospel Parallels,* p. 26.
13. Hopkins, Richard R., *How Greek Philosophy Corrupted the Christian Concept of God,* p. 156.
14. Bacchiocchi, Samuele, p. 157.
15. Ibid., p. 154, note 63.
16. Fruchtengaum, Arnold, *Hebrew Christianity - Its Theology, History and Philosophy,* p. 40.
16a. Ibid.
17a. Sheldon, Henry C. *A History of the Christian Church, Volume I,* p. 220.
17b. Latourette, Kenneth Scott, *A History of Christianity: Volume I, Beginnings to 1500,* pp. 319–326.
17c. Nichols, Aidan, *Rome and the Eastern Churches: A Study in Schism,* p. 63.
18. McBirnie, William Stewart, *The Search for the Twelve Apostles,* p. 147.
19. Moffett, Samuel Hugh, *Christianity in Asia, Volume I, Beginnings to 1500,* pp. 169–179.
20. Burgess, Stanley, M., *The Holy Spirit: Ancient Christian Traditions,* p. 49.
21. Moffett, Samuel Hugh, *Christianity in Asia, Volume I,* p. 177.
22. Barth, Karl, *Church Dogmatics, Volume I: The Doctrine of God,* p. 475.
23. Froom, L. E., *The Conditionalist Faith of Our Fathers, Vol. II,* p. 108–109.
24. Moffett, Samuel Hugh, p. 31.
25. McBirnie, William Stewart, *The Search for the Twelve Apostles,* pp. 144–173.
26. Lapide, Pinchas, E., *Hebrew in the Church: The Foundation of Jewish-Christian Dialogue,* p. 2.
27. Kummel, Werner Georg, Kee, Howard Clark, trans., *Introduction to the New Testament,* p. 526.
28. Isichei, Elizabeth, *A History of Christianity in Africa: From Antiquity to the Present,* p. 18.

29. Fitzmyer, Joseph A., *The Semitic Background to the New Testament,* p. 103.
30. Beckwith, Roger, *The Old Testament Canon of the New Testament Church and Its Background in Early Judaism,* p. 185.
31. Ferguson, Everett, et al, eds., *The Encyclopedia of Early Christianity,* pp. 690–691.
32. Ibid.
33. Buchanan, George Wesley, *Worship, Feasts and Ceremonies in the Early Church, New Testament Studies: An International Journal, Vol. 26, No. 3,* p. 19.
34. Goodenough, Erwin R., *Jewish Symbols in the Greco-Roman Period,* p. 61.
35. Ibid., pp. 45–115.
36. Freedman, David Noel, *Anchor Bible Dictionary, Vol. 2,* p. 1055.
37. Stauffer, Ethelbert, *New Testament Theology,* p. 253.
38. Throckmorton, Burton H., Jr., *Gospel Parallels,* p. 26.
39. Isichei, Elizabeth, *A History of Christianity in Africa,* p. 49.
40. Ibid., p. 5.
41. Marshall, David, *The Celtic Connection,* pp. 39–40.
42. Ibid., p. 38.
43. Wellesz, Egon, *A History of Byzantine Music and Hymnography,* p. 65.
44. Bultmann, Rudolf, *Theology of the New Testament,* p. 53.
45. Ibid.
46. Ibid., pp. 119–120.
47. Wellez, Egon, *A History of Byzantine Music and Hymnography,* p. 66.
48. Frankfurter, David, *Elijah in Upper Egypt - The Apocalypse of Elijah and Early Egyptian Christianity,* pp. 209–210.
49. Ibid.
50. Ibid., pp. 209–212.
51. Ferguson, Everett, et al., eds., *The Encyclopedia of Early Christianity,* p. 291.
52. Robbins, Vernon K., *Jesus, The Teacher,* p. 147–148.
53. Hardinge, Leslie, *The Celtic Church in Britain,* pp. 50–51.
54. Maxwell, C., Mervyn, *God Cares, Volume I: The Message of Daniel for You and Your Family,* p. 139.
55. Buchanan, George Wesley, *Worship, Feasts and Ceremonies in the Early Jewish-Christian Church, New Testament Studies: An International Journal, Vol. 26, No. 3,* p. 297.

Chapter 7

1. Roberts, Alexander and Donaldson, James, *Ante-Nicene Fathers, Volume I,* p. 198.

2. Froom, L. E., *The Conditionalist Faith of Our Fathers, Vol. 1,* p. 936.
3. Roberts, Alexander and Donaldson, James, *Ante-Nicene Fathers, Volume 2, Chap. II,* p. 67.
4. Ibid., p. 91.
5. *Ante-Nicene Fathers, Vol. 6,* p. 439.
6. *ANF, Vol. 3, Book VI, Chap. 1,* p. 555.
7. *ANF, Vol. 1. Against All Heresies,* p. 309–310, 312.
8. *ANF, Vol. 5, Chap. 1, A Treatise Concerning the Treaty,* p. 611–612.
9. *ANF, Vol. 9, Chap. XXVI, The First Epistle of Clement to the Corinthians,* p. 237.
10a. Froom, L. E., Vol. 1, pp. 703–852.
10b. Schaff, Philip, *History of the Christian Church, Volume II: Ante-Nicene Christianity A. D. 100–325,* p. 751.
10c. *Ante-Nicene Fathers, Vol. I, Irenaeus, Book IV, Chap. 25–26,* pp. 533–555.
10d. *ANF, vol. 1, Book 4, Chap. 39,* pp. 522–523.
10e. *Encyclopedia Britannica, 11th Edition, Vol. 2., Athenagorus,* p. 602.
10f. *ANF, Vol. 2, Chap. 19, Anthenagorus,* p. 137.
10g. *ANF, Vol. 2, Chap. 12,* p. 155.
10h. *ANF, Vol. 2, Athenagorus, Chap. 36, 31, 4, 22, 25* p. 162.
10i. *ANF, Vol. 3, Tertullian, Chap. 1,* p. 545.
10j. Schaff, Philip and Wace, Henry, eds., *Nicene and Post-Nicene Fathers, Vol. 1, Eusebius, Church History, Book IV, Chap. XXVI,* pp. 203–205.
11. Froom, L. E., Vol. 1, pp. 909–910.
12. Ali, Maulana Muhammed, *Holy Quran: Arabic Text, English Translation and Commentary,* p. xxi.
13. Jenni, Ernst and Westernmann, Claus, Biddle, Mark E., trans, *Theological Lexicon of the Old Testament,* p. 15.
14. *ANF, Vol. 6, Book II, Chap. 3,* p. 434.
15. *ANF, Vol. 9, Book II, Chap. 2, Origen's Commentary on John,* p. 323.
16. Stead, Christopher, *Divine Substance,* p. 229.
17. Harvey, Van A., *A Handbook of Theological Terms,* p. 226.
18. Froom, L. E., Vol. 2, p. 877.
19. Tillich, Paul, *A Complete History of Christian Thought,* p. 119-121.
20. Leon-Dufour, Xavier, *Life and Death in the New Testament, The Teaching of Jesus and Paul,* p. 17.
21. Ibid., p. 26–27.
22. Fudge, Edward William, *The Fire That Consumes,* p. 23.
23. Brown, Colin, gen. ed., *The New International Dictionary of New Testament Theology, Vol. 3,* p. 303.
24. Achtemeier, Paul J., *Hermania: 1 Peter,* p. 272.
25a. Ibid., p. 273.
25b. Garrett, H. Dean, ed., *The New Testament and the Latter-Day Saints, Sperry Symposium, 1987,* pp. 295–317.

26. Schaff, Philip, *The Creeds of Christendom, Volume II: The Greek and Latin Creeds,* pp. 44–55.

Chapter 8

1. Finn, Thomas H., *It Happened One Saturday Night: Ritual and Conversion in Augustine's North Africa, Journal of the American Academy of Religion, Volume LVIII, Number 4,,* p. 602.
2. Aland, Kurt, ed., *Synopsis of the Four Gospels - Greek-English Edition of the Synopsis Quattor Evangeliorum,* p. 335.
3. *Gal. 3:13, The Zondervan Parallel New Testament in Greek and English,* p. 713.
4. Bacchiocchi, Samuele, *The Time of the Crucifixion and Resurrection,* pp. 125–127.
5. Schillebeechx, Edward, *Jesus, An Experiment in Christology,* p. 303.
6. Reling, J. and Swellengrebel, J. L. *A Handbook on the Gospel of Luke,* p. 762.
7. Laymon, Charles, E., ed., *The Interpreter's One-Volume Commenty on the Bible,* p. 837.
8. Hengel, Martin and Schwerner, Anna Maris, *Paul - Between Damascus and Antioch: The Unknown Years,* p. 167.
9. Mann, Jacob, *The Bible as Read and Preached in the Old Synagogue, Volume I, the Palestian Triennial Cycle: Genesis and Exodus, Prolegomenon,* Ben Zion Wacholder, *The Library of Biblical Studies,* P. XVI.
10. Ibid.
11. Brooten, Bernadette, *Women Leaders in the Ancient Synagogue,* pp. 139–140.
12. Conybeare, Rev. W. J. and Howson, Very Rev. J. S., *The Life and Epistles of St. Paul,* pp. 389–390.
13. Robertson, Archibald Thomas, *Word Pictures in the New Testament,* p. 114.
14. Ibid.
15. Souter, Alexander, *A Glossary of Later Latin to 600 A.D.,* p. 147.
16. Souter, Alexander, *Earliest Latin Commentaries on the Epistles of St. Paul,* p. 242.
17. Rogers, Cleon L., Jr., and Rogers, Cleon L., III, *The New Linguistic and Exegetical Key to the Greek New Testament,* p. 357.
18. Conybeare, Rev. W. J. and Howson, Very Rev. J. S., *The Life and Epistles of St. Paul,* footnote 5, pp. 389–390.
19. Ellingworth, Paul and Matton, Howard, *A Translator's Handbook on Paul's First Letter to the Corinthians,* p. 102.

20. Bacchiocchi, Samuele, *From Sabbath to Sunday*, p. 105–106.
21. Davis, W. D., *Jewish and Pauline Studies*, pp. 99–100.
22a. Raisanen, Heikki, *Paul and the Law*, p. 53.
22b. Schreiner, Thomas R., *The Law and Its Fulfillment - A Pauline Theology*, p. 136.
22c. Davis, W. D., *Jewish and Pauline Studies*, p. 112–122.
23. Martin, Troy, *Pagan and Judeo-Christian Time-Keeping Schemes in Gal. 4.10 and Col. 2.16, Journal of Biblical Literature*, pp. 108–109.
24. Bacchiocchi, Samuele, *From Sabbath to Sunday*, pp. 354–355.
25. Martin, Troy, *But Let Everyone Discern the Body of Christ, (Colossians 2.17), Journal of Biblical Literature*, p. 249.
26a. Odom, Robert, *Sabbath and Sunday in Early Christianity*, p. 63, note 2.
26b. Barnes, Albert, *Barnes' Notes on the New Testament*, pp. 1070–1071.
27. Bacchiocchi, Samuele, p. 353.
28. Pokomy, Petr, *Colossians, A Commentary*, p. 144.
29. Lenski, R. C. H., *The Interpretation of St. Paul's Epistles*, pp. 122–123.
30. Martin, Troy, *But Let Everyone Discern the Body of Christ (Colossians 2.17), Journal of Biblical Literature*, p. 254.
31. Pokomy, Petr, *Colossians: A Commentary*, p. 114.
32. Martin, Troy, p. 255.
33. Ladd, George Eldon, *A Theology of the New Testament*, pp. 391–392.
34. Tarazi, Paul Hadim, *Galatians, A Commentary*, p. 266.
35. Daube, David, *The New Testament and Rabbinic Judaism*, p. 282–283.
36. Ibid., p. 444.
37. Dorothy, Charles V., *Colossians: Then and Now, Part III, Association for Christian Development Newsletter, August 1991*, pp. 4–8.
38. Bacchiocchi, Samuele, *Immortallity or Resurrection? A Biblical Study on Human Nature and Destiny*, pp. 177–188.
39a. Pinnock, Charles H., *Four Views on Hell - Conditional.* Crockett, William gen. ed, pp. 135–140.
39b. Brower, Kent E. and Elliott, Mark W., *Eschatology in Bible and Theology: Evangelical Essays at the Dawn of a New Millennium*, pp. 231–241.
39c. Kung, Hans, *Eternal Life? Life After Death as a Medical Philsophical and Theological Problem*, pp. 129–142.
40. Berstein, Alan E., *The Formation of Hell: Death and Retribution in the Ancient and Early Christian Worlds*, p. 227.
41. Harris, Murray J., *Raised Immortal: Resurrection and Immortality in the New Testament*, pp. 159–162.
42. Bruner, Frederick Dale, *Matthew: A Commentary, Volume 2: The Churchbook Matthew 13–28*, p. 791.
43. Ibid., p. 790.
44. Collin, Rodney, *The Theory of Eternal Life*, p. 67–68.
45. McDannell, Colleen and Lang, Bernhard, *Heaven: A History*, p. 43.

46. Martin, Troy, *Pagan and Judeo-Christian Time-Keeping Schemes in Gal. 4.10 and Col. 2.16, Journal of Biblical Literature,* p. 112.
47. Taylor, Edward, *Upon the Types of the Old Testament,* p. 533.
48. Van Orden, Bruce A. and Top, Brent L., eds., *The Lord of the Gospels - The 1990 Sperry Symposium on the New Testament,* p. 201.
49. Schnachenburg, Rudolf, *The Gospel According to St. John,* pp. 138–139.
50. Martin, Troy, p. 108.
51. Bacchiocchi, Samuele, p. 357.
52. Wellesz, Egon, *A History of Byzantine Music and Hymnography,* pp. 89–90.

Chapter 9

1. Holbrook, Brank B., ed., *Symposium on Revelation,* pp. 190–191.
2. Robertson, A. T., *Word Pictures in the New Testament, VI - General Epistles,* pp. 220–221.
3. Ibid., pp. 190–191.
4. Coggins, R. J. and Houlden J. L, eds., *Dictionary of Biblical Interpretation,* p. 380.
5. Byolan, Patrick, *Throth, the Hermes of Egypt,* p. 143.
6. Ibid., p. 379.
7. Ibid.
8. Gianotti, Charles, R., *The New Testament and the Mishnah, A Cross-Reference Index,* p. 34.
9. Coggins, R. J. and Houlden, J. L., eds., *A Dictionary of Biblical Interpretation,* p. 343.
10. Alter, Robert and Kermode, Frank, eds., *The Literary Guide to the Bible,* p. 527.
11. Bacchiocchi, Samuele, *God's Festivals in Scripture and History, Part 2. The Fall Festivals,* p. 165.
12. Ibid., p. 105.
13. Hoyt, Edyth Armstrong, *Studies in the Apocalypse of John of Patmos,* p. 116.
14. Doukhan, Jacques, *Daniel, The Vision of the End,* p. 62–63.
15. Smyth, Piazzi, *The Great Pyramid - Its Secrets and Mysteries Revealed,* pp. 464–465.
16. Frankfurter, David, *Elijah in Upper Egypt - The Apocalypse of Elijah and Early Egyptian Christianity,* p. 230.
17. Ibid., p. 231.
18. Pate, C. Marvin, *Communities of the Last Days—The Dead Sea Scrolls, the New Testament and the Story of Israel,* pp. 155–178.

19. Draper, Richard D., *Opening the Seven Seals, Vision of John the Revelator,* p. 255.
20. Ford, Desmond, *Crisis,* p. 599.
21. Walvoord, John F., *The Revelation of Jesus Christ: A Commentary,* p. 215.
22. Nicoll, W. Robertson, *Expositor's Greek New Testament, Volume 5,* p. 444.
23. Ford, Desmond, *Crisis,* p. 595–596.
24. Ibid., p. 609.
25. Martinez, Florentino Garcia and Tigchelaar, Eibert J. C., *The Dead Sea Scrolls, Study Edition, Volume 1–1Q1–4Q273,* p. 469.
26a. Holbrook, Frank F., ed., *Symposium of Revelation—Book II,* p. 391.
26b. Martinez, Florentino Garcia, *The Dead Sea Scrolls Translated: The Qumran Texts in English,* p. 419.
27. Doukhan, Jacques, *Daniel, The Vision of the End,* p. 95.
28. Gaskell, G. S., *The Dictionary of Scripture and Myth,* p. 112.
29. Kittel, Gerhard, ed., *Theological Dictionary of the New Testament,* pp. 674–675.
30. Chaney, William A., *The Cult of Kingship in Anglo-Saxon English—The Transition from Paganism to Christianity,* pp. 248–249.
31. Flanagan, Marie Therese, *Irish Society, Anglo-Norman Settlers, Angevin Kingship-Interactions in Ireland in the Late 12th Century,* p. 197.

Summary and Conclusion—Notes

1. Parry, Donald W., *Temples of the Ancient World,* p. 501.

Bibliography

Acharya, B. *The Christ Conspiracy, The Greatest Story Ever Told,* Adventures Unlimited Press, Kempton, Illinois, 1999.

Achtemeier, Paul J., Epp, Eldon Jay, ed., *Hermania—A Critical and Historical Commentary on the Bible, A Commentary on 1 Peter.* Fortress Press, Minneapolis: 1996.

Aland, Kurt, ed., *Synopsis of the Four Gospels—Greek-English Edition of the Synopsis Quattor Evangeliorum,* Seventh Edition, German Bible Society, Stuttgart, 1984.

Allen, Willoughby C., *A Critical and Exegetical Commentary on the Gospel According to S. Matthew,* third edition, T & T. Clark, Edinburgh: 1912.

Ali, Maulana Mohammed, *Holy Quran—Arabic Text—English Translation and Commentary.* Ahmaniyyah Anjuman Isha'at Islam, Lahore, Inc., USA: 1995.

Allison, Dale, C., Jr., *The Jesus Tradition in Q.* Trinity Press International, Harrisburg, Pennsylvania: 1997.

Alter, Robert, *The World of Biblical Literature.* Basic Books, A Division of HarperCollins Publishers, 1992.

Alter, Robert, and Kermode, Frank, eds., *The Literary Guide to the Bible,* The Belknap Press of Harvard University Press, Cambridge, Massachusetts: 1987.

Angus, S., *The Reglious Quests of the Graeco-Roman World—A Study in the Historical Background of Early Christianity,* John Murray, Albemarle Street, W., London: 1929.

Arndt, W. F., Gingrich, F. W., trans. & eds., *A Greek-English Lexicon of the New Testament and Other Early Christian Literature—A Translation and Adaption of Walter Bauer's Grieschish-Deutches*

Worterbuch zu den Schriften des Neuen Testaments und der ubrigen urchristlichen Literatur. Fourth Revised and Augmented Edition, University of Chicago Press: 1952.

Bacchiocchi, Samuele, *God's Festivals in Scripture and History, Part II. The Fall Festivals,* Biblical Perspectives, Berrien Springs, Michigan: 1996.

Bacchiocchi, Samuele, *Immortality or Resurrection? A Biblical Study on Human Nature and Destiny.* Biblical Perspectives, Berrien Springs, Michigan: 1997.

Barker, Margaret, *The Great Angel, A Study of Israel's Second God.* Westminster/John Knox Press, Louisville, Kentucky: 1992.

Barnes, Albert; Cobbin, Ingram, ed., *Barnes's Notes on the New Testament.* Kregel Publications, Grand Rapids, Michigan: 1974.

Bartels, Robert A., *Kerygma or Gospel Tradition—Which Came First?* Augsburg Publishing House, Minneapolis: 1961.

Barth, Karl, Bromiley, G. W., Torrance, T. F., eds., Parker, Rev. T.H.L., Johnston, Rev. W.B., Knight, Rev. Harold, Haire, Rev. Prof. J. L. M., trans., *Church Dogmatics, Volume II, The Doctrine of God.* T & T Clark, Edinburgh, Charles Scribner's Sons, New York: 1957.

Barthelemy, Dominique; Hulst, A. R., Lohfink, Norbert; McHardy, W. D.; Ruger, H. P. Sanders, James A., committee members, Schenker, Adrian, Thompson, John A., secretaries, *Preliminary and Interim Report on the Hebrew Old Testament Text Project, Compte Rendu Preliminaire Et Provisoire Sur Le Travail D'Analyse Textuelle De L'Ancien Testament Hebreu, Volume 5, Prophetical Books II, Ezekiel, Daniel. Twelve Minor Prophets, Livres prophetiques II, Exechiel., Daniel, les douse petits prophetes.* United Bible Societies, Alliance Biblique Universelle, New York, 1980.

Bartsch, Hans Werner, ed., Fuller, Reginald H., trans., *Kerygma and Myth: A Theological Debate.* Herbert Reich, Ev. Verlag G. m. b. H., Hamburg-Volksdorf, Germany, S.P.C.K., London: 1957.

Beasley-Murray, G. R., *Jesus and the Kingdom of God.* William B. Eerdmans Publishing Company, Grand Rapids, Michigan, and The Paternoster Press, Carlisle, Cumbria, U.K.: 1986.

Beckwith, Roger, *The Old Testament Canon of the New Testament Church: Its Background in Early Judaism.* William B. Eerdmans Publishing Co., Grand Rapids, Michigan: 1986.

Bimson, John J., *Redating the Exodus and Conquest.* The Almond Press, Sheffield, England, second edition, 1981.

Boeeterweck, G. Johannes, and Ringgren, Helmer, eds., trans., Wiles, John T. Froniley, Geoffrey Ward, and Green, David E., *Theological Dictionary of the Old Testament, Volume III.* Wiliam B. Eerdman's Publishing Company, Grand Rapids, Michigan: 1978.

Boylan, Patrick, *Thoth, The Hermes of Egypt: A Study of Some Aspects of Theological Thought in Ancient Egypt.* Oxford University Press, Inc., New York, special edition for Sandpiper Books, Ltd.: 1999.

Bradford, Charles E., *Sabbath Roots, The African Connection: A Biblical Perspective,* L. Brown and Sons Printing, Inc., Barre, Vermont: 1999.

Bratcher, Robert G., and Reyburn, William D., *A Translator's Handbook on the Book of Pslams.* United Bible Societies, New York: 1991.

Brenton, Charles Lee, *The Septuagint Version of the Old Testament and Apocrypha with an English Translation: and with Various Readings and Critical Notes with Apocrypha: Greek and English,* Zondervan Publishing House: 1978.

Breuggermann, Walter, *The Message of the Psalms: A Theological Commentary,* Augsburg Publishing House, Minneapolils: 1984.

Bright, John, *A History of Israel.* The Westminster Press, Philadelphia, Pennsylvania, second edition, 1976.

Bright, John, *The Kingdom of God: The Biblical Concept and Its Meaning for the Church.* Abingdon Press, Nashville, Tennessee: 1953, 1981.

Bronkamn, Gunther; Barth, Gerhard; Heinz, Joachim Held; Scott, Perry, trans., *Tradition and Interpretation in Matthew, Ungerlieferung und Auslegung in Mattausevangelium.* SCM Press, Ltd., The Westminster Press, Philadelphia, Pennsylvania: 1963.

Brough, R. Clayton, *The Lost Ten Tribes—History, Doctrine, Prophecies and Theories About Israel's Lost Ten Tribes.* Horizon Publishers & Distributors, Inc., Bountiful, Utah: 1999.

Brower, Kent E., and Elliott, Mark W., eds., *Eschatology in Bible and Theology: Evangelical Essays at the Dawn of a New Millennium.* InterVarsity Press, Downers Grove, Illinois: 1997.

Brown, Colin, gen. ed., *The New International Dictionary of New Testament Theology, Volume 3: Pri-Z. Translated, with additions and revisions, from the German, Theologisches Begriffslezidon Zum Neuen Testament* Coenen, Lothar, Beyrether, Erich and Bietendard, Hans, eds., Theologisher Verlag Rolf Brockaus, Wuppertal, 1967, 1969, 1971; Zondervan Publishing House, Grand Rapids, Michigan, 1978, 1986.

Bruner, Federick, Dale, *Matthew: A Commentary, Volume 2. The Churchbook, Matthew 13–28.* Word Publishing, Dallas, Texas: 1990.

Budge, E. A. Wallis, *The Book of the Dead: The Hieroglyphic Transcript and Translation into English of the Ancient Egyptian Papyrus of Ani, with a Comprehensive Introduction and Commentary,* Gramercy Books, New York: 1960.

Burgess, Stanely M., *The Holy Spirit: Ancient Christian Traditions.* Hendrickson Publishers, Peabody, Massachusetts: 1994.

Burgess, Stanley M., *The Holy Spirit: Eastern Christian Traditions.* Hendrickson Publishers, Peabody, Massachusetts: 1989.

Butler, Alfred J., *The Arab Conquest of Egypt and the Last Thirty Years of the Roman Dominion* containing also *The Treatise of Misr in Tabari* (1913) and *Babylon of Egypt* (1914), edited by Fraser, P. M. *with a critical bibliography and additional documentation,* Oxford at the Clarendon Press, Oxford, second edition, 1978.

Butlmann, Rudolf, *Theology of the New Testament, Volume 1.* Charles Scribner's Sons, New York: 1951.

Buttrich, George Arthur; Bowie, Walter Russell; Scherer, Paul; Knox, John; Terrier, Samuel; and Harmon, Nolan B., editorial board, *The Interpreter's Bible: The Holy Scriptures in the King James and Revised Standard Versions with General Articles and Introduction, Exegesis, Exposition for Each Book of the Bible in Twelve Volumes, Volume V: The Book of Ecclesiastes, The Song of Songs, The Book of Isaiah and the Book of Jeremiah.* Abingdon Press, New York, Nashville: 1956.

Carter, Howard, and Mace, A. C., *The Tomb of Tut-ankh-Amen, Discovered by the Late Earl of Carnarvon and Howard Carter.* George H. Doran Company, New York: 1923.
Cathcart, Kevin, Maher, Michael, and McNamara, Martin, eds., *The Aramaic Bible—The Targums, Volume 15—The Targum of Job, The Targum of Proverbs, The Targum of Qohelet.* A Michael Glazier Book, The Liturgical Press, Collegeville, Minnesota: 1991.
Chaney, Wiliam A., *The Cult of Kingship in Anglo-Saxon England—The Transition from Paganism to Christianity.* Manchester University Press, special edition for Sandpiper Books, Ltd.: 1999.
Charles, R. H., trans., *The Book of Enoch or 1 Enoch: Translated from the Editor's Ethiopic Text and Edited with the Introduction Notes and Indexes of the First Edition Wholly Together Recast, Enlarged and Rewritten Together with a Reprint from the Editor's Text of the Greek Fragments.* Oxford at the Clarendon Press, Oxford: 1912, reprinted 1964 by Health Reserach, Mokelumne Hill, California.
Charlesworth, James H., ed., *The Old Testament Pseudepigrapha, Volume 1, Apocalyptic Literature & Testaments.* Doubleday, New York: 1983.
Child, Brevard S., *Biblical Theology in Crisis.* The Westminister Press, Philadelphia, Pennsylvania: 1974.
Childs, Brevard S., *Biblical Theology of the Old and New Testaments: Theological Reflection on the Christian Bible.* Fortress Press, Minneapolis, Minneosta: 1992.
Childs, Brevard S., *Introduction to the Old Testament as Scripture.* Fortress Press, Philadelphia, Pennsylvania: 1982.
Ching, Julia, *Confusianism and Christianity: A Comparative Study,* Kondansha International, Tokyo, New York, and San Francisco in cooperation with The Institute of Oriental Religions, Sophia University, Tokyo: 1977.
Coggins, R. J., and Houlden, J. L., eds., *A Dictionary of Biblical Interpretation,* SCM Press, London, Trinity Press International, Philadelphia, Pennsylvania: 1990.
Collin, Rodney, *The Theory of Eternal Life.* Samuel Weiser, New York: 1974.

Collins, John J., ed.; Cross, Frank Moore, *Hermeneia, A Critical and Historical Commentary on the Bible: A Commentary on the Book of Daniel.* Fortress Press, Minneapolis, Minnesota: 1993.
Conybeare, Rev. W. J., and Howson, Very Rev., J. S., *The Life and Epistles of St. Paul.* Wm. B. Eerdmans Publishing Company, Grand Rapids, Michigan: 1983.
Crockett, William, gen. ed., *Four Views on Hell.* Zondervan Publishing House, Grand Rapids, Michigan: 1996.
Cross, Frank Moore, *Canaanite Myth and Hebrew Epic: Essays in the History of the Religion of Israel.* Harvard University Press, Cambridge, Massachusetts, and London, England, First Harvard University Press paperback edition: 1997.
Cryer, Tom, *Visual Testament and the Israelite Indian.* Tom Cryer, 1999.
Currid, John D., *Ancient Egypt and the Old Testament.* Baker Books, a division of Baker Book House Co., Grand Rapids, Michigan: 1997.
Dahood, Mitchell, trans. & ed., *The Anchor Bible—Volume 17: Psalms II, 51–100.* Doubleday & Company, Inc., Garden City, New York: 1968.
Dankenbring, William F., *The First Genesis: The Saga of Creation vs. Evolution,* Trimuph Publishing, Altadena, California: 1979.
Dankenbring, William F., *Satan's Fate.* Triumph Publishing Company, Altadena, California: 1982.
Daube, David, *The New Testament and Rabbinic Judaism.* Hendrickson Publishers, Peabody, Massachusetts: 1956.
Davies, W. D., *Jewish and Pauline Studies.* Fortress Press, Philadelphia, Pennsylvania: 1984.
Deissman, Adolf; Strachan, Lionel R. M., trans. *Light from the Ancient East: The New Testament Illustrated by Recently Discovered Texts of the Graeco-Roman World.* Hendrickson Publishers, Peabody, Massachusetts, reprinted from the 1927 edition originally published by George H. Doran Co., New York: 1995.
Deuel, Leo, *Testaments of Time—The Search for Last Manuscripts and Records,* Alfred A. Knopf, New York: 1965.
Doukhan, Jacques, *Daniel, the Vision of the End.* Andrews University Press, Berrien Springs, Michigan, revised edition, 1989.

Doukhan, Jacques, trans, Beach, Walter R, and Johnston, Robert M., *Drinking at the Sources: An Appeal to the Jew and the Christian to Note Their Common Beginnings.* Pacific Press Publishing Association, Mountain View, California: 1981.

Draper, Richard D., *Opening the Seven Seals: Vision of John the Revelator.* Deseret Book Company, Salt Lake City, Utah: 1991.

Driver, S. R., *A Treatise on the Use of the Tenses in Hebrew and Some Other Syntactical Questions,* first published Oxford University Press, London: 1874; third edition published 1892, Oxford University Press, London. This edition with New Introduction by W. Randall Garr published jointly by William B. Eerdmans Publishing Company, Grand Rapids, Michigan/Cambridge, U.K. and by Dove Booksellers, Livonia, Michigan: 1998.

Dummelow, Rev. J. R., ed., *A Commentary on the Holy Bible by Various Writrers Complete in One Volume with General Articles.* Macmillan Publishing Co., Inc., New York: 1936.

Durant, Will, *The Story of Civilization: Part 1, Our Oriental Heritage: Being a history of civilization in Egypt and the Near East to the death of Alexander and in India, China and Japan from the beginning to our own day; with an introduction on the nature and foundations of civilizations.* Simon and Schuster, New York: 1954.

Edelman, Diana Vikander, ed., *The Triumph of Elohim: From Yahwisms to Judaisms,* William B. Eerdman's Publishing Company, Grand Rapids, Michigan: 1996 through special arrangement with Kok Pharos Publishing House, Kampen, The Netherlands: 1995.

Ehrman, Bart D., *The Orthodox Corruption of Scripture—The Effect of Early Christological Controversies on the Text of the New Testament.* Oxford University Press, New York, Oxford: 1993.

Eibfeldt, O., *"Liber Gensis," Biblia Hebraica Stuttgartensia.* Elliger, K. et Rudolph, W., Textum Masoreticum curavit H. P. Ruger, Masoram Elaboravit, G. E. Weil, Wurttembergische, Bibelanstalt, Stuttgart: 1969.

Eichrodt, Warner, *Theology of the Old Testament, Volume One*, translated by J. A. Baker from the German, *Theologie des Alten Testaments, Teil I,* sixth edition, 1959, published by Ehrenfried Klotz Verlag, Stuttgart, in association with Vandenhoeck & Ruprecht,

Gottingen, with the author's revisions to November 1960; The Westminster Press, Philadelphia, Pennsylvania, S.C.M. Press, Ltd., 1961.

Elliger, K., and Rudolph, W., eds., *Encyclopedia Judaica, Volume 15. Sm-Un,* Keter Publishing House, Jerusalem, Ltd., Israel, corrected edition, 1996.

Ellingsworth, Paul, and Matton, Howard., *A Translator's Handbook on Paul's First Letter to the Corinthians.* United Bible Societies, London, New York, Stuttgart: 1985.

Encyclopaedia Britannica, 11th Edition, Volume 2. The University of Chicago, Encyclopaedia Britannica, Inc., Chicago, London, Toronto: 1947.

Faulker, R. O., trans., *Ancient Egyptian Pyramid Texts.* Oxford at the Clarendon Press, 1969, Special edition for Sandpiper Books Ltd., 1998.

Fell, Barry, *American B.C.—Ancient Settlers in the New World.* A Wallaby Book, Published by Pocket Books, New York: 1978.

Ferguson, Everett, ed., McHugh, Michael P., and Norris, Frederick W., assoc. ed., Scholer, David M., cons. ed., *The Encyclopedia of Early Christianity.* Garland Publishing, Inc., New York & London: 1990.

Finegan, Jack, *Light From the Ancient Past: The Archaeological Background of the Hebrew-Christian Religion.* Princeton University Press: 1949.

Fitzmyer, Joseph A., *The Semitic Background of the New Testament: Combined Edition of Essays on the Semitic Background of the New Testament and A Wandering Aramean: Collected Aramaic Essays.* Wiliam B. Eerdmans Publishing Company, Grand Rapids, Michigan/Cambridge, U.K., Dove Booksellers; Livonia, Michigan: 1997.

Flanagan, Marie Therese, *Irish Society, Anglo-Norman Settlers, Angevin Kingship—Interactions in Ireland in the Late 12th Century,* Clarendon Press, Oxford: 1989; Special edition for Sandpiper Books, Ltd., 1998.

Ford, Desmond, *Crisis: A Commentary on the Book of Revelation, Volume II: A Verse by Verse Commentary.* Desmond Ford Publications, Newcastle, California: 1982.

Frankfurter, David., *Elijah in Upper Egypt—The Apocalypse of Elijah and Early Egyptian Christianity,* Fortress Press, Minneapolis: 1993.

Frazer, Sir James G., *Folklore in the Old Testament: Studies in Comparative Religion, Legend and Law,* abridged edition, Avenel Books, New York: 1988.

Freedman, David Noel, editor-in-chief, Herion, Gary A., Graf, David F., and Pleins, John David, assoc. eds., Beck, Astrid B., managing ed., *The Anchor Bible Dictionary, Volume 1: A-C, Volume 5:0–Sh,* Doubleday, New York: 1992.

Friedman, Richard Elliot, *Who Wrote the Bible,* Summit Books, New York: 1987.

Froom, Le Roy Edwin, *The Conditionalist Faith of Our Fathers: The Conflict of the Ages Over the Nature and Destiny of Man, Volume I: The Biblical Norm and Origin, Development and Penetration of Innate Immortality (900 B.C. to A.D. 500).* Review and Herald Publishing Association, Washington, D.C.: 1966.

Froom, Le Roy Edwin, *The Conditionalist Faith of Our Fathers: The Conflict of the Ages Over the Nature and Destiny of Man, Volume II: From Repression and Obscurity to Restoration, Gathering Momentum and Status, Accelerated Acceptance and Expansion Spiritualism Climaxes the Conflict.* Review and Herald Publishing Association, Washington, D.C., 1965.

Fruchtengaum, Arnold G., *Hebrew Christianity—Its Theology, History and Philosophy,* Canon Press, Washington, D.C.: 1974.

Fudge, Edward William, Cousins, Peter, revising ed. *The Fire That Consumes—The Biblical Case for Conditional Immortality.* The Paternoster Press, Carlisle, U.K.: 1994.

Fujita, Neil S., *The Crack in the Jar—What Ancient Jewish Documents Tell Us About the New Testament,* Paulist Press, New York/ Mahwah: 1986.

Funk, Robert W., *Honest to Jesus: Jesus for a New Millennium,* A Polebridge Press Book, HarperSanFrancisco, HarperCollins Publishers, New York: 1996.

Funk, Robert W., Hoover, Roy W., and the Jesus Seminar, *The Five Gospels—What Did Jesus Really Say? The Search for the Authentic Words of Jesus.* HarperSanFrancisco, HarperCollins Publishers, New York: 1993.

Gaebelein, Frank E., gen. ed., *The Expositor's Bible Comentary in Twelve Volumes, Volume I,* Zondervan Publishing House, Grand Rapids, Michigan: 1979.
Gamble, Harry, Jr., *The Textual History of the Letter to the Romans: A Study in Textual and Literary Criticism,* Studies and Documents, Volume 42, Sparks, Irving Alan, ed. Wm. B. Eerdmans, Grand Rapids, Michigan: 1977.
Gammie, John G., *Holiness in Israel,* Fortress Press, Minneapolis, Minnesota: 1989.
Gaskell, G. S., *The Dictionary of Scripture and Myth,* Dorset Press, New York: 1988.
Gehman, Henry Snyder, ed., *The Westminister Dictionary of the Bible,* The Westminister Press, Philadelphia, Pennsylvania: 1976.
Gerstenberger, Erhard, S., *Psalms, Part I with an Introduction to Cultic Poetry,* Knierim, Rolf, and Tucker, Gene M., eds., *The Forms of the Old Testament Literature, Volume XIV.* William B. Eerdmans Publishing Company, Grand Rapids, Michigan: 1991.
Gianotti, Charles R., *The New Testament and the Mishnah—A Cross-Reference Index,* Baker Book House, Grand Rapids, Michigan: 1983.
Gileadi, Avraham, *The Literary Message of Isaiah,* Hebraeus Press, New York: 1994.
Goldingay, John, *Theological Diversity and the Authority of the Old Testament,* William B. Eerdmans Publishing Company, Grand Rapids, Michigan: 1987.
Goodenough, Erwin R., edited and abridged by Jacob Neusner, *Jewish Symbols in the Graeco-Roman Period,* Bolligen Series, Princeton University Press, Oxford: 1988.
Gordis, Robert, *The Book of God and Man: A Study of Job,* The University of Chicago Press, Chicago & London, 1965.
Gordis, Robert, *The Book of Job: Commentary, New Translation and Special Studies,* The Jewish Theological Seminary of America, New York City, 1978.
Gordon, Cyrus, H., *Before Columbus - Links Between the Old World and Ancient America,* Crown Publishers, Inc., New York, 1971.
Gordon, Cyrus H. and Rendsburg, Gary A., *The Bible and the Ancient Near East,* W. W. Norton & Company, New York, London, 1997.

Halioni, David Weiss, *Revelation Restored, Divine Writ and Critical Responses,* Westview Press, Boulder, Colorado, 1997.

Hallio, William W., Moyer, James C., and Perdue, Leo G., *Scripture in Context II: More Essays on the Comparative Method,* Eisenbrauns, Winona Lake, Indiana, 1983.

Hanson, Paul D., *The Dawn of Apocalyptic: The Historical and Sociological Roots of Jewish Apocalayptic Eschatology,* Fortress Press, Philadelphia, Pennsylvania, revised edition, 1979.

Hanson, Paul D., *The Diversity of Scripture: A Theological Interpretation,* Fortress Press, Philadelphia, 1982.

Hanson, Paul D., *The People Called: The Growth of Community in the Bible,* Harper & Row Publishers, San Francisco, 1986.

Hardinge, Leslie, *The Celtic Church in Britain,* first published in 1972, Church Historical Society Series, reprinted 1973, Teach Services, Inc., Brushton, New York, 1995.

Harris, Murray, J., *Raised Immortal: Resurrection and Immortality in the New Testament,* published through special arrangement with Marshall, Morgan & Scott, England by William B. Eerdmans Publising Company, Grand Rapids, Michigan, 1983.

Harrison, Everett F., *Introduction to the New Testament,* Wm. B. Eerdmans Publishing Company, Grand Rapids, Michigan, revised edition, 1971.

Harrison, R. K., *Introduction to the Old Testament with a Comprehensive Review of Old Testament Studies and a Special Supplement on the Apocrypha,* William B. Eerdmans Publishing Company, Grand Rapids, Michigan, 1973.

Harvey, Van A., *A Handbook of Theological Terms,* Macmillan Publishing Co., Inc. New Collier Macmillan Publishers, London: 1964.

Hatch, Edwin Fairbairn, A. M., ed., *The Influence of Greek Ideas and Usages Upon the Christian Church,* reprinted from the fifth edition originally published by Williams and Norgate, London: 1985; Hendrickson Publishers: 1995.

Hengel, Martin; Bowden, John, trans., *Judaism and Hellenism: Studies in their Encounter in Palestine during the Early Hellenistic Period, Volume 1 and 2. Judenium and Hellenismus. Studien zu iber*

Begegnung unter besonderer Berucksichtigung Palastins bis zur Mitte des 2 Jh. s. v. Chr., no. 10 in the series Wissenschaftliche Untersuchungen zum Neuen Testament, Jeremiah, Joachim and Michel, Otto, eds., J. C. B. Mohr (Paul Siebeck), Tubingen, second revised and enlarged edition, 1973; Fortress Press, Philadelphia, Pennsylvania, first one-volume edition, 1981.

Hengel, Martin, and Schwemer, Anna Maris; Bowden, John, trans., *Paul—Between Damascus and Antioch, The Unknown Years,* Westminister John Knox Press, Louisville, Kentucky: 1997.

Hengstenberg, E. W., *Christology of the Old Testament,* Kregel Publications, Grand Rapids, Michigan: 1970.

Hess, Richard S., Wenham, Gordon J., and Satterthwaite, Philip E., eds. *He Swore an Oath: Biblical Themes from Genesis 12–50,* second edition, The Paternoster Press, Carlisle, U.K., Baker Book House, Grand Rapids, Michigan: 1994.

Hester, H. L., *The Heart of Hebrew History—A Study of the Old Testament,* Broadman Press, Nashville, Tennessee: 1962.

Hislop, Rev. Alexander, *The Two Babylons,* Loizeaux Brothers, 1959.

Holbrook, Frank B., ed., *Symposium on Revelation—Book 2: Daniel and Revelation Committee Series, Volume 7,* Biblical Research Institute, Silver Spring, Maryland: 1992.

Hopkins, Richard R., *How Greek Philosophy Corrupted the Christian Concept of God,* Horizon Publishers & Distributors, Inc., Bountiful, Utah: 1998.

Horne, Charles F., *The Sacred Books & Early Literature of the East, Volume 2 with Historical Surveys of the Chief Writings of Each Nation,* Park, Austin and Lipscomb, Inc. New York, London: 1917.

Howe, Bruce, with Stearns, Charles E., contrib., Arambourg, Camille, and Briggs, Lloyd Cabot, contrib., Briggs, Lloyd Cabot, and Hencken, Hugh, eds., *The Palaeolithic of Tangier, Morocco: Excavations at Cape Ashakar, 1939–1947,* Bulletin No. 22, American School of Prehistoric Research, Peabody Museum, Harvard University, Published by the Peabody Museum, Cambridge, Massachusetts: 1967.

Hoyt, Edyth Armstrong, *Studies in the Apocalypse of John of Patmos: A Non-Interpretive and Literary Approach to the Last Book of the English Bible,* Columbus, Ohio: 1950.

Hurtado; Larry W., *One God, One Lord—Early Christain Devotion and Ancient Jewish Monotheism,* Fortress Press, Philadelphia, Pennsylvania: 1988.

Isichei, Elizabeth, A., *A History of Christianity in Africa From Antiquity to the Present,* William B. Eerdman's Publishing Company, Grand Rapids, Michigan; Africa World Press, Inc. Lawrenceville, New Jersey: 1995.

Jackson, F. J. Foakes, Lake, Kirsop, and Cadbury, Henry J., eds., *The Beginnings of Christianity, Part I, The Acts of the Apostles, Vol. V: Additional Notes to the Commentary,* originally published 1932, Baker Book House, Grand Rapids, Michigan: 1979.

Jamme, Albert, *1974–75 Yemen Expedition,* Carnegie Museum of Natural History Special Publication No. 2., Pittsburgh, Pennsylvania: 1976.

Jenni, Ernst, and Westermann, Claus, Biddle, Mark E., trans., *Theological Lexicon of the Old Testament, Volume I,* translated from the *Theologisches Handworterbuch zum Alten Testament,* Chr. Kaiser Verlag, Munich, and Theologischer Verlag, Zurich: 1971, 1976; Hendrickson Publishers, Peabody, Massachusetts: 1997.

Kelber, Werner, H., *The Oral and the Written Gospel: The Hermeneutics of Speaking and Writing in the Synoptic Tradition, Mark, Paul, and Q.,* Fortress Press, Philadelphia, Pennsylvania: 1983.

Kent, Charles Foster, *The Growth and Contents of the Old Testament,* Charles Scribner's Sons, New York: 1926.

Kittel, Gerhard, ed. Bromiley, Geoffrey W., trans. and ed., *Theological Dictionary of the New Testament: Volume I A—I,* translated from *Theologisches Wortenbuch zum Nueum Testament: Erster Bank: A–I.* W. Kohlhammer Verlag, Stuttgart, Germany: 1964; Wm. B. Eerdmans Publishing Company, Grand Rapids, Michigan: 1993.

Kittell, Rud., ed., Kahle, P., textum maasoreticum curavit, *Biblia Hebraica, Adjuvantibus, Editionem Tertaim Denuo Elaboratuam Ad Finem Perduxerunt Editionem Septimam Auxerunt Et Emendaverunt, O. Eissfeldt, Editio Nona Emendata Typis Editionis Septimae Expressa,* for the American Bible Society, New York, Published by Privileg, Wurtt. Bibelanstalt, Stuttgart: 1954.

Klein, Ernest, *A Comprehensive Etymological Dictionary of the Hebrew Language for Readers of English,* Macmillan Publishing

Company, New York, Collier Macmillan Publishers, London: 1987.

Koehler, Ludwig, and Baumgartner, Walter, ed., *Lexicon in Veteris Testamenti Libros, Editio Photomechanice Iterata Cui Adjectum Est Supplementum Lexicon Germanico-Hebraicum (aramaicum) Et Correctiones Additamentaque I. A Continens: Worterbuch Zum Hebraischen Alten Testament in Deutscher und Englischer Sprache, A Dictionary of the Hebrew Old Testament in English and German; Worterbuch Zum Aramaischen Teil Des Alten Testaments in Deutscher und Englisher Sprache, A Dictionary of the Aramaic Parts of the Old Testament in English and German,* E. J. Brill, Leiden, Netherlands: 1958.

Kummel, Werner Georg; Kee, Howard Clark, trans, *Introduction to the New Testament, Einleitung in das Neue Testament,* 17th edition, Abingdon Press, Nashville, Tennessee: 1975.

Kung, Hans; Quinn, Edward, trans., *Eternal Life? Life After Death as a Medical, Philosophical and Theological Problem.* Doubleday & Company, Inc., Garden City, New York: 1984.

Laetsch, Theodore, *Jeremiah,* Concordia Publishing House, St. Louis, Missouri: 1952.

Lapide, Pinchas E., Rhodes, Errol, F., trans., *Hebrew in the Church: The Foundation of Jewish-Christian Dialogue,* William B. Eerdmans Publishing Company, Grand Rapids, Michigan: 1984.

Lang, Bernhard, *Monotheism and the Prophetic Minority: An Essay in Biblical History and Sociology,* The Almond Press, Sheffield, England: 1983.

Lange, John Peter, *Commentary on the Holy Scriptures: Critical Doctrinal and Homiletical—Job,* translated from the German, and edited, with additions, by Philip Schaff, Zondervan Publishing House, Grand Rapids 2, Michigan: 1874.

La Rondelle, Hans K., *Deliverance in the Psalms: Message of Hope for Today,* First Impresions, Sarasota, Florida: 1983.

Latourette, Kenneth Scott, *A History of Christianity, Volume I, Beginnings to 1500,* Harper & Row, Publishers, San Francisco: 1953, 1975.

Layman, Charles M., ed., *The One Volume Commentary on the Bible: Introduction and Commentary for Each Book of the Bible Including the Apocrypha, with General Articles,* Abingdon Press, Nashville, Tennessee: 1971.

Lenski, R. C. H., *The Interpretation of St. Paul's Epistles to the Colossians to the Thessalonians to Timothy, to Titus and to Philemon,* Lutheran Book Concern, 1937, The Wartburg Press, 1946; Augsburg Publishing House, Minneapolis, Minnesota: 1961.

Leon-DuFour, Xavier; Prendergast, Terrence, trans., *Life and Death in the New Testament—The Teaching of Jesus and Paul, Face A La Mort, Jesus et Paul,* Editons du Seuil, 1979; Harper & Row, Publishers, Inc., New York: 1986.

——— translated from the second (revised) French edition by Terrence Prendergast, *Dictioinary of the New Testament,* Harper & Row Publishers, San Francisco, 1980.

Leslie, Elmer A., *The Psalms, Translated and Interpreted in the Light of Hebrew Life and Worship,* Abingdon-Cokesbury Press, New York, Nashville: 1949.

Lincoln, Andrew T., *Paradise Now and Not Yet: Studies in the Role of the Heavenly Dimension in Paul's Thought with Special References to His Eschcatology,* Baker Book House, Grand Rapids, Michigan: 1981.

Ludlow, Daniel H., *A Comparative to Your Study of the New Testament: The Four Gospels,* Deseret Book Company, Salt Lake City, Utah: 1982.

Ludlow, Victor L., *Isaiah—Prophet, Seer, and Poet,* Deseret Book Company, Salt Lake City, Utah: 1982.

Lundquist, John M., and Ricks, Stephen D., eds., *By Study and Also by Faith, Volume I,* Deseret Book Company, Salt Lake City, Utah, and Foundation for Ancient Research and Mormon Studies, Provo, Utah: 1990.

Maier, John, and Toller, Vincent, eds., *The Bible in its Literary Milieu,* William G. Eerdmans Publishing Company, Grand Rapids, Michigan: 1979.

Malina, Bruce, J., *The New Testament World: Insights from Cultural Anthropology,* John Knox Press, Louisvile, Kentucky: 1981.

Mann, Jacob, *The Bible as Read and Preached in the Old Synagogue: A Study in the Cycles of the Readings from Torah and Prophets, as well as from Psalms, and in the Structure of the Midrashic Homilies, Volume 1—The Palestian Triennial Cycle: Genesis and Exodus with a Hebrew Section Containing Manuscript Material of Midarshim of These Books,* KTAV Publishing House, Inc., New York: 1940, 1971.

Marshall, Rev. Alfred, *The Zondervan Parallel New Testament in Greek and English,* Zondervan Bible Publishers, Grand Rapids, Michigan: 1976.

Marshall, David, *The Celtic Connection: The Story of the Beginnings of Christianity in Ireland and Britain,* The Stanborough Press, Ltd., England: 1994.

Martinez, Florentino Garcia; Watson, Wilfred G. E., trans., *The Dead Sea Scrolls Translated: The Qumran Texts in English,* original title *Textos de Qumran,* Editorial Trotts SA, Madrid, Spain, 1992, English edition (with corrections and additions) E. J. Brill, Leiden, The Netherlands: 1994.

Martinez, Florentino Garcia, and Tigchelaar, Eibert J. C., *The Dead Sea Scrolls, Study Edition, Volume I: 1Q1–4Q273,* paperback edition published jointly, E. J. Brill, Leiden, The Netherlands and William B. Eerdmans Publishing Company, Grand Rapids, Michigan/Cambridge, U.K.: 2000.

Martinez, Florentino Garcia, and Tigchelaar, Eibert J. C., *The Dead Sea Scrolls, Volume 2: 40274–11031,* paperback edition published jointly, E. J. Brill, Leiden, The Netherlands and William B. Eerdmans Publishing Company, Grand Rapids, Michigan/Cambridge, UK: 2000.

Maspero, Gaston, Sayce, A. H., ed. and McClure, M. L. trans., *The Dawn of Civilization: Egypt and Chaldea,* fifth edition, Society for Promoting Christian Knowledge, London: 1910.

Maspero, Gaston; Sayce, A. H., ed., McClure, M. L., trans., *The Struggle of the Nations: Egypt, Syria and Assyria,* second edition, Society for Promoting Christian Knowledge, London: 1910.

Maxwell, C. Mervyn, *God Cares, Volume I: The Message of Daniel for You and Your Family,* Pacific Press Publishing Association, Boise, Idaho; Oshawa, Ontario, Canada: 1981.

McBirnie, William Steuart, *The Search for the Twelve Apostles,* Tyndale House Publishers, Wheaton, Illinois: 1977.
McDannell, Colleen, and Lang, Bernhard, *Heaven: A History,* Yale University Press, New Haven, Connecticut and London, England: 1988.
McKenzie, John L., *Myths and Realities: Studies in Biblical Theology,* The Bruce Publishing Company, Milwaukee, Wisconsin: 1963.
Meier, John P., *A Marginal Jew, Rethinking the Historical Jesus, Volume One: Roots of the Problem and the Person,* Doubleday, New York: 1991.
Mendenhall, George E., *The Tenth Generation: The Origins of the Biblical Traditions,* The Johns Hopkins University Press, Baltimore, Maryland, and London: 1974.
Menzies, Allan, ed. *Ante-Nicene Fathers: The Writings of the Fathers Down to* A.D. *325, Volume 9: The Gospel of Peter, The Diatessaron of Tatian, The Apocalypse of Peter, The Vision of Paul, The Apocalypses of the Virgin and Sedrach, The Testament of Abraham, The Acts of Xanthippe and Polyxena, The Narrative of Zosimus, The Apology of Aristotles, The Epistles of Clement (Complete text), Origen's Commentary on John, Books 1–10 and Commentary on Matthew, Books 1, 2, and 10–14,* Fourth Edition, Christian Literature Publishing Company, 1896, 1897, Hendrickson Publishers, Peabody, Massachusetts: 1994.
Merling, David, ed., *To Understand the Scriptures: Essays in Honor of William H. Shea,* Institute of Archaeology, Seigfried H. Horn Archaeological Museum, Andrews University, Berrien Springs, Michigan: 1997.
Metzger, Bruce M., *The Early Versions of the New Testament: Their Origin, Transmission and Limitations,* Clarendon Press, Oxford: 1977.
Metzger, Bruce M., *The Text of the New Testament: Its Transmission, Corruption and Restoration,* third, enlarged edition, Oxford University Press, New York, Oxford: 1992.
Meyer, Marvin, *The Gospel of Thomas—The Hidden Sayings of Jesus: Translation with Introduction, Critical Edition of the Coptic Text & Notes,* with interpretation by Harold Bloom, HarperSanFrancisco, HarperCollins Publishers, New York: 1992.

Meyers, Eric M., editor in chief, *The Oxford Encyclopedia of Archaeology in the Near East, Volume 2.* Prepared Under the Auspices of the American School of Oriental Research; Oxford University Press, New York, Oxford, 1997.

Moffett, Samuel Hugh, *A History of Christianity in Asia, Volume I: Beginnings to 1500,* HarperSanFrancisco, HarperCollins Publishers, New York: 1992.

Moore, Carey, A., *Daniel, Esther and Jeremiah: The Additions—A New Translation with Introduction and Commentary.* Doubleday & Company, Inc., Garden City, New York: 1977.

Nestle, Eberhard, ed., *Novum Testamentum Graece,* Editio Photomechanmice in Maiorem Formam Producta, for the American Bible Society, New York, published by Privileg. Wurtt. Bibelanstalt, Stuttgart: 1953.

Neusner, Jacob, trans. & ed., *Genesis and Judaism: The Perspective of Genesis Rabah, An Analytical Anthology,* Scholars Press, Atlanta, Georgia: 1985.

Neusner, Jacob, *Genesis Rabbah: The Judaic Commentary to the Book of Genesis, A New American Translation, Volume II: Parashiyyot Thirty-Four through Sixty-Seven on Genesis 8:15 to 28:9,* Scholars Press, Atlanta, Georgia, 1985.

Nibley, Abraham, Gillum, Gary P., ed., *Abraham in Egypt: The Collected Works of Hugh Nibley: Volume 14 Pearl of Great Price,* second edition, Deseret Book Company, Salt Lake City, Utah and Foundation for Ancient Research and Mormon Studies at Brigham Young University, Provo, Utah: 1981.

Nibley, Hugh; Ricks, Stephen, D., ed., *Enoch, The Prophet: The Collected Works of Hugh Nibley: Volume 2,* Deseret Book Company, Salt Lake City, Utah and Foundation for Ancient Research and Mormon Studies, Provo, Utah: 1986.

Nibley, Hugh, *Nibley on the Timely and the Timeless: Classic Essays of Hugh W. Nibley,* Religious Studies Center, Brigham Young University, Provo, Utah: 1978.

Nibley, Hugh; Welch, John W.; Gillum, Gary P., and Norton, Don E., eds., *Old Testament and Related Studies: The Collected Works of Hugh Nibley: Volume I,* Deseret Book Company, Salt Lake

City, Utah, and Foundation for Ancient Research and Mormon Studies, Provo, Utah: 1986.

Nibley, Hugh; Welch, John W., gen., ed., *Since Cumorah: The Collected Works of Hugh Nibley: Volume 7. The Book of Mormon,* second edition, Deseret Book Company, Salt Lake City, Utah, and Foundation for Ancient Research and Mormon Studies, Provo, Utah: 1988.

Nibley, Hugh; Norton, Don E., ed., *Temple and Cosmos: The Collected Works of Hugh Nibley: Volume 12 Ancient History,* Deseret Book Company, Salt Lake City, Utah, and Foundation for Ancient Research and Mormon Studies, Provo, Utah: 1992.

Nichol, Francis D., ed., Cottrell, Raymond F., and Neufeld, Don F., assoc. eds., Neuffer, Julia, asst. ed., *Seventh-Day Adventist Bible Commentary in Seven Volumes: The Holy Bible with Exegetical and Expositiory Comment, Volume 4: Isaiah to Malachi,* Review and Herald Publishing Association, Washington, D.C.: 1955.

Nichols, Aidan, *Rome and the Eastern Churches: A Study in Schism,* A. Micheal Glazier Book, The Liturgical Press, Collegeville, Minnesota: 1992.

Nicoll, W. Robertson, ed., *Expositor's Greek New Testament, Volume V,* Wm. B. Eerdmans Publishing Company, Grand Rapids, Michigan: 1980.

Neibuhr, H. Richard, *Radical Monotheisim and Western Culture with Supplementary Essays,* Harper & Row, Publishers, New York: 1960.

Nyman, Monte S., ed. Tate, Charles D., assoc. ed., *Isaiah and the Prophets: Inspired Voices from the Old Testament,* Religious Studies Center, Brigham Young University, Provo, Utah: 1984.

Odom, Robert, *Sabbath and Sunday in Early Christianity,* Review and Herald Publishing Association, Washington, D.C.: 1977.

Olsen, Benjamin D., *Ages of Creation and Sabbatical Times, with Ordinances in Type and Antitype,* Vantage Press, New York: 1983.

Olsen, S. Gusten, *The Incredible Nordic Origins,* Nordica S.F. Ltd., Borough Green, Sevenoaks, Kent, England: 1981.

Padinjarekara, Joseph, *Christ in Ancient Vedas (An exciting, surprising and edifying discovery from the ancient Vedas, the sacred books of the Hindus, written between the period 2000 and 1200* B.C.), India Mjkti Mission, Kerala, India; Welch Publishing Company, Inc., Burlington, Ontario, Canada: 1991.

Paine, Lauren, *The Hierarchy of Hell,* Hippocrene Books, Inc., New York: 1972.

Parry, Donald W., *Temples of the Ancient World: Ritual and Symbolism,* Deseret Book Company, Salt Lake City, Utah, and Foundation for Ancient Research and Mormon Studies, Provo, Utah: 1964.

Parry, Donald W., and Ricks, Stephen D., eds., *The Temple in Time and Eternity,* The Foundation for Ancient Research and Mormon Studies at Brigham Young University, Provo, Utah: 1999.

Pate, C. Marvin, *Communities of the Last Days, The Dead Sea Scrolls, The New Testament & the Story of Israel,* InterVarsity Press, Downers Grove, Illinois: 2000.

Perdue, Leo G., Toombs, Lawrence E., and Johnson, L. eds., *Archaeology and Biblical Interpretation: Essays in Memory of D. Glenn Rose,* John Knox Press, Atlanta, Georgia: 1987.

Perry, T. A., *Wisdom Literature and the Structure of Proverbs*, The Pennsylvania State University Press, University Park, Pennsylvania: 1993.

Pokomy, Petr; Schatzmann, Siegfried S., trans., *Colossians: A Commentary,* German edition, *Der Brief des Paulus an die Kolasser,* Theologischer Handkommentar zum Neuen Testament 10/1, Evangelische Verlagsanstalt GmbH Berlin, 1987, Hendrickson Publishers, Inc., Peabody, Massachusetts: 1991.

Pritchard, James B., ed. *The Ancient Near East: Volume II. A New Anthology of Texts and Pictures,* Princeton University Press, Princeton and London: 1975.

Rahlfs, Alfred, ed., *Septuginta: Id est Vetus Testamentum graece iauxta LXX interpretes: Duo volumina in uno,* Deutsche Biblgesellschaft, Stuttgart: 1979.

Rahner, Karl, ed., *The Encyclopedia of Theology; The Concise Sacramentum Mundi,* Herder KG Freiburg-im-Breisgau, 1975; Crossroad Publishing Company, New York: 1975.

Raisanen, Heikki, *Paul and the Law,* Fortress Press, Philadelphia, Pennsylvania: 1986.

Rawlingson, George, *The Five Great Monarchies of the Ancient Eastern World; or, The History, Geography and Antiquities of Chaldea, Assyria, Babylon, Media, and Persia in Three Volumes, Volume I,* second edition, Dodd, Mead & Company, New York: 1870.

Reling, J., and Swellengrebel, J. L., *A Handbook on the Gospel of Luke,* UBS Handbook Series, United Bible Societies, New York: 1971.

Reumann, John; Fitzmyer, Joseph A. and Quinn, Jerome D. respondents, *"Righteousness" in the New Testament: "Justification" in the United States Lutheran-Roman Catholic Dialogue,* Fortress Press, Philadelphia; Paulist Press, New York/Ramsey: 1982.

Ricks, Stephen D., Parry, Donald W., and Hedges, Andrew H., *The Disciple as Scholar: Essays on Scripture and the Ancient World in Honor of Richard Lloyd Anderson.* The Foundation of Ancient Research and Mormon Studies at Brigham Young University, Provo, Utah: 2000.

Ridderbos, Herman, de Jongste, H., trans., and Zorn, Raymond O., ed., *The Coming of the Kingdom,* The Presbyterian and Reformed Publishing Company, Philadelphia, Pennsylvania: 1962.

Riken, Leland; Wilhoit, James C. and Longman, Tremper II, gen. eds., *Dictionary of Biblical Imagery,* InterVarsity Press, Downers Grove, Illinois: 1998.

Robbins, Vernon K., *Jesus The Teacher: A Socio-Rhetorical Interpretation of Mark,* Fortress Press, Philadelphia, Pennsylvania: 1984.

Roberts, Alexander, and Donaldson, James, eds., *Ante-Nicene Fathers: The Writings of the Fathers Down to A.D. 325, Volumes 1: The Apostolic Fathers, Justin Martyr, Irenaeus,* revised and chronologically arranged, with brief prefaces and occasional notes by Coxe, A. Cleveland, Christian Literature Publishing Company, 1985, Hendrickson Publishers, Peabody, Massachusetts: 1994.

Roberts, Alexander, and Donaldson, James, *Ante-Nicene Fathers: The Writings of the Fathers Down to A.D. 325, Volume 2: Fathers of the Second Century: Hermas, Tatian, Athenagoras, Theophilus, and Clement of Alexandria (Entire),* revised and chronologically arranged with brief prefaces and occasional notes by Cove, A.

Cleveland, Christian Literature Publishing Compoany, 1885, Hendrickson Publishers, Peabody, Massachusetts: 1994.

Roberts, Alexander, and Donaldson, James, *Ante-Nicene Fathers: The Writings of the Fathers Down to A.D. 325, Volume 3: Latin Christianity: Its Founder, Tertullian, I. Apologetic; II. Anti-Marcion; III. Ethical,* revised and chronologically arranged, with brief prefaces and occasional notes by Coxe, A. Cleveland, Christian Literature Publishing Company, 1885, Hendrickson Publishers, Peabody, Massachusetts: 1994.

Roberts, Alexander, and Donaldson, James, *Ante-Nicene Fathers: The Writings of the Fathers Down to A.D. 325, Volume 5: Hippolytus, Cyprian, Caius, Novatian, Appendix,* revised and chronologically arranged, with brief prefaces and occasional notes by Coxe, A. Cleveland, Christian Literature Publishing Company, 1885; Hendrickson Publishers, Peabody, Massachusetts: 1994.

Roberts, Alexander, and Donaldson, James, *Ante-Nicene Fathers: The Writings of the Fathers Down to A.D. 325, Volume 6: Gregory Thaumaturgus, Dionysius The Great, Julius Africanus, Anatolius and Minor Writers, Methodius, Arnobius,* revised and chronologically arranged, with brief prefaces and occasional notes by Coxe, A. Cleveland, Christian Literature Publishing Company, 1886; Hendrickson Publishers, Peabody, Massachusetts: 1994.

Robertson, A. T., *A Grammar of the Greek of the New Testament in Light of Historical Research,* Broadman Press, Nashville, Tennessee: 1934.

Robertson, Archibald Thomas, *Word Pictures in the New Testament Volume VI-General Epistles and The Revelation of John,* Baker Book House, Grand Rapids, Michigan: 1933, renewal 1960.

Robinson, James M., *A New Quest of the Historical Jesus and Other Essays,* SCM Press, Ltd., London: 1959; Fortress Press, Philadelphia: 1983.

Rogers, Cleon L., Jr. and Rogers, Cleon L., III, *The New Linguistic and Exegetical Key to the Greek New Testament,* Zondervan Publishing House, Grand Rapids, Michigan: 1998.

Rushdooney, Rousas John, *The Institutes of Biblical Law,* The Presbyterian and Reformed Publishing Company, 1973.

Russell, D. S., *Between the Testaments,* Fortress Press, Philadelphia, Pennsylvania: 1960, 1965.

Russell, D. S., *The Method and Message of Jewish Apocalyptic: 200* BC—AD *100,* The Westminster Press, Philadelphia, Pennsylvania: 1964.

Saenz-Badillos, Angel, *A History of the Hebrew Language,* translated by John Elwolde, Originally published in Spanish as *Historia de la Lengua Hebrea,* Editorial ASUA, Sabadell, 1988, Cambridge University Press, First paperback edition, 1996.

Sanders, James A., *Torah and Canon,* Fortress Press, Philadelphia, Pennsylvania: 1972.

Sayce, A. H., and Peterson, R., *Race in Ancient Egypt and the Old Testament,* Scott-Townsend Publishers, Washington, D.C.: 1993.

Schaff, Philip, *The Creeds of Christendom with a History and Critical Notes—Volume II: The Greek and Latin Creeds with Translations.* Baker Book House Company, Grand Rapids, Michigan, reprinted 1996.

Schaff, Philip, *History of the Christian Church, Volume II: Ante-Nicene Christianity* A.D. *100–325,* Wm. B. Eerdmans Publishing Company, Grand Rapids, Michigan: reprinted 1994.

Schaff, Philip, and Wace, Henry, eds., *Nicene and Post-Nicene Fathers: A Select Library of the Christian Church, Volume 1: Eusebius: Church History, Life of Constantine the Great, and Oration in Praise of Constantine,* Second Series, Christian Literature Publishing Company, 1890, Hendrickson Publishers, Peabody, Massachusetts: 1994.

Schillebeecx, Edward, Hoskins, Herbert, trans., *Jesus, An Experiment in Christology, Jesus, het verhaal van een lavende,* Uitgeverij H. Nelissen B. V. Bloemendaal, 1974; The Crossroads Publishing Company, New York: 1979.

Schmithals, Walter; Steely, John E., trans., *The Apocalyptic Movement: Introduction and Interpretation, Die Apokalyptik: Einfuhrung Und Deutung,* Vandenhoeck & Reprecht, Gottingen: 1973; Abingdon Press, Nashville, New York: 1975.

Schnachenburg, Rudolf, *The Gospel According to St. John, Volume 2: Commentary on Chapters 5-12,* original edition *Das Johannesevangelium, Part II, Herdes theologischer Kommentar zum Neuen*

Testament IV/2, Verlag Herder KG, 1971; A Crossroad Book, The Seabury Press, New York: 1980.

Schreiner, Thomas R., *The Law and Its Fulfillment—A Pauline Theory on Law,* Baker Book House Co., Grand Rapids, Michigan: 1993.

Schurer, Emil; Taylor, Sophia, and Christie, Peter, trans., *A History of the Jewish People in the Time of Christ, Second Division: The Internal Condition of Palestine and of the Jewish people in the Time of Jesus Christ, Volume II,* being a second and revised edition of a "Manual of the History of New Testament Times", reprinted from the edition originally published by T & T Clark, Edinburgh: 1890; Hendrickson Press, Peabody, Massachusetts, 1994.

Schweitzer, Albert; Montgomery, B. D., trans., *Quest of the Historical Jesus: A Critical Study of Its Progress from Reimarus to Wrede, Von Reimarus zu Wrede,* 1906, Macmillan Publishing Co., Inc., New York: 1961.

Sheldon, Henry C., *History of the Christian Church, Volume I: The Early Church,* Hendrickson Publishers, Peabody, Massachusetts: 1988.

Scott, J. Julius, Jr., *Jewish Backgrounds of the New Testament,* Baker Book House Co., Grand Rapids, Michigan: 1995.

Skousen, W. Cleon, *The Fourth Thousand Years,* Bookcraft, Salt Lake City, Utah: 1966.

Smith, George, and Sayce, A. H., *The Chaldean Account of Genesis Containing the Description of The Creation, The Deluge, The Tower of Babel, The Destruction of Sodom, The Times of the Patriarchs, and Nimrod: Babylonian Fables, and Legends of the Gods; From the Cuneiform Inscriptions,* Charles Scribner's Sons, New York: 1880.

Smyth, Piazzi, *The Great Pyramid: Its Secrets and History Revealed,* fourth and much enlarged edition, Bell Publishing Company, New York: 1990.

Souter, Alexander, *A Glossary of Later Latin to 600* A.D., Oxford at the Clarendon Press, Special edition for Sandpiper Books, Ltd., 1996.

Souter, Alexander, *Earliest Latin Commentaries on the Epistles of St. Paul, a Study,* Oxford at the Clarendon Press, Special for Sandpiper Books, Ltd., 1999.

Stauffer, Ethelbert; Marsh, John, trans., *New Testament Theology*, translated from the fifth edition from *Die Theologie Des Neuen Testaments*, W. KohlhammerVerlag, Stuttgart: 1955; The McMillan Company, New York: 1961.
Stead, Christopher, *Divine Substance*, Oxford at the Clarendon Press, 1977.
Steinberg, Naomi, *Kinship and Marriage in Genesis: A Household Economics Perspective*, Fortress Press, Minneapolils, Minnesota: 1993.
Strand, Kenneth H., ed., *The Sabbath in Scripture and History*, Review and Herald Publishing Association, Washington, D.C.: 1982.
Tanner, Obert C., Rogers, Lewis M., and McMurrin, Sterling M., eds., *Toward Understanding the New Testament*, Signature Books, Salt Lake City: 1990.
Tarazi, Paul Nadim, *Galatians: A Commentary*, St. Vladimir's Seminary Press, Crestwood, N.Y.: 1994.
Taylor, Edward, *Upon the Types of the Old Testament: Volume II*, University of Nebraska Press, Lincoln and London: 1989.
Telushkin, Rabbi Joseph, *Biblical Literacy: The Most Important People, Events and Ideas of the Hebrew Bible*, William Morrow and Company, Inc., New York: 1997.
Thiele, Edwin R., *The Mysterious Numbers of the Hebrew Kings*, new revised edition, Zondervan Publishing House, Grand Rapids, Michigan: 1983.
Thiele, Edwin, and Margaret, *Job and the Devil*, Pacific Press Publishing Association, Boise, Idaho; Oshawa, Ontario, Canada: 1988.
Thiering, Barbara, *Jesus and the Riddle of the Dead Sea Scrolls: Unlocking the Secrets of His Life Story*, HarperSanFrancisco, HarperCollins Publishers, New York: 1992.
Throckmorton, Burton H., Jr., *Gospel Parallels; A Comparison of the Synoptic Gospels*, fifth edition, Thomas Nelson Publishers, Nashville, Tennessee: 1992.
Tillich, Paul, Braaten, Carl E., ed., *A Complete History of Christian Thought*, Harper & Row Publishers, New York and Evanston: 1968.
Trymer-Kinsky, Tikva, *In the Wake of the Goddesses: Woman, Culture and the Biblical Transformation of Pagan Myth*, Fawcett Columbine, New York: 1992.

Van der Tourn, Karel, Becking, Bob, van der Horst, Pieter, eds., *Dictionary of Dieties and Demons in the Bible, DDD,* second extensively revised edition, Brill, Leiden, Boston, Koln; William B. Eerdmans Publishing Company, Grand Rapids, Michigan, Cambridge, U.K., 1999.

Van Orden, Bruce A., and Top, Brent L., eds., *The Lord of the Gospels—The 1990 Sperry Symposium on the New Testament,* Deseret Book Company, Salt Lake City, Utah: 1991.

Vine, W. E., Bruce, F. F., ed. Old Testament., *Vine's Expository Dictionary of Old and New Testament Words,* Fleming H. Revell Company, Old Tappan, New Jersey: 1981.

Waddell, L. A., *The Makers of Civilization in Race and History Showing the Rise of the Aryans or Sumerians, Their Origination & Propagation of Civilization, Their extension of it to Egypt & Crete, Personalities & Achievements of Their Kings, Historical Originals of Mythic Gods & Heroes with Dates From the Rise of Civilization about 3380 B.C. Reconstructed from Babylonian, Egyptian, Hittite, Indian & Gothic Sources,* Omni Christian Book Club, Hawthorne, California: 1929.

Wallenkampf, Arnold V., Lesher, W, Richard, eds., *The Sanctuary and the Atonement: Biblical, Historical and Theological Studies,* The Review and Herald Publishing Association, Washington, D.C.: 1981.

Walvoord, John F., *The Revelation of Jesus Christ: A Commentary,* Moody Press, Chicago: 1969.

Wansbrough, Henry, gen. ed., *The New Jerusalem Bible,* Doubleday, New York: 1985.

Watson, Alan, *Jesus and the Law,* The University of Georgia Press, Athens, Georgia: 1996.

Waxman, Meyer, *A History of Jewish Literature, Volume I: From the Close of the Canon to the End of the Twelfth Century,* South Brunswick, New York: 1960.

Weiser, Artur, Hartwell, Herbert, trans., *The Psalms: A Commentary, Die Psalmen (Da Alten Testament Deutsch 14/15),* fifth revised edition, Vandenhoeck & Rupreseht, Gottingen, 1959, The Westminster Press, Philadelphia, Pennsylvania: 1962.

Welesz, Egon, *A History of Byzantine Music and Hymnography,* second edition, revised and enlarged, Oxford at the Clarendon Press, Special Edition for Sandpiper Books, Ltd., 1998.
Wenham, Gordon, J., *Word Biblical Commentary, Volume I: Genesis 1–15,* Word Books Publishers, Waco, Texas: 1987.
Whiston, William, trans., *Josephus: Complete Works,* Kregel Publications, Grand Rapids, Michigan: 1960.
Wilkinson, Benjamin George, *Truth Triumphant: The Church in the Wilderness,* Teach Services, Inc., Brushton, New York: 1994.
Wisse, Frederik, *The Profile Method for Classifying and Evaluating Manuscripit Evidence as Applied to the Continuous Greek Text of the Gospel of Luke,* Studies and Documents, Volume 44, Sparks, Irving Alan, ed., Wm. B. Eerdmans, Grand Rapids, Michigan: 1982.
Wofters, David, *Deep Things Out of Darkness: The Book of Job, Essays and a New English Translation,* Kok Pharos, The Netherlands, William B. Eerdmans Publishing Company, Grand Rapids, Michigan: 1995.
Wright, Dennis A., Ostler, Craig J., Pike, Dana M., Darling, Dee R., Smith, Patty A., Symposium Committee, *Voices of Old Testament Prophets: The 26th Annual Sidney B. Sperry Symposium,* Deseret Book Company, Salt Lake City, Utah: 1997.
Zerwick, Max, and Grosvenor, Mary, *A Grammatical Analysis of the Greek New Testament,* unabridged, 5th revised edition, Editrice Pontifico, Istituto Biblico, Roma: 1996.

Dissertations

Bacchiocchi, Samuele, *From Sabbath to Sunday—A Historical Investigation of the Rise of Sunday Observance in Early Christianity.* The Pontifical Gregorian University Press, Rome: 1977.
Baker, D. L., *Two Testaments: One Bible, A Study of Some Modern Solutions to the Theological Problem of the Relationship Between Old and New Testament,* InterVarsity Press, Downers Grove, Illinois: 1976.

Beaudean, John Wiliam, Jr., *Paul's Theology of Preaching,* Dissertation Series Number 6, Mercer University Press, Macon, Georgia: 1988.

Brooten, Bernadette, *Women Leaders in the Ancient Synagogue, Inscriptual Evidence and Background Issues, Brown Judiac Studies 36,* Scholars Press, Chico, California: 1982.

Doukhan, Jacques B., *The Literary Structure of the Genesis Creation Story,* Andrews University, UMI Dissertation Services, Ann Arbor, Michigan: 197, reprinted 2000.

Knight, Douglas A., *Rediscovering the Traditions of Israel: The Development of the Tradio-Historical Research of the Old Testament, with Special Consideration of Scandinavian Contributions,* Second Edition, Society of Biblical Literature and Scholars Press, Dissertation Series, Number Nine, University of Montana, Missoula: 1975.

Lazaroff, Allan, *The Theology of Abraham Bibago: A Defense of the Divine Will, Knowledge and Providence in Fifteenth Century Spanish-Jewish Philosophy,* The University of Alabama Press, University, Alabama: 1981.

Mikels, Leroy, *The Kenosis (An Exegetical Analysis),* Triune Biblical Institute and Seminary, 1982.

Articles

Buchanan, George Wesley, *"Worship, Feasts and Ceremonies in the Early Jewish-Christian Church" New Testament Studies, An International Journal, Vol. 26, No. 3, April 1980.*

Cameron, Grant, *"To Depart and Be With Christ: What Does This Popular Text Really Mean?" Resurrection, An International Magazine, Winter, 1987.*

De Jone, Henk, *"Sonship, Wisdom, Infancy, Luke II 41–51a" New Testament Studies: An International Journal, Vol. 24, No. 3, April, 1978.*

Dorothy, Charles V., *"Colossians: Then and Now, Part III," Association for Christian Development Newsletter,* Auburn, Washington: August 1991.

Dorothy, Charles V., *"Did Ezra Edit or Author the Law? The Law of God—Part 4," Association for Christian Development Newsletter,* Rolling Bay, Washington: July 1985.
Dorothy, Charles, V., *"Recent Trends in Biblical Studies, Part 2: Canon Criticism and Canonical Criticism: Two Recent Whole-Bible Approaches—Are They Big Guns or Loose Canons on the Deck of Theology?" Association for Christian Development Newsletter,* Rolling Bay, Washington: August 1989.
Eibfeldt, O., *"Liber Gensis," Biblia Hebraica Stuttgartensia,* Elliger, K., et Rudolph, W., Textum Masoreticum curavit H. P. Ruger, Masoram Elaboravit, G. E. Weil, Wurttembergische, Bibelanstalt, Stuttgart, 1969.
Finn, Thomas H., *"It Happened One Saturday Night; Ritual and Conversion in Augustine's North Africa," Journal of the American Academy of Religion, Volume LVIII, Number 4, Winter, 1990.*
Kimbrough, S. T., Jr., *"Theological Table Talk: Bible Translation and the Gender of God," p. 196, Theology Today, Vol. XLVIU, No. 2, July 1989.*
Martin, Troy, *"But Let Everyone Discern the Body of Christ" (Colossians 2.17) Journal of Biblical Literature, Vol. 114, No. 2, 1995.*
Martin, Troy, *"Pagan and Judeo-Christian Time-Keeping Schemes in Gal. 4.10 and Col. 2:16"* Cambridge University Press, 1996.
Martini, Rev. Prof. Carlo M., *"Is There a Late Alexandrian Text of the Gospels?" New Testament Studies, An International Journal, Vol. 24, No. 3, April 1978.*
Rollins, Rev. G. S. *"The Principle of Adaptation in Revelation,"* reprint, *The Biblical World—July-December 1990.*